Boundaries of Authority

Boundaries of Authority

A. JOHN SIMMONS

OXFORD
UNIVERSITY PRESS

OXFORD
UNIVERSITY PRESS

Oxford University Press is a department of the University of Oxford. It furthers the University's objective of excellence in research, scholarship, and education by publishing worldwide. Oxford is a registered trade mark of Oxford University Press in the UK and certain other countries.

Published in the United States of America by Oxford University Press
198 Madison Avenue, New York, NY 10016, United States of America.

Library of Congress Cataloging-in-Publication Data
Names: Simmons, A. John (Alan John), 1950– author.
Title: Boundaries of authority / A. John Simmons.
Description: New York, NY : Oxford University Press, [2016]
Identifiers: LCCN 2015039691 | ISBN 9780190603489 (hardcover)
Subjects: LCSH: Territory, National—Philosophy. | Jurisdiction, Territorial—Philosophy. | Nation-state.
Classification: LCC JZ3675 .S56 2016 | DDC 320.1/2—dc23
LC record available at http://lccn.loc.gov/2015039691

CONTENTS

PART III PROPERTY AND TERRITORY

PREFACE

This book has, in a way, been in progress for nearly two decades, though it took me almost that long to decide that there was a book lurking where I had thought there were only some related chunks of argument. As a result of this lengthy process, many pieces, bits, and revised portions of a large number of essays and lectures, some from quite a few years ago, have found their way into this final version, often intertwined with material that was composed very recently. During so many years of work on a project, one naturally receives help from many, many people. Alas, but just as inevitably, there were many more than I can now recall. To those of you whose assistance I've managed to forget, my sincere apologies along with my genuine gratitude.

Here, though, are at least a few of those helpful groups, events, and individuals that I'm still able to remember. My thanks to the audiences, respondents, and participants at Virginia Tech, the Eighteenth Annual Greensboro Symposium in Philosophy, Bowling Green State University, the University of Virginia Law School, the University of Toronto Law School, the Chapel Hill (University of North Carolina) Workshop on Political Authority, the International Colloquium on Political Authority and Obligation, Royal Netherlands Academy of Arts and Sciences (University of Amsterdam), Harvard University, University of Arizona, University of Virginia Philosophy Department, Princeton University, the University of Pennsylvania Law School, the London School of Economics, Wake Forest University, the University of Maryland, and the Workshop for Oxford Studies in Political Philosophy. Among the individuals who've supplied written (or sustained verbal) comments on parts of the book, my thanks to Annie Stilz, David Copp, Sahar Akhtar, John Christman, Barbara Levenbook, George Sher, Randy Barnett, Chris Morris, Daniel Shapiro, Geoff Sayre-McCord, Dave Estlund, Tim Scanlon, Nahshon Perez, Mike Otsuka, Jody Kraus, Susanne Sreedhar, Bas Van Der Vossen, Matthew Adams, Leif Wenar, Massimo Renzo, John Arras, and Arthur Ripstein. Margaret Moore and Cara Nine, as readers for

Oxford University Press, generously provided comments on (almost) the whole manuscript. Try as I might, I could think of no plausible way to escape responsibility for the mistakes and confusions that remain in the text, despite the help of all these smart people.

My wife and friend, Nancy Schauber, and my daughter, Sarah Simmons, are owed a different kind and order of gratitude. Nancy's consistent support and advice, both philosophical and non-, have been invaluable throughout the course of this project. But equally important have been the calm and happy environments that she and Sarah have made possible, where they have both tolerated with grace and good humor my many hours of solitary work. As I complete this book in Paris, accompanied again by them both, my sense of undeserved good fortune—along, of course, with incomparable walks, art, architecture, food, and drink—has been the steady purlieu of an unusually gratifying writing process.

Portions of the following articles, some very heavily revised and frequently discontinuous, are included in this book:

"Historical Rights and Fair Shares," *Law and Philosophy* 14 (1995), 149–84.

"On the Territorial Rights of States," *Philosophical Issues* 11 (Social, Political, and Legal Philosophy) (2001), 300–26.

"Disobedience and Its Objects," *Boston University Law Review* 90 (2010), 1805–31.

"States' Resource Rights: Locating the Limits," Territory and Justice Symposium (Edition on Resource Rights), C. Nine (ed.) (January 2012). Published online at *Territory and Justice: A Research Network*, http://eis.bris.ac.uk/~plcdib/territory/papers/SimmonsMooreReply.pdf.

"Authority," in D. Estlund (ed.), *The Oxford Handbook of Political Philosophy* (Oxford: Oxford University Press, 2012), 23–39.

"Democratic Authority and the Boundary Problem," *Ratio Juris* 26 (2013), 325–56.

"Territorial Rights: Justificatory Strategies," in D. Sobel, P. Valentine, and S. Wall (eds.), *Oxford Studies in Political Philosophy*, vol. 1 (Oxford: Oxford University Press, 2015), 145–72.

Introduction

States are defined in international law as entities with permanent populations and *fixed territories* under government control.[1] Henry Sidgwick, anticipating such definitions, was surely correct when he wrote that "it seems essential to the modern conception of a State that its government should exercise supreme dominion over a particular portion of the earth's surface . . . Indeed, in modern political thought the connection between a political society and its territory is so close that the two notions almost blend."[2] Most of us think of nation-states in terms of their territories, first learning about our own and other nations by locating their colored territorial shapes on maps. Exactly *where* the territorial lines defining these shapes are drawn is obviously a matter of considerable importance to states, and the history of the conflicts in which modern states have engaged has regularly involved attempts, often successful, to redraw those lines by force.[3]

States, of course, not only occupy and identify themselves with particular territories, they almost always claim to do so *rightfully*. Such claims may sometimes seem to amount to nothing more than claims of *legality*, claims made in accordance with the (disturbingly imprecise) international laws of territory. But usually states' claims to their particular territories have a more distinctively *moral* tone to them. And it will be on the possible *moral* justifications of states'

[1] For instance, under the 1933 Montevideo *Convention on the Rights and Duties of States* (Article 1), states are defined as having these properties, along with the capacity to enter into relations with other states. The *territorial state* is the principal type of "legal person" recognized in international law. For a more sophisticated, but closely related, *philosophical* definition of the state, see Kavka (1986), 158.

[2] Sidgwick (1897), 221, 222 ([chap.] 14, [sec.] 2).

[3] Abraham Lincoln told Congress that a nation consists "of its territory, its people, and its laws. The territory," he claimed, "is the only part which is of certain durability" (Second Annual Message, December 1862). Lincoln was fortunate not to have had to consider the prospect of portions of his nation's territory being lost under steadily rising oceans. But he certainly knew what we all know: that the durability of national *territory*—as opposed to the reasonable durability of *land*—has throughout the modern state's history proved to be anything but certain.

territorially based claims that I will concentrate in this book. We all know, of course, that the actual means by which existing states have established their claimed territories have seldom been morally exemplary. Boundaries have expanded and contracted by simple seizures or annexations, by military conquest and intimidation and expulsion, and by negotiation under duress. The international community has generally accepted such changes after a suitable period of mourning.[4] Powerful states have tended to lay claim to by force (and to then defend by force) all territory extending to salient, useful, or defensible geographical features (like coastlines, rivers, or mountains), regardless of whether they extend services to those areas or whether those areas are used or inhabited by their subjects. Even where new territories have been acquired by settlement or by uncoerced agreement between states, these processes have frequently involved displacement of (or other severe impact on) native peoples.

Despite these disturbing histories, it is commonly assumed that the territorial rights that many modern states claim to possess and exercise are not chimerical, nor are they merely conventional or legal rights. They are, at least sometimes, also *moral* rights over territories (or morally justified legal rights). This book aims to clarify and explore the territorial dimensions of the authority states claim, examining the available justifications for states' claimed "dominion" over particular portions of the earth (and beyond) and the relations between those claims to territory and states' claims to political authority over sets of persons. Obviously, territorial rights are only one category of the rights claimed by modern states. The total set of rights they claim is minimally that which states must exercise if they are to retain effective control over their territories and populations in a world composed of numerous autonomous states. Often the rights states are trying to claim in asserting their legitimacy go far beyond this minimum.

But whether a state's claims are modest or extravagant, the rights claimed invariably fall into three categories.[5] The first category is a set of rights held over or against those persons who fall within the state's claimed legal jurisdiction—what I will call *rights over subjects.* The second is a set of rights claimed against those persons *without* the state's jurisdiction—what we can call *rights against aliens.* And the third category is the set of rights held over a particular geographical

[4] While many such acquisitions are prohibited under widely accepted principles of law, the legal force of subsequent international recognition in effect undermines those principles. The rules of international law have often "had the effect of legitimising the results of the exercise of power . . . Law must come to terms with power and force . . . The international community has accepted the results of illegal aggression in many cases by virtue of recognition" (Shaw [1997], 332, 340). See also Wallace (1997), 98–9.

[5] These categories correspond roughly to the three sorts of rights noted in Copp (1999), 18. I characterize the categories slightly differently and suggest a different set of constituent rights for them than does Copp.

territory (whose extent largely determines the scope of the state's claimed jurisdiction)—call these *territorial rights.* The rights states claim in these three categories jointly define their conception of the sovereignty[6] that they (or their peoples, governments, or institutions) enjoy, sovereignty that is more extensive (strong, absolute) as the rights asserted in these categories are more numerous and wide-ranging.[7]

In the first category ("rights over subjects"), decent states claim: (a) the right to coercively regulate the conduct of all subjects by making and enforcing legal rules and other state directives; (b) the right to be obeyed by their subjects (i.e., the right to have subjects perform their imposed legal duties); and (c) the right to reasonable assistance from subjects in the enforcement of law. These rights—which collectively are often referred to as the state's legislative and executive powers—are generally taken to be limited to making and enforcing only tolerably just (or, at the very least, procedurally legitimate) law.

These rights in the first category—the rights to make and enforce law and to be obeyed by those subject to that law—are normally taken to correlate with

[6] Sovereignty is thus often characterized in international law as consisting of that set of rights normally exercised by modern states. Jurisdiction is then defined as that particular set of rights that entitles a state to govern persons and property by the state's municipal law. See, e.g., Brownlie (1998), 106, and Wallace (1997), 111. "International law is based on the concept of the state. The state in its turn lies upon the foundation of sovereignty, which expresses internally the supremacy of the governmental institutions and externally the supremacy of the state as a legal person" (Shaw [1997], 331). A good philosophical discussion of the concept of sovereignty is in Morris (1998), chap. 7.

[7] In my view, both state legitimacy and state sovereignty consist in the state's possession of complex and internally related sets of these three kinds of right. A state is sovereign if it possesses the highest or final political authority over a citizenry and territory—that is, if it possesses a reasonably extensive (but not necessarily absolute) authority that consists in rights both to have the final word in matters of internal control (in that territory) and to independence from external control and interference. A state (like any other institutional arrangement) is legitimate if it actually possesses the rights to do what it does (or what it attempts to do). Since the rights modern states claim and try to exercise add up to various kinds of sovereignty, discussions of legitimacy and sovereignty will naturally tend to converge. But the differences in the concepts allow the possibility of legitimate but nonsovereign political institutions (which might or might not qualify as "states"). The old (sixteenth- and seventeenth-century) debates about sovereignty concerned principally questions of internal sovereignty (e.g., who has de jure authority over whom within a political society, the limits on political authority, etc.). More recent debates have concerned primarily external sovereignty (e.g., when and why nations have a right to self-determination, when international intervention is justified, etc.). The arguments of this book bear on both aspects of state sovereignty. I will, however, henceforth mostly try to avoid in the book the vexed language of sovereignty. While sovereignty refers only to supremacy or finality of rule (within a jurisdiction), it is still common to associate the idea of sovereignty with the kind of absolute or unlimited rule described by Bodin and Hobbes. Few serious philosophers today believe that absolute political sovereignty can be justified; but the Hobbesian argument that limited sovereignty is no sovereignty at all—because a limit implies a superior power that imposes the limit—continues, I think, to influence thinking about the concept.

the *obligations* of other persons, groups, or states. Some of the correlative obligations are the obligations of subjects: obligations not to attempt rival legislation or enforcement, to fulfill lawfully imposed requirements, and not to resist the state's lawfully employed coercive powers. Other such correlative obligations, however, are the obligations of *non*subjects, of those *without* the state's claimed jurisdiction.

Here the first category of rights makes obvious contact with the second, with the "rights against aliens" claimed by states. States claim the right not to be interfered with or usurped by alien persons, groups, or states in the exercise of those rights claimed in the first category. States claim rights to noninterference, self-determination, self-government, or external sovereignty. This is generally intended to include not only obligatory alien respect for the state's exercise of its first-category legislative and executive powers, but also for the state's exercise of what is sometimes called its *federative* power—what Locke describes as "the power of war and peace, leagues and alliances, and all the transactions with all persons and communities without the commonwealth" (II, 146).[8] States claim the right to "do business" in the world as a legal person, as an autonomous, equal corporate entity—including the "business" of conducting just war—without alien interference. This business may even be taken to include the enforcement against aliens of "natural law," God-made law, or "human rights," which will, of course, inevitably bring the rights claimed by some states in category two ("rights against aliens") into conflict with those claimed by other states in category one ("rights over subjects").

Finally, every modern state identifies itself with and claims a set of exclusive (third category) "territorial rights" over a particular geographical area.[9] These include at least rights to exclusive legal jurisdiction over the territory, rights to exclusive control of movement (of persons and materials) over the boundaries of the territory, and rights to exclusive control over the nonhuman things and beings contained in (or constitutive of) the territory. More specifically, states saliently claim: (a) the right to coercively regulate the conduct of all within the territory by means of enforcing all legal rules and directives of the state; (b) the right to reasonably full control over the land and resources within the territory that are not privately owned; (c) the right to tax and regulate privately owned

[8] My (frequent) references in this book to Locke's *Two Treatises of Government* will be indicated by "I" or "II," followed by paragraph or section number. All quotations are from Locke (1960), spelling modernized.

[9] I should emphasize that the list below is intended only as a list of the principal rights actually *claimed* by modern states. Cara Nine, oddly, objects to an earlier version of my list of "the rights claimed by states" in relation to territory on the grounds that not all of these rights are necessary elements "of the *concept* of territorial rights" (Nine [2012], 11; my emphasis). I of course agree that they are not.

land and resources within the territory; (d) the right to control or prohibit movement across territorial boundaries; (e) the right to determine the standing of those within the territory (by, e.g., establishing rules governing residency, diplomatic status, or citizenship); and (f) the right to prohibit individual or group territorial secession or alienation of territory to nonmember persons or groups.

Some of these claimed rights, notice, are primarily *jurisdictional* in nature—that is, they are claims primarily to regulate and *control* a particular territory, rather than claims to *exclude* persons from entering or using it. Other such territorial claims states make are more *property-like*, exclusionary claims over a region, claims to choose who or what may pass over its boundaries and who may use (and how they may use) the land and resources located within those boundaries.[10] States' territorial claims thus interact or overlap with both the "rights over subjects" in our first category—since most of those within the territory will normally be subjects—and the "rights against aliens" in our second category, since it is primarily aliens who are excluded from entering and using state's land and resources. The jurisdictional claims that states make are not, of course, merely claims they make with respect to the geographical space itself; they are primarily claims over the human beings located in that space. States claim authority over those within their territories, the rights to make and enforce laws and directives for them and the right to peaceful compliance from them. States claim the right to "speak the law" to a set of persons—as the literal meaning of "jurisdiction" suggests—and the relevant set of persons is in the modern world primarily located in territorial terms. As a result, the word "jurisdiction" now refers as well to the geographical area over which legal authority is thought to extend.

This is not to say that states' claimed jurisdictions coincide *precisely* with their claimed territories, nor is it to say that the kind of authority claimed over those within the territory is uniform throughout. States typically exercise only a truncated form of legal authority over noncitizens—e.g., visitors, resident aliens, and foreign diplomats—who, while generally held to the observance of the laws establishing "peace and good order," may not be subject to other laws (such as parking or traffic, tax, or military service laws); and even such truncated authority is normally asserted only when these noncitizens are physically within the state's territorial domain. States also enforce some rights against their

[10] See Nine (20012), 11. As we will see, cosmopolitan skeptics about the defensibility of the modern state system, that system's most relentless critics, are largely united in rejecting states' property-like claims to decide as they like who shall pass over their territorial borders and to exercise exclusive control over natural resources in their territories. But most cosmopolitans appear prepared to accept something like the current districted division of jurisdictional rights over persons among a multiplicity of states. I will raise more systematic doubts about states' claims in both of these areas.

own citizens wherever they may be, just as they enforce the law with respect to some kinds of wrongs, regardless of where those wrongs occur or who commits them (as in cases of piracy on the high seas). Similarly, the rights states claim against alien persons and nations are *primarily*, but not exclusively, territorial in nature—that is, they are mostly rights not to be interfered with in exercising an autonomous state's territorial jurisdiction. States do claim a variety of rights against aliens not to be harmed in their nonterritorial (e.g., economic) interests, not to have territorial interests (e.g., security) harmed in ways that involve no territorial incursions, and not to have their citizens unlawfully harmed while abroad. So we can most accurately say that actual states' authority claims are territorially *centered*; and the rights states claim against aliens are *principally* rights not to be harmed or interfered with in exercising their *territorial* jurisdiction or control.[11]

I should add here a quick clarification of my assertions above about rights being claimed and exercised by *states*. In describing states as claiming territorial rights, I intend to deny neither the possibility of federal governance *within* nation-states nor the possibility of voluntary renunciation, transfer, or collective exercise (e.g., in unions or federations) of these rights by nation-states. The rights I listed above (and discuss further below) should be thought of only as those to which autonomous nation-states take themselves to be entitled, prior to or independent of any voluntary reduction or sharing of those rights within or between states. Further, I intend nothing particularly controversial in identifying *states*, rather than (say) nations or peoples or communities, as the bearers of these (and especially of territorial) rights. Longstanding rules of international law, of course, also identify traditional nation-states as the relevant class of territorial right-bearers; but more recent additions to those rules suggest as well that certain other "nonstate" peoples may also have valid territorial claims. My use of "state" here is in fact intended to be consistent with both kinds of claims. By "state" (or "political society"[12]), I mean only an incorporated group of persons (which can thus act as a single agent) who have legitimately structured their interactions under effective institutions of government and law. And on the Lockean model of the state that I endorse, both familiar modern states and

[11] States thus claim jurisdiction not only under the "territorial principle," but also under the "nationality principle" (which determines jurisdiction by an *offender's* nationality) and the "passive personality principle" (which can determine jurisdiction by a *victim's* nationality). Other nonterritorial principles of jurisdiction include the "protective principle" (according to which those who threaten or injure state security are held liable) and the "universality principle" (which makes, e.g., pirates, war criminals, and perpetrators of genocide subject to every state's jurisdiction). See, e.g., Wallace (1997), 111–19.

[12] See the account of political society in Simmons (2008), 6–8.

some (apparently) "nonstate" peoples could qualify as "states" and hold territorial rights.[13]

Return with me for a moment, now, to our three categories of states' claimed rights. Much has been written in recent political and legal philosophy and theory dealing with the first category of rights claimed by states—that is, the state's rights over its subjects. The large contemporary literature on political obligation and authority, and civil or uncivil disobedience is centrally concerned with the nature and extent of the state's rights over subjects. Most contemporary discussions of state (or governmental) legitimacy likewise concentrate on this first category of rights. Similarly, there is a significant body of contemporary writing that deals with the second category of claimed rights, the state's rights against aliens. Concerns about the extent of states' rights over those within their claimed jurisdictions have led naturally to discussion of the rights of groups (principally, minority groups) to secede or to otherwise limit their subjection; and concerns about the rights of groups to secede have naturally focused attention on groups' rights of self-determination, leading inevitably to discussion of

[13] Nine has forcefully opposed the view (advanced primarily by contemporary Kantians) that territorial rights are held specifically by *states*. Because Nine understands a state as "merely a set of institutions" (Nine [2012], 15), and because mere institutions can't be rightholders, she takes it to follow that states can't hold territorial rights. She also takes our conviction that groups in failed states can retain territorial (including resource) rights to show that such groups must be the real rightholders, even in successful and legitimate states (14–15, 55). My own view takes neither side (or perhaps both sides) in that debate. In Lockean political philosophy, only *morally legitimate* social organizations or groupings can count as "states" (or genuinely "civil" societies); all other coercive social arrangements are *merely* coercive, not properly *political*. What creates a "political" society or "state," on the Lockean model, is the unanimous consent of each member to help make (or to join) an enduring society—a consent that implicitly includes (as we will see in chapter 5) consent to be governed by some nonunanimity rule for dispute resolution, as well as consent to bind together members' holdings in land (if any) under the society's territorial jurisdiction. States are not, on this view, *necessarily* territorial entities, though all modern states in fact take territorial form. Migratory societies or societies on space stations could count as "states" in the relevant sense. Political societies with failed or overthrown formal institutional structures (or with "informal" structures) can also hold or retain this status as "states." Consenting members can remain morally bound by their consents to membership in their political society. They can remain a "state," in this sense, and can collectively hold territorial rights. Even without "standard" institutions of government and law, they can remain a governed people—their government being, as Locke calls it, a "perfect democracy" (under their chosen decision rule)—and they can remain subject to law—that is, bound by their collective commitment to enable an enduring society together by enforcing among themselves (at least) the moral "law of nature." Aboriginal groups may or may not be (or have been) political societies or "states" of this sort. But even if they are (or were) not, they may hold individual or group *property* rights in land, rights that stand as powerful moral barriers to attempted *territorial* acquisitions by *states*. Locke himself seldom used the language of "states." But his account of "civil society" follows Pufendorf's account of "states": "by such pacts as these a multitude of men unite to form a state, which is conceived as a

states' rights of independence and self-government, held against alien persons, groups, and states. But theorists have only quite recently begun examining the kinds of particular *territorial* rights that modern states claim;[14] and their discussions have seldom illuminated—as I will try to do in this book—the ways in which the many moral limits to states' claimed political authority over subjects must seriously affect the kinds of claims states can justifiably make with respect to particular geographical territories. Similarly, relevant sources of international law have largely left such questions unaddressed.[15]

The reasons for this general cross-disciplinary neglect do not seem particularly obscure. Recent political philosophy and theory, largely following the extraordinarily influential example of John Rawls, has focused primarily on problems concerning the *internal* institutional structure of the state—that is, on the domestic justice (so understood) of its basic structure. But in doing so, it has been necessary to assume (at least *arguendo*) that the territorially limited sets of persons governed by the institutions of the state are *legitimately* so governed, that the territories over which states claim jurisdiction and control are *legitimately* so claimed. Critical examination of that core assumption is left for later, once we have solved the puzzle of domestic justice. Rawls, remember, begins with the idea that "political society is closed: we come to be within it and we do not, and indeed cannot, enter or leave it voluntarily . . . The government's authority cannot be evaded except by leaving the territory over which it governs, and not always then."[16] For Rawls, the fundamental question of political philosophy is: how can political power ("which is always coercive power"[17]) be justifiably wielded over such a "captive audience"?

But there is a logically prior question to be asked: what is the nature and basis of states' claims over those territories within which each of us comes

single person with intelligence and will, performing other actions peculiar to itself and separate from those of individuals" (Pufendorf [1934], 983 [{bk.} 7, {chap.} 2, {sec.} 13]).

[14] When I first explored the topic of territorial rights in print (in 2001), almost nothing had been written on the subject. Of the great historical philosophers, only John Locke spilled more than a thimble-full of ink on the problem; and even his account of state's territorial rights is extraordinarily brief. Between Locke's time and ours, philosophers seem mostly to have either taken for granted that current states' territorial claims can be easily justified, or have not thought the problem of justification worth the effort of stating and questioning.

[15] As Malcolm Shaw argues, "the problem of how a state actually acquires its own territory in international law is a difficult one . . . With long-established states one may dismiss the question on the basis of recognition and acceptance." With respect to new states, "there has been relatively little discussion of the method by which the new entity itself acquires the legal rights to its lands. The stress has instead been on compliance with factual requirements as to statehood coupled with the acceptance of this by other states" (Shaw [1997], 335).

[16] Rawls [1993], 136, 222.

[17] Ibid., 136.

nonvoluntarily to be? An answer to this prior question seems necessary before Rawls's question can be persuasively answered; and a sufficiently skeptical answer to this prior question can make Rawls's question seem otiose. For surely most would agree that even the most just or reasonable sort of political authority cannot be justifiably wielded by a state over territory (and the persons on it) to which that state has no legitimate claim. No matter how just its constitution and its policies might be made, the United States could still not justifiably extend its political power to include, say, Pakistan or Antarctica within its jurisdiction. The question of states' territorial rights, I will argue here, must be answered *simultaneously* with the question of states' rights over subjects. And both must be convincingly answered before we can identify the proper reach of even a perfectly just basic structure.

This book will explore, then, the *boundaries* of states' justified political authority, examining the ways in which states' claimed authority over those persons that states treat as their subjects bears on the plausibility of states' claims to territorial authority—and vice versa. The basic view defended here is that states' claims to authority over persons have *normative priority* over their claims to authority over territory, in the sense that claims over territory rest on and presuppose legitimate authority over the persons who live and work in the claimed geographical spaces. I will begin, in chapter 1, with some necessary preliminaries. I attempt there first to present clearly the basic idea of practical authority over persons, then to distinguish the various other forms of practical authority from the genuinely political authority claimed by states, and finally to discuss the ways in which states' claimed political authority over persons relate to their claims of political authority over geographical territories. In the following two chapters of part I, I go on to argue (first, in chapter 2) that the historical wrongs done by states to persons and peoples in their acquisitions of territory constitute a legitimate basis for legal disobedience, in part because those wrongs must be understood to limit the territorial authority that states can justifiably claim. And I argue as well (in chapter 3) that the dominant strain in contemporary political philosophy and theory—what I call Kantian functionalism—is unable to plausibly answer questions about the boundaries of the legitimate territorial authority of contemporary states precisely because of its systematic denial of the continuing moral importance of those historical wrongs. In parts II and III, I then examine the capabilities of the various proposed theories of states' territorial rights—Kantian functionalism included—to yield plausible answers about states' claimed jurisdictional and property-like rights. And I defend there as well a Lockean voluntarist theory that I believe answers such questions far more convincingly than do any rival approaches to those issues.

PART I

POLITICAL AUTHORITY AND STATE BOUNDARIES

1

Authority

Practical, Political, Territorial

The Concept of Authority

Thomas Hobbes, writing in the middle of the seventeenth century, offered this definition of authority: "the right of doing any action is called AUTHORITY."[1] Hobbes was in this passage exploring the concept of authority at work in his account of the *political* authority of the sovereign person (or body) in a society. In another, slightly later, work, Hobbes wrote, "I call authorities anyone in any subject whose precept or example is followed, because one hath been led thereto by a belief in their wisdom."[2] Here Hobbes was enumerating the six sources of "men's inclinations," one of which is our disposition to conform our conduct to the teachings of those we regard as wise. The two quite different notions of authority utilized by Hobbes in these two passages correspond to what contemporary theorists call *practical* authority and *theoretical* (or *epistemic*) authority.

Practical authorities are those whose commands or pronouncements give us distinctive kinds of reasons to act in accordance with them. Theoretical authorities are experts on their subjects. In both cases, our recognition of a pronouncement as issuing from an authority provides us with reasons to act or to believe that are both *peremptory* and *content-independent*.[3] When accepted authorities tell us what to do or to believe, we have reason to simply comply. Their status as authorities gives us reasons even where we cannot ourselves discern or confirm or appreciate the reasons they have for what they tell us. Similarly, pronouncements by authorities give us reasons that are independent of the actual content of the pronouncement. We have reason to believe an expert even where what he

[1] Hobbes (1968), 218 (*Leviathan* [chap.] 16, [para.] 4).
[2] Hobbes (1972), 67 (*De Homine* [chap.] 13, [sec.] 7).
[3] Hart (1982), 261.

asserted turns out to be false. Again, it is the mere status of the pronouncement as authoritative that establishes its reason-giving force.

The distinction between theoretical and practical authority is usually drawn in terms of the kinds of reasons given us by exercises of those two kinds of authority: "expert advice gives reason for belief, not action."[4] It is only exercises of practical authority that give us reasons to *act*. Some theorists have tried to minimize this difference, characterizing practical authority as really just a complicated kind of theoretical authority.[5] While that is mistaken (since practical authorities, such as political authorities, need not be experts on any subjects at all), the connection between theoretical and practical authority is actually stronger than it might at first seem. Most of us believe that those who have practical authority over us—our political or religious leaders, our military commanders, our judges or police officers—ought also to be experts or to possess genuine wisdom in their relevant domains. And reasons for belief regularly provide us with reasons for action, especially when they are reasons for believing that something is best done in a recommended fashion. What merely theoretical authority *cannot* give the expert, it seems, is a *right* that we act on those reasons. No expert has any special right that we act in one way or another merely in virtue of their expert pronouncements or could claim to be *wronged* by someone's utterly disregarding their expert "precepts or examples."[6]

If practical authority—our primary concern here—does in fact consist in having a special right with respect to the actions of others, how should we understand that right? First, the right in question must indeed be some kind of *special* right, not a right shared by all or most people. While I, along with all of my fellow citizens, have a legal right to practice my preferred religion—and, in consequence, a right that others refrain from interfering with that practice—it would be deeply odd to say that this amounts to my possessing legal authority in that domain. But even when we focus on special, not generally shared rights, not all such rights seem to constitute authority. Suppose that I have made a promise to lend you my car on Friday. While we would then say that you have a special right to use my car on that day (and that I have a special obligation to permit you to use it), we would be unlikely to say that you as a result "have authority over me (or over my car)" for the day. We might at most say that I had "authorized" your use of the car.

Suppose, by contrast, that I promise to spend the weekend helping you in whatever ways (within reason) you say would be most useful to you. While we might still simply say that you had a right to my help, it would in this case be

[4] Green (1988), 27.

[5] See the discussions in ibid., 27–8, and Raz (1986), 28–31.

[6] Green (1988), 27.

more natural (than in the previous case) to say that you had acquired a kind of authority over me—and particularly if the promise were not a friendly or gratuitous promise, but, say, were made in payment of a debt. While the "authority" in question is plainly severely limited in both duration and content, what makes it natural to call it authority in the first place is that it consists in a right to *specify* what the precise content of the promissory obligation will be (by specifying what kinds of help will be most useful). While the authority arises from or is grounded in the promise, the precise content of the promise is left open for specification by the one to whom that authority is granted. When I authorize my financial adviser to use her judgment in making investments for me, I make myself responsible for the financial consequences of her decisions. She acquires through my consent the authority to specify what the precise contents of my financial obligations will be.

While practical authority is often characterized as the right to *create* new obligations for others, it is better characterized as the right to specify the content of their already-created, but unspecific, obligations. The authority of a state or government to impose on me a specific (and likely changing) set of legal obligations would most naturally be said to be grounded in some fact about its relationship to me (e.g., that I consented to its authority, or that it benefitted me in ways requiring reciprocation) or in some fact about its virtues (e.g., that it was just or democratic). My generic obligation to the state would have its source in such performances or facts. The state's correlative authority would consist in its right to dictate (no doubt, within limits) what the precise content of my unspecific obligation—my generic obligation to obey the law, or to support and comply with my government—shall be.

However, even agreement on this—on the concept of practical authority as a special right to specify the content of the unspecific or generic obligations of others—leaves ample room for substantive disagreement about the concept of authority, since the term "right" can be used in a variety of ways. Following Hohfeld[7]—whose well-known analysis of legal rights is applicable as well to the analysis of *moral* rights—"right" can refer either simply to the absence of an obligation or duty (on the rightholder) to refrain from doing something—a "privilege" or "liberty right" to act—or to a claim for the rightholder that correlates with the obligations of others not to interfere: a "claim right." Or the right in question could be what Hohfeld called a "power"—namely, a right to alter existing normative relations by changing others' (or one's own) rights or duties. So practical authority could simply be a liberty right to command and coerce others, which others were free to resist if able. Or it might be a claim right to command, which others had a duty to permit the authority to exercise, but with

[7] Hohfeld (1964), 35–64.

those commanded having no duty to comply with the commands. Or, more plausibly, it might be a power to specify binding duties that includes as well a right not to be interfered with (or competed with) in that task. Political authority, for instance, is most often thought of as the state's (or government's, or society's) moral power to specify citizens' legal and political duties (which citizens are morally bound to discharge), free from interfering or competing efforts by other nations (or their citizens) or by rival individuals or groups within the state. This moral power is commonly referred to as the state's or government's "right to rule."

We must draw one final distinction in order to precisely identify the concept of political authority with which we will be dealing below. The term "authority" can refer either to de jure authority—where those with authority actually *possess* the rights in which we have said practical authority consists—or only to de facto authority, where possessing authority consists merely in claiming, exercising, or being generally *believed* (by those subject to the authority or by suitable officials) to possess those rights. When we refer to "the authorities" (in speaking of "the [political and legal] powers that be"), we are usually referring to those who (or those bodies which) possess de facto practical authority, and usually without our making any implicit commitment as to their de jure status. Indeed, "the authorities" may refer only to those assigned authority by the prevailing structure of institutional rules, even where few believe that the institutional structure itself is legitimate (or, worse, only to those who merely wield physical power while *claiming* to possess the authority to do so). De facto authority is nonetheless distinguishable from the *mere* exercise of physical power, where a right to specify duties is neither claimed nor acknowledged.

It is not difficult to find treatments of political and legal authority that focus on de facto authority. For instance, Max Weber's famous discussion of "the three pure types of legitimate authority"—rational or legal authority, traditional authority, and charismatic authority[8]—is a discussion of the unmixed forms of de facto practical authority acknowledged in modern societies. The three types are distinguished according to the kinds of claims to legitimacy made by the different kinds of authority and by the kinds of beliefs of those who regard themselves as subject to the authority. Authority here is simply power accepted as legitimate by those subject to it (and "legitimacy" is correspondingly equated with a general belief in legitimacy[9]). If we are interested in issues of political

[8] Weber (1947), 328.

[9] On the idea of (de jure) political legitimacy that I favor, see Simmons (2001a). While I will employ my account of legitimacy at various points later in this book, I will not discuss legitimacy further in this chapter. Some contemporary authors *identify* political legitimacy with political authority (e.g., Wolff [1998], 4–12), while others try to sharply distinguish the two (e.g., Buchanan [2004],

stability, we will no doubt be interested in questions about de facto authority that is "legitimate" in this sense—that is, in understanding what kinds of claims to authority are regularly accepted as legitimate by subjects.[10] But if we are interested in political *right*—in the moral standing of states or governments and in the moral rights and duties of political life—then we will focus (as we do here) on the idea of de jure authority.

Varieties of Practical Authority: Hobbes and Locke

Instances of practical authority vary considerably in terms of duration, comprehensiveness, and inevitability. Employers, for instance, normally exercise practical authority over their employees, but the domains within which they have authority and the duration of that authority seem almost infinitely variable—compare, say, servants, day-laborers, accountants, federal judges, and so on. Practical authority can be isolated or part of an elaborate and rigid hierarchical structure—as in the hierarchies of legal, military, or religious authority.[11] Our subjection to some kinds of authority is easy to avoid, while subjection to (e.g.) parental or political authority seems virtually inevitable (and subjection to God's authority would be absolutely inevitable). Some philosophers have tried to impose order on this apparent chaos by advancing unified accounts of practical authority—accounts that purport to explain the sources of all of these instances of authority in the same way. And because so many of these kinds of practical authority have been taken to flow from the *consent* of those subjected to them, a consent-based account of authority is a natural candidate for such unification.

Hobbes's theory of (practical) authority is a good example of such a unified, consent-based view. Hobbes writes that "by authority is always understood a right

234–8). Where legitimacy and authority are taken to be identical, of course, accounts of de jure legitimacy vary in the same ways as do the accounts of authority discussed here.

[10] Theories of de jure authority and legitimacy will also, of course, need to consider the stability of the various possible forms and structures of political society. We may, for instance, refuse to count inherently unstable arrangements as legitimate or as yielding genuine practical authority. But authority and legitimacy will not here be simply *equated* with general belief in claims to authority or legitimacy.

[11] In most political societies, practical authority is hierarchical, with political or legal authority establishing the set of duties and rights within whose constraints lower-order practical authorities (such as church leaders, employers, or parents) may permissibly exercise their authority. Genuinely rival practical authorities within the same domains—for instance, lord, king, and pope in medieval society—become unintelligible without some (at least implicit) priority rules or domain rules to preclude rival specifications of the same persons' duties.

of doing any act; and *done by authority*, done by commission or license from him whose right it is."[12] When persons act "with authority," Hobbes suggests, they exercise rights that were originally held by others, rights conferred by those others on the person(s) they authorize to act in their stead. Once authorities are thus created, their actions (in their authorized capacities) should be understood as in fact the actions of those who authorized them: the "words and actions [of authorities are] owned by those whom they represent."[13] Authorization makes us the authors of others' actions, as if those other persons were our puppets or were performing parts we had written for them in a play. But in this case, unlike a real play or a puppet show, "authoring" another's actions instead amounts to our acting *as if* that other's acts were our own by taking responsibility for them in advance: "he is called the author [and] . . . hath declared himself responsible for the action done by another according to his will."[14] So we can hardly complain when our authorities act (or decline to act) within the terms of their "commissions"; their acts (or omissions) are "owned" by us. In the political case, for example, "every subject is . . . author of all the actions and judgments of the sovereign instituted," so that whatever the sovereign chooses to do "can be no injury to any of his subjects."[15]

That authority is created by "license" or "commission," of course, suggests that all authority is grounded in the *consent* of those "for whom" authorities act. This *authorization* view of authority, however, will surely seem an odd view to be embraced by Hobbes, the champion of absolute, unlimited monarchy and apparent proponent of the view that "might makes right." This odd conjunction of views in Hobbes's philosophy is explained by another oddity—by Hobbes's peculiar ideas about when consent may be "presumed" to have been given to the actions of an authority. Consent for Hobbes must, of course, be given *freely*. Otherwise, it is not an act by an agent at all, but only behavior of that agent's body. So "unfree consent" is unintelligible. But freedom, for Hobbes, is the "absence of *external* . . . impediments of motion."[16] *Internal* impediments—such as fear, even if caused by external agents—do not limit freedom. But this means, of course, that *consent* given to another's authority, even if given at sword-point and only out of fear for one's life, is nonetheless *free*, hence binding, consent.[17]

Further, Hobbes's (in)famous mechanistic materialism commits him, he thinks, to a broadly egoistic psychological theory according to which each person is motivated (either always or "predominantly") by her own perceived best

[12] Hobbes (1968), 218 (*Leviathan* 16, 4); see also Hobbes (1972), 84 (*De Homine* 15, 2).

[13] Hobbes (1968), 218 (*Leviathan* 16, 4).

[14] Hobbes (1972), 84 (*De Homine* 15, 2).

[15] Hobbes (1968), 232 (*Leviathan* 18, 6).

[16] Ibid., 261 (*Leviathan* 21, 1 [my emphasis]).

[17] Ibid., 262–3 (*Leviathan* 21, 2–4).

interest.[18] And, for Hobbes, this implies especially that each person, unless confused by religious (or other) claptrap, seeks above all to stay alive. Finally, we are, Hobbes thinks, entitled to infer that, since each always seeks his own continued existence, each may be *presumed* to consent to any arrangement that is necessary to staying alive. If others seek authority over us and are able to *kill* us, we may therefore be presumed to consent to their authority over us: "every man is supposed to promise obedience to him in whose power it is to save or destroy him."[19] And such presumed consent to the authority of the powerful still counts as free and binding, since the only "impediment" to our will is the *internal* (even if supremely influential) impediment of our fear of death. Thus, Hobbes's reputation as a defender of the doctrine that "might makes right" turns out to be a half-truth. Another's might (i.e., his power to dispose of us at will) in fact "makes" our binding (even if only presumed) consent to his authority; and that authority, in turn, renders his actions toward us rightful. All *political* consent, Hobbes claims, "proceed[s] from fear of death," whether the society begins in a "free" contract (by "institution") or in conquest (by "acquisition").[20]

Hobbes applies this same authorization account of authority to all varieties of practical authority, not just political authority. But as a political philosopher, Hobbes is primarily interested in instances of practical authority that—like political authority—are quite comprehensive and largely inevitable. Thus, the central cases he considers (other than political authority) are the practical authority possessed by conquerors, parents, and God. The "despotical" authority (or "dominion") of the conqueror over the conquered derives from the conquered person's agreement to accept servitude in order "to avoid the present stroke of death": "it is not . . . the victory that giveth the right of dominion over the vanquished, but his own covenant."[21] The parental authority of mother over child is based in the child's presumed promise "to obey her, rather than any other," in response to the fact that "the infant is first in the power of the mother, so as she may either nourish or expose it."[22] Even the authority of God is derived by Hobbes from God's "irresistible power," to which "the dominion of all men adhereth naturally."[23]

One of the principal aims of John Locke's *Two Treatises of Government* is precisely to *distinguish* these varieties of de jure practical authority[24] (or moral

[18] Kavka (1986), 50–51.

[19] Hobbes (1968), 254 (*Leviathan* 20, 5).

[20] Ibid., 252 (*Leviathan* 20, 2).

[21] Ibid., 255–6 (*Leviathan* 20, 10–11); Hobbes (1972), 205–8 (*De Cive* 8, 1–5).

[22] Hobbes (1968), 254 (*Leviathan* 20, 5); Hobbes (1972), 211–13 (*De Cive* 9, 1–3).

[23] Hobbes (1968), 397 (*Leviathan* 31, 5); Hobbes (1972), 292 (*De Cive* 15, 5).

[24] Locke does not routinely use the word "authority" in the *Second Treatise*, mostly preferring to use the word "power" to convey the idea of practical authority. He uses the word "authority" often

"power") from one another, both in terms of their sources or grounds and in terms of their contents and limits. And in doing so, Locke rejects Hobbes's unified authorization account of authority, accepting that legitimate practical authority can flow from sources other than an authorizer's explicit or presumed consent. He resists in the process the temptation—to which both Hobbes and Robert Filmer succumbed—to conflate the salient categories of practical authority. Hobbes and Filmer had, in Locke's view, confused both parental and political authority with despotical authority. Hobbes supposed that both parental and political authority must be absolute (like despotical authority), since both arise from a presumed choice of absolute subjection over death. Filmer likewise viewed both as absolute, with both deriving from God's grant to Adam of absolute (despotical) dominion over the earth (with all subsequent political authority—including that of the Stuart monarchs—understood as the inherited political and paternal authority of Adam's descendants). But in fact, Locke argues, parental authority "comes as far short of" political authority, as despotical authority "exceeds it" (II, 174).

For Locke, God's authority over humankind is perfectly *sui generis*, God being the only one with a creator's authority over (or property in) human beings. But the other important kinds of practical authority are different not only from God's, but from each other. Parental authority is that of parents over their children "to govern over them for the children's good, till they come to the use of reason," and it is thus a nonabsolute, severely limited right. God entrusts children to their parents' care, giving parents only those rights over their children that they need to do the "duty which is incumbent on them to take care of their offspring during the imperfect state of childhood" (II, 170, 58). Despotical authority, by contrast, actually is "an absolute, arbitrary power . . . over another"; but it can derive neither simply from superior power nor "from compact" with a powerful conqueror. Rather, "it is the effect only of forfeiture," where an aggressor who makes war on the innocent forfeits all moral standing and makes himself "liable to be destroyed," like "any other wild beast or noxious brute" (II, 172). It is rather *political* authority that "has its original only from compact and agreement, and the mutual consent of those who make up the community." And that consensual authority is limited (by the "voluntary agreement" that creates it) to use "by governors for the benefit of their subjects [and] to secure them in the possession and use of their properties" (II, 171, 173).

in its theoretical (or epistemic) sense in his *An Essay Concerning Human Understanding* and in his writings on religion. The *First Treatise* often contrasts "regal (kingly, royal) authority" and "fatherly (paternal) authority" (e.g., I, 6), while the *Second Treatise* uses "authority" primarily in defining the state of nature and in characterizing our "natural freedom" in terms of the *absence* of authority.

Locke's position on practical authority is in part a response to natural worries about the authorizing force of consent, once one's account of practical authority is no longer conjoined with Hobbes's peculiar conception of freedom. Even if (with Hobbes) we presume consent to one-sided terms by those vanquished in war or by vulnerable children, when we more reasonably (with Locke) take coerced consent or consent by prerational beings to be unfree, and so not to be morally binding (or perhaps not even to count as consent at all, properly understood), any plausible analysis of despotical or parental authority that we give will have to abandon the idea of authority as authorization. If all de jure practical authority derived from the consent of those subject to it, we would need to accept the conclusion that parents have no such authority over their minor children—a conclusion that Locke, with most of his audience, finds unacceptable. Only in the case of political authority does Locke preserve the authorization account favored by Hobbes.[25]

The Grounds of Political Authority: Some Theories

We should not exaggerate, however, the extent to which Locke abandoned Hobbes's authorization account of practical authority. While he offered nonconsensual accounts of divine, despotical, and parental authority, Locke was very much committed to the authorization view—as are most contemporary persons—with respect to the many more mundane instances of practical authority in our lives, such as the authority of employers over their employees, teachers over their students, or military superiors over those of inferior rank. Locke's foundational assertion of our "natural freedom," of our natural moral right to govern ourselves within the bounds of morality, implies that consent-based authority is the most "natural" sort. For while authority always in one way limits our freedom (by making the specification of our duties subject to the will of another), authority that has been authorized by those subject to it can be characterized as "freedom freely surrendered," and so as a *use* of freedom rather than simply an abridgment of it. Indeed, Locke's accounts of divine, despotical, and parental authority, while exceptions to this general rule, are in fact similarly motivated by his focus on individual freedom. Parental authority must be nonconsensual, because children are incapable of genuinely free (rational) choice

[25] For the time being, at least, we can work with the standard notion of "political authority" (or "the right to rule") mentioned above. Political authority, in this sense, is the state's (limited) moral right to specify citizens' legal and political duties, free from interfering or competing efforts by other nations (or their citizens) or by rival individuals or groups within the state.

and can become capable of it only by their subjection to parental rule (II, 61). Despotical authority is the consequence of persons freely abandoning the life of freedom and reason, and their personhood along with it. And the exercise of divine authority over us is what gives us our rights to freedom in the first place.

The consent-based accounts of political authority that drive much of the social contract tradition thus flow from a concern to reconcile a strong presumption in favor of individual freedom with a reasonably comprehensive and inevitable state authority. Consent to authority allows unfreedom to nonetheless flow from the exercise of freedom. The primary question for early modern theorists of authority was not whether freely undertaken restrictions on freedom were binding (or adequately respected individual liberty), but rather just how much freedom could be legitimately surrendered by free consent: whether, for example, slavery or absolute political authority could be legitimated by free consent. But if we assume (with Locke) that there are limits to what free consent can legitimate, the ideal of a voluntary political association yields a natural and compelling account of political authority, along with a correlative account of the political obligations of citizens[26]—understood as obligations to accept the state's (government's, society's) specifications of the general, consensually (or contractually) undertaken moral obligation to support and comply with the state.

Many rival theories of political obligation not based on consent have attempted either to extend the idea of "freely undertaken unfreedom" that motivates consent theories or to identify uncontroversial limits to individuals' rights to freely govern themselves—limits within whose range the state's authority might then be taken to fall. Thus, for instance, accounts that base political obligation on the principle of fairness (or fair play) originally did so by emphasizing that free cooperative activity, even without any consent or promises, can produce obligations to do one's fair share within the cooperative scheme. And reciprocation and associative theories of political obligation argue that individual liberty does not extend so far that it allows us (in the first case) to take the benefits that flow to us from the efforts of others without responding to this benefaction in kind or (in the second case) to ignore the moral requirements of relationships like those with family or friends. These kinds of theories have been discussed extensively,

[26] It is possible, of course, to try to defend an account of political authority that completely decouples it from citizens' political obligations. Robert Ladenson understands political authority (or "the right to rule") as a mere "justification right" (what we called above a Hohfeldian "liberty right") to use coercion against members of the society. As such, political authority implies no duties of allegiance or compliance for those members (Ladenson [1980], 138–41). This is the "thinnest" possible conception of de jure authority, one that actually challenges the distinction between de facto and de jure authority. Most who have commented on Ladenson's views find this conception *too* thin to count as a conception of authority at all—as opposed to simply an account of the justified use of force (e.g., Raz [1986], 25–8).

and I will not explore their relative strengths and weaknesses here.[27] Let us focus instead on another, different way in which political authority might be thought to be potentially in conflict with individual freedom.

Suppose we think of individual freedom as not only a right, which persons may retain or freely transfer (or lay down), as they please—thus creating freely undertaken unfreedom—but also as a *responsibility* belonging to all persons. Since "taking responsibility involves attempting to determine what one ought to do,"[28] the price of real freedom—or *autonomy*—is an obligation to ourselves examine and weigh the reasons that bear on our actions and to follow where the balance of reasons leads. This more robust idea of freedom appears to be suggested in Rousseau and utilized centrally in Kant. If we think we have an obligation to be autonomous, though, we may well think that the demands of practical authority—and, in particular, of political authority—are in direct conflict with this obligation of autonomy: "The defining mark of the state is authority, the right to rule. The primary obligation of man is autonomy, the refusal to be ruled."[29] The Lockean idea that political consent can "preserve and enlarge freedom"—by a free acceptance of general restrictions on freedom (II, 57)—appears suspect if by "freedom" we now mean "autonomy" of the Kantian sort. Political authorities require us to act as and because commanded, which we cannot do while judging for ourselves how best to act.

The central question of political philosophy now becomes: can the exercise of genuine political and legal authority be consistent with lives in which each citizen can still "obey only himself and remain as free as before"?[30] And R. P. Wolff defends a negative answer to this question. There is no "viable form of political association which will harmonize the moral autonomy of the individual with the legitimate authority of the state." Given our primary obligation, we should "embrace philosophical anarchism and treat *all* governments as non-legitimate bodies whose commands must be judged and evaluated in each instance before they are obeyed."[31]

This conclusion, of course, rests on our being bound by an exceptionally strong moral obligation of autonomy. As even Wolff admits, an ideal of *perfect* autonomy might well seem a dubious goal, given that our ability to live our lives well would then be dependent on our acquiring a personal mastery of the myriad practical disciplines within whose domains we all now regularly rely

[27] For discussion of these (and other) theories of political obligation, see Simmons (2008), chap. 3, and Simmons and Wellman (2005), chaps. 5–8.

[28] Wolff (1998), 12.

[29] Ibid., 18.

[30] Rousseau (1997), 49–50 (*Social Contract,* book 1, chap. 6, para. 4).

[31] Wolff (1998), 69, 71.

on the testimony of experts. Worse, even making a simple promise in everyday life appears to violate such an obligation to remain perfectly autonomous, for it gives another the right to determine how we shall act, thus preempting our own judgment about how it is best to act. But neither Rousseau nor Kant, of course, thought that we breached a basic moral obligation by making a promise or contract, nor do the vast majority of moral or political philosophers. Indeed, neither Rousseau nor Kant thought that even mutual promises that create a political society (to which all in consequence owe obligations of support and compliance) necessarily involve any moral wrongdoing. This suggests that Wolff's conception of our obligation of autonomy is too strong to be plausible, that many voluntary sacrifices of autonomy—and the authority for others that these sacrifices may create—are perfectly innocent and uncontroversial.[32]

The defender of one of the most widely discussed contemporary accounts of practical authority accordingly concludes that what is most problematic about authority is *not* that it seems irreconcilable with autonomy. Rather, he argues, the real problem about authority that needs to be addressed is a distinct, though closely related, one. The claims of authority appear, on their face, to require of us a kind of *practical irrationality*. Joseph Raz suggests that what is troubling about authority is that we take authoritative pronouncements as reasons for action of a special sort, a sort that preempts our own judgments about where the balance of reasons lies. We should obey authorities even when we think them mistaken in their commands, thus acting contrary to the perceived balance of reasons that apply to us.[33] Authority seems to require individual irrationality.

Raz responds that this appearance rests on an impoverished (and mistaken) conception of practical reason. Some valid reasons for action are "second order" and "exclusionary"—that is, we sometimes have reasons to act contrary to the "balance of first-order reasons," to exclude their weight in determining what to do.[34] This can be true, for example, where authoritative directives are at issue. Such directives claim to replace and exclude the ordinary reasons for action that should otherwise govern our deliberations. Where there are good grounds for believing that we will do better by complying with an authority's directives than

[32] Indeed, Wolff seems himself unable to resist the apparent moral legitimacy of consensual arrangements, concluding that "a contractual democracy is legitimate, to be sure, for it is founded upon the citizens' promise to obey its commands. Indeed, any state is legitimate which is founded upon such a promise" (Wolff [1998], 69). This, despite his earlier insistence that "the concept of the *de jure* legitimate state would appear to be vacuous" (19).

[33] Raz (1990), 5.

[34] Raz (1979), 27. In order to *apply* such a view, of course, one needs a reasonably detailed account of the relative "weights" of various kinds of reasons (in order to determine just where the "balance" lies).

we would do by relying on the balance of reasons as we perceive it, it is rational to comply with authority, rather than doing what seems best independent of its directives. Authority is then justified or legitimate. In this we see the strongest similarity between practical and theoretical authority. In both cases we can have exclusionary reasons (to act or to believe), because someone's being an authority attests to the existence of such reasons even where we cannot perceive or weigh those reasons.

In the case of *political* authority, of course, we are only likely to do better by complying with its directives where the authorities are in fact aiming to "serve" those subject to authority (Raz's "service conception" of authority) by designing their commands and rules to help their subjects conform their conduct to the reasons that independently apply to them. But where this is the case, treating the government's directives as binding may be the best way to conform to those reasons. Authoritative political or legal directives can then supply reasons that preempt and replace subjects' ordinary reasons for action. Compliance with authority is then practically rational (and obligatory); indeed, it is practically rational even when governmental directives are mistaken and fail to achieve their service-oriented aim.[35] And the authority claimed by government is then justified or legitimate (de jure).

Raz argues that political authority can in fact be justified in this "normal" fashion in several kinds of cases: where the authority is "wiser" than the subject (possessing special expertise the subject lacks); where it has a "steadier will" (one less prone to weakness, bias, etc.) than the subject; where the authority can establish solutions to coordination problems that subjects have difficulty solving for themselves; where self-direction by subjects is very costly or time-consuming (and guidance by the authority has few drawbacks); and where the authority can solve prisoners' dilemma–style problems, in which no individually rational paths to collectively rational solutions are possible.[36]

One obvious consequence of this Razian position on de jure political authority, of course, is that claims to authority, even by apparently similar states or governments, may vary dramatically in terms of their justifiability. Different governments (or the same governments at different times) may have very different ranges of expertise, and their success at generating salient solutions to coordination problems may vary as well. Similarly, different citizens will have both different levels of personal expertise (in various domains) and different kinds of reasons that apply to them independent of authoritative pronouncements. This means, as Raz concedes, that we will have to think about the justification

[35] These remarks have (very) briefly summarized what Raz calls the "dependence" thesis, the "normal justification" thesis, and the "pre-emptive" or "pre-emption" thesis (Raz [1986], 46–59).

[36] Ibid., 75.

of political authority rather differently than we are used to doing.[37] We can no longer think that political authority is either justified or not *simpliciter*. Various aspects of the authority claimed by states may be justified where others are not; and that authority may, in individual states, be justified with respect to some subjects but not others. Perhaps, though, Raz is correct that the all-or-nothing approach in our thinking about political authority needed to be abandoned in any event.

What is less easy to abandon, however, is the idea of a tight connection between justified or legitimate authority and our ordinary understanding of *moral obligation or duty*. For Raz, justified (de jure) authority is (de facto) authority whose directives it is individually rational to *treat as* authoritative.[38] But simple practical rationality is in many cases not regarded by us as *mandatory*. We regularly make and act on choices that are not maximally rational, and we are often taken to be perfectly *entitled* to do so. Unless we think that independent obligations or duties owed *to others* are thereby breached, we do not normally think that any *wrong* is done in so acting. But the Razian "normal justification" of authority makes no distinction between other-regarding and self-regarding reasons for compliance with authority. As a result, in some cases where we would normally think an action only the one most rational for us—but in no way mandatory for us—Raz's theory implies that we are morally required to act, that authorities are justified in "imposing duties" to act. Further (and relatedly), we normally suppose that political authorities are entitled to *enforce* the duties they impose by using coercion; and it is not obvious why Razian "normal justification"—especially where it lacks any entailed wrong to others, involving merely a superior "balance of reasons"—should be thought to legitimate the use of coercion.

One way to try to recapture both the connection with duty or obligation and the justification for coercive enforcement might be to focus on Raz's apparent neglect of the connection between *democracy* and authority, and to try to link authority's binding force and its warrant for coercion to its democratic origins (and thus more firmly to reasons of collective good). Scott Shapiro, for instance, argues that "Raz's theory of authority is flawed because of the inadequate justificatory role that it accords to democratic decision making."[39]

[37] Ibid., 73–8, 100, 104.

[38] Whether it *can* be rational to allow a generalization (that is, *indirect* reasoning) about compliance with reasons—such as the claim that obedience to an authority is likely to better secure such reason-compliance than would individual efforts at compliance—to *exclude* deliberation about any particular acts' direct compliance with those same reasons, is a separate question which I will not attempt to address here. If it cannot, of course, Raz's views on authority must be rejected.

[39] Shapiro (2002), 431.

He rejects Razian "mediation models" of authority (according to which authorities are justified in virtue of serving effectively as "the mediation between reasons and persons") in favor of an "arbitration model," according to which "authorities are legitimate for a given subject just in case acceptance of the process as binding by some of the parties generates a moral obligation for the subject to abide by the outcome." Democratic procedures can produce legitimate, authoritative results because the majority's acceptance of those results gives all parties "reason to accept the outcome of the process."[40] That reason is that democratic procedures "represent power-sharing arrangements that are fair."[41] This arbitration model of political authority, Shapiro claims, "has surely been the dominant account of authority in modern liberal theory," including in its ranks the "social contract theorists" ("such as Hobbes, Locke, and Kant") and "fair play theorists."[42]

While both traditions of thought may involve some notion of "arbitration," there is nonetheless something initially odd about thus grouping together the theories of political authority at work in the classical social contract theories and those from theories of democracy. For there is surely an important difference between grounding authority in subjects' *actual acceptance* of a process and grounding it in their having *reason to accept* that process (which is Shapiro's actual position on the subject). Further, of course, Hobbes, Locke, and Kant all denied that there was anything *naturally* authoritative about democratic decision procedures. Hobbes and Locke both viewed such procedures as producing binding results only for those who had given prior *consent* to membership in a democratically governed group; and even Rousseau, that great champion of democracy, never suggested that democratic procedures produce binding results prior to the social contract which creates political society.

Shapiro's grouping of social contract and democratic theories looks less odd, however, when we consider some contemporary offspring of social contract theory—and, in particular, the political philosophy of John Rawls. Rawls describes his theory of justice as one "which generalizes and carries to a higher level of abstraction the familiar theory of the social contract."[43] But while he finds the contractarian ideal of a fully voluntary political association attractive, Rawls claims that no political society can be a voluntary scheme "in a literal sense."[44] Indeed, as we have seen, Rawls's theory proceeds on the assumption that

[40] Ibid., 433.
[41] Ibid., 432.
[42] Ibid., 432–3.
[43] Rawls (1971), 11.
[44] Ibid., 13.

"political society is closed: we come to be within it and we do not, and indeed cannot, enter or leave it voluntarily."[45] But a society that is just—that offers its members *fair* terms of cooperation—"comes as close as a society can to being a voluntary scheme."[46] So "power-sharing arrangements that are fair" will generate results that are binding on everyone in the society, since each of us has a "natural duty . . . to support and to comply with just institutions that exist and apply to us."[47] The "fundamental organizing idea" of Rawls's theory thus becomes that of "society as a fair system of cooperation between free and equal persons viewed as fully cooperating members of society over a complete life."[48]

Rawls extends here, of course, not the Lockean but the Kantian branch of social contract theory. In Kant's view, we have a basic obligation to join with others to support—or to create where none exist—the political institutions that alone make justice possible, that allow each person "to enjoy his rights."[49] Because the tasks of making justice possible and of resolving basic social disagreements are "urgent" or "necessary"[50]—and because democratic procedures are the best way for a social group to do those tasks—democracy seems to produce legitimate political authority and binding duties of compliance even without individual (or even general) consent to democratic arrangements. Indeed, refusal to consent to such arrangements may itself be morally wrong, as Kant argued.[51]

This Kantian tradition of thought on the subject of political authority will be explored at considerable length in the remainder of this book, as will the Lockean position on political authority with which we began this section. In chapter 2, for instance, we will examine Rawls's theory of the limits on political authority (as these are revealed, primarily, in his account of the justifications for legal disobedience). We will see there the ways in which Rawls's (and Kantians') focus on the justice or injustice of the basic structure of political and economic institutions in society ignores important limits to the state's authority (over both persons and territories) that are set instead by nonstructural *historical* wrongs. Then, in chapter 3, we will see how Kantian "structuralism" or "functionalism"—in which, importantly, I mean to include the wing of Kantian political philosophy that emphasizes the authority inherent in specifically democratic political institutions—finds itself unable to adequately motivate the most intuitively plausible placement of the moral *boundaries* of political societies. These two

[45] Rawls (1993), 136.

[46] Rawls, (1971), 13.

[47] Ibid., 115.

[48] Rawls (1993), 9.

[49] Kant (1991), 120.

[50] Anscombe appeals to "the necessity of a task" to try to explain both political and parental authority (Anscombe [1990]). For doubts about such appeals, see Simmons (2005), 127–42.

[51] Kant (1991), 122.

basic problems—the problems of historical wrongs and of boundary drawing—in turn motivate (in part II) my critique of all of the currently prominent theories of states' territorial rights and my defense of a rival, Lockean theory (which is introduced in chapter 5 and more fully fleshed out in part III). Before proceeding to those tasks, however, I should conclude this chapter with just a few quick words about the relationship between our discussion above of practical and political authority and the understanding of authority in *territorial* terms that will figure centrally in the remainder of the book.

Political Authority and Territory

As we saw above in the introduction, some of the most important rights claimed by states are *territorial* in nature—that is, they are claims to authority over a territory, claims to regulate and control the people and things within a particular geographical space. Thus far, however, we have examined only views of practical authority that treat it as a relation strictly between persons, in which one party (the one in authority) has a right to impose new duties—or, better, to specify the content of unspecific, preexisting duties—on another. The distance between such interpersonal notions of authority and the modern state's claimed territorial authority is in fact neither very great nor very complicated.

Political authority, of course, need not be wielded territorially. Political superiors could (despite the various inconveniences involved) have the right to make and enforce laws for (and demand peaceful compliance from) sets of persons named one by one and without geographical qualification, with claims to land or resources being grounded (if at all) by separate considerations. Prior to the rise of the modern state, political relationships of authority and subjection sometimes approximated this interpersonal model, with allegiances sworn to particular sovereign lords rather than to (territorial) states, countries, or nations.[52] And even today, the authority of the state over its citizens is thought to extend to them "nongeographically"—that is, even when they are outside of the state's claimed domains. The authority of political superiors can also (and was often believed to) extend to individuals not one by one, but *qua* members of some tribe, people, ethnic group, or nation, but again, without specifying any exact or fixed geographical criteria for subjection.

By contrast, part of what makes the modern state distinctive is its use of relatively precise, bounded geographical criteria to specify both the (primary) scope of its authority over persons and the extent of its property-like claims to land and

[52] See Morris (1998), esp. 32–8, and Miller (2007), 215.

other resources. First and foremost, modern states claim jurisdictional political authority over all persons who are within (or, indeed, who are under or over) its claimed territory. As we have seen, there are typically various categories (or degrees of comprehensiveness) of authority at work, which distinguish (e.g.) citizens from tourists, resident aliens, foreign diplomats, or illegal aliens. And these claimed geographical criteria for authority are typically combined with claims to nongeographical ones (such as the authority to punish those who commit crimes against that state's citizens or to punish international criminals on the high seas). But states principally and uniformly claim the jurisdictional right to (in one way or another) make law for and regulate the conduct of—to authoritatively create or specify the duties of—all who come within their territories. It is that geographical conception of political authority on which we will focus in this study.

Exactly how we might *justify* the transition from an interpersonal to a geographical conception of practical (political) authority is, of course, theoretically controversial. There is no doubt that wielding political authority territorially is vastly more convenient than attempting to rule a set of persons who are not territorially concentrated. But administrative convenience and enhanced social utility (through the improved delivery of public goods) are thought by many to be insufficient to establish new claims (or new kinds) of authority. Hobbes and Locke, consequently, took territorial authority to arise not from utility but from tacit consent: the consent that persons give to a political authority when they choose to enter or remain in the geographical territory within which a particular government's law is effectively enforced (this choice being understood to be a choice to "enjoy" the public goods that this government provides for all who come within the areas that the state claims by such provision). Kantians take the state's administration of justice to be sufficient by itself (without individuals' consent) to ground political authority over all within the territory whose affairs are in fact governed by its right-enforcing (and property-defining) institutions. And we will consider still other possibilities as we proceed.

The claim to govern or rule the people within a geographical area is, of course, only part of the right of territorial control claimed by states, with (as we've seen) other claims looking more like property-style claims over the land and resources in or comprising that area. The two sorts of claims to territory—jurisdictional and property-like claims—of course combine in obvious ways in the state's regulation of the uses of land and resources by those who are within its boundaries. Most of this book will focus on the jurisdictional territorial claims made by states, with only part III addressing at length the more property-like territorial claims states make. My hope is that once we fully understand the alleged grounds of states' jurisdictional authority, the answers to our questions about states' property-like claims will be far easier to approach.

2

Disobedience, Nonideal Theory, and Historical Illegitimacy

Justifying Disobedience

Morally legitimate political authorities have the right to impose morally binding legal duties and directives on all who are rightly subject to their authority. There are, of course, both "internal" and "external" limits to such political authority. Internally, there are moral limits to the kinds of laws or policies that may be legitimately imposed, set by the requirements of minimal justice (however that notion is understood). When laws or policies fail to respect these limits, subjects may be justified in disobeying the law. And when those limits are exceeded systematically or egregiously, the moral authority to impose binding duties may be lost altogether. But there are also, of course, "external" limits to a legitimate state's authority that are determined by the "boundaries" of that authority. Only a particular set of persons is subject to any particular state's authority, no matter how just or virtuous that state and its laws may be; outside the boundaries of this group, persons are not "spoken to" by that state's commands, regardless of the character or force of those commands. As we've seen, these external limits to political authority are generally thought to correspond closely, in modern polities, to the state's acknowledged geographical boundaries. By and large, only those persons within a state's claimed territories are claimed as subjects of that state's authority, as bound by its laws.

As we have also seen, due largely to the influence of John Rawls, the preeminent political philosopher of the twentieth century, recent political philosophy has focused primarily on concerns about the internal limits on political authority. Rawls's regular contributions on the subject of civil disobedience within a near-just society were his only substantial philosophical engagements with the problem of limits to the state's authority. But this concentration on the internal limits to authority produced in Rawls, I believe, a theoretical orientation that left his view incapable of dealing adequately with questions about the external limits to authority. And these same problems—caused by an unremittingly "structuralist" or "functionalist" approach to the problem of political authority[1]—are replicated in the contemporary explosion of broadly Kantian political philosophy that followed in Rawls's wake. Or so I will argue, looking in this chapter at Rawls's orientation and in the next at that of the "new Kantians" who followed the theoretical trail Rawls blazed.

When Rawls reinvigorated the contemporary philosophical debate about civil disobedience with his 1969 essay, "The Justification of Civil Disobedience,"[2] he also largely set the terms for subsequent discussions of that subject. Rawls, of course, went on to refine and further defend his account of the nature and justification of civil disobedience in chapter 6 of *A Theory of Justice*; but the basics of the account remained the same as in his earlier essay. Rawls's theory of civil disobedience is firmly embedded in his overall theory of justice, and he discusses civil disobedience only as an issue in "near-just" societies—which for Rawls means constitutional democracies whose basic institutional structures[3] are mostly "well ordered" by the correct (Rawlsian) principles of justice, but which still contain some serious injustices.

According to Rawls, the natural duty of justice (along with what he calls the "duty of civility"[4]) requires that we comply with those laws that apply to us in near-just societies.[5] This implication of the duty, he believes, is uncontroversial in the case of just laws.[6] And legal obedience is generally required even if the

[1] While my meaning in using these terms will become clear as we proceed, I understand them as follows: functionalist theories aspire to ground the state's political authority (its rights) solely in its successful performance of its morally mandated functions. Structuralist theories attempt to ground political authority in the moral character of the structure of the state's basic political and legal institutions. In Kantian (and neo-Kantian) political philosophy, the two views come together: the state's moral mandate is to do justice (or to make justice possible) by imposing a just basic structure of political, legal, and economic institutions. "Functionalist" is the name given to such theories by Annie Stilz in Stilz (2011), 576.

[2] Rawls (1999b), 176–89.

[3] A society's "basic structure" is its "major social institutions," that is its "political constitution and the principal economic and social arrangements" (Rawls [1971], 7).

[4] Ibid., 355.

[5] Exactly when a society counts as being "nearly just" is left extremely vague by Rawls; and that vagueness is accentuated by Rawls's further qualifications, such as "making due allowance for what it is reasonable to expect in the circumstances" and "reasonably just, as estimated by what the current state of things allows" (ibid., 351). Another complication is that a society can be "nearly just" in either of two ways: by having institutions and laws that fall slightly short of a defensible shared public sense of justice (say, a Rawlsian one), or by having institutions and laws that conform perfectly to a defective public sense of justice (352). Rawls focuses on the former case. Of the latter case—where one cannot hope to repair injustice by appealing to the public's sense of justice—Rawls says that we must consider exactly *how* unreasonable the defective sense of justice is; and if it is not *too* unreasonable, we may in fact have a duty to live with our society's injustices and do the best we can.

[6] I challenge even this initial claim in Simmons and Wellman (2005), 158–9, 168–70.

laws in question are unjust, as some laws will inevitably be, even with a nearly just constitution and just legislative procedures. Compliance is here simply part of the cost of making a constitutional democracy work, and all must share this burden—at least, if the injustice in question is not too severe and if the burdens of injustice do not fall too regularly on the same people (e.g., minority groups). This duty to comply, however, appears to conflict with our duty to oppose injustice (along with our right to defend our own liberties). So the central question of Rawls's theory of civil disobedience becomes: when does injustice in a near-just constitutional regime establish a right of (and, further, a justification for) disobedience to unjust law?

Rawls's answer is that one has a *right* to disobey unjust law in a near-just state only when one's disobedience is *civil*—where disobedience takes the form of nonviolent, political, conscientious protest, done openly and addressed to the majority's sense of justice—and only where the injustice in question is clear and substantial, where normal legal appeals have already been made in good faith, and where disobedience will not lead to a breakdown in respect for law. Disobedience so characterized is principled (not merely self-interested) and political (and so a possible part of, rather than antithetical to, ordinary political processes).[7] One is *justified* in acting on this right of civil disobedience only when legal disobedience is conducted reasonably so as to actually assist in achieving the aim of eliminating the injustice in question. Disobedience to law that is limited by these conditions will, Rawls thinks, be consistent with the idea of a constitutional democracy, helping to strengthen the just institutions of society (by making them more just) and focusing public attention on the principles of justice according to which their institutions are structured. Such disobedience cannot endanger the society, for it is undertaken in ways that demonstrate a broader allegiance to law and an acceptance of society's near-just character.[8]

Even operating within the very limited scope of Rawls's account, there are several obvious questions that ought to be raised about it. First, in concentrating solely on the idea of legal disobedience as a way of addressing the public in political terms, Rawls seems to ignore two motives for legal disobedience that seem both perfectly justifiable and to frequently guide the choices of actual practitioners of civil disobedience: namely, the desire to frustrate evil (as in Gandhi's

[7] Rawls contrasts "civil disobedience," so understood, with what he calls "conscientious refusal"—that is, "noncompliance with a more or less direct legal injunction or administrative order," where the noncompliance is "not necessarily based on political principles" and is not "a form of address appealing to the sense of justice of the majority" (Rawls [1971], 368–9).

[8] The paragraph above summarizes (with nearly unconscionable brevity) the arguments of *A Theory of Justice*, sections 55, 57, and 59.

campaigns) and the desire to avoid complicity in injustice or wrongdoing (as in Thoreau's disobedience). Is it obvious that "nonpolitical" legal disobedience originating in such concerns, even in a near-just state, will always be morally indefensible? Second, if such reasons for noncompliance are (as I believe them to be) often defensible, it is further unclear why legal disobedience (in a nearly just state) should always be open and public, with "fair notice" given in advance. Our morally respectable desire (or perhaps our moral duty) to avoid complicity in wrongdoing (by, say, refusing to pay a legally prescribed tax that supports an unjust policy) seems adequate by itself to justify legal disobedience. Why should open acceptance of (perhaps quite harsh) legal punishment be necessary to justify it? And the laudable goal of frustrating evil or unjust policies is seldom very effectively advanced by announcing in advance the time, place, and manner of planned legal disobedience.

Further, it seems possible to question even the most basic (and perhaps the most widely shared) of Rawls's assumptions—that disobedience in a near-just state must always be nonviolent. Rawls's own commitment to this view is not motivated by any prior commitment to pacifism (like that of Gandhi or King). It is motivated rather by his other requirements that legal disobedience be a political act, addressed to the public. One cannot, Rawls thinks, address the public with violence; violence constitutes an assault, not a conversation. And violent acts, far from being political (that is, "fitting" usefully within a framework of basically just political institutions), in fact are antithetical to and express contempt for law and politics (which are premised on limiting threats and uses of violence to the legal institutions charged with maintaining order).

However, once we question (as we have just done) the Rawlsian requirements that defensible legal disobedience be public and political, we also threaten Rawls's principal rationale for the non-violence clause. But even if we instead accept Rawls's ("public and political") requirements, it is simply not at all clear why violent acts could not be addressed to the public in the right way—as an attempt, say, to get the majority to reconsider its position on the justice of some policy. Indeed, it is not evident (to me at least) why an act of violence must always fail the test of counting as an appropriately political act, by necessarily expressing contempt or diminished respect for law and politics—especially if the violent act is carefully presented to the public as protest, if it is isolated (an unusual act in an otherwise nonviolent life), if it has been preceded by passive political efforts, and if it is followed by nonevasion and acceptance of punishment. Further, it just seems generally implausible to suppose that in the face of significant injustice, even in an otherwise just society, violence—and especially violence against *property* only—could never be morally justified if it were likely to be effective in its aims. Violence against *persons* will obviously always be harder to morally justify. But it again seems far from obvious that some such violence—say, kidnaping a public official who is instrumental in administering an unjust policy—could never be both effective and morally justifiable.

All of this can be argued even within the primary Rawlsian terms of the debate over civil disobedience. David Lyons has characterized those terms as follows:

> True civil disobedients are supposed by theorists to regard the systems under which they live as morally flawed but basically just and requiring modest reform rather than fundamental change. Evidence of this outlook is seen in the disobedients' nonviolent methods and use of moral suasion rather than violent rebellion. Their submitting to arrest and punishment is taken as further evidence of respect for legal authority and recognition of a moral obligation to obey.[9]

But, as Lyons goes on to show, these assumptions about their positions and attitudes were in fact false with respect to the paradigmatic practitioners of civil disobedience, including Thoreau, Gandhi, and King. Since Gandhi was not confronting a constitutional democracy—and since King's position has been ably discussed by Lyons—I will in this chapter use Thoreau's "civil disobedience" as my principal example. But my aim here will not be merely to demonstrate the ways in which Thoreau's stance departs from that of the "true civil disobedient," aptly characterized above by Lyons. Rather, I aim to use the example of Thoreau to demonstrate the broader inadequacy of the Rawlsian conception of nonideal theory within which Rawls's account of civil disobedience is developed.

Accordingly, I discuss Thoreau's position as an illustration in the next section. I then use that illustration to motivate my exploration of the nature and limits of the Rawlsian nonideal theory of justice in the following two sections. To be clear: my intention here is to discuss only deliberate, principled, plainly illegal conduct. I will not be considering cases of lawful protest or resistance, unintentional disobedience, disobedience flowing from confusion or factual error, disobedience to "laws" which have unclear status, or plainly unprincipled (e.g., merely self-interested or malicious) illegal conduct. I shall also leave to one side the more difficult case of "principled" disobedience that is based on plainly invalid principles, such as the white supremacist's legal disobedience aimed at changing racially equitable social policies. I shall ask only: supposing that the disobedient person is correct in her diagnosis of the relevant social ills and is acting in the name of defensible moral or political principles, how should we understand the possible objects of any justified legal disobedience?

[9] Lyons (1998), 39.

An Example: Thoreau on the State's Authority

Henry David Thoreau, the person generally credited with coining the term "civil disobedience"—and the person whose writings were identified by both Gandhi and King as a significant influence on their own thought—was neither practicing nor trying to justify the kind of "civil disobedience" discussed by Rawls.[10] In Thoreau's 1849 essay "Civil Disobedience,"[11] he is, of course, protesting injustice—in particular, the injustices done by his nation in its legal recognition of human slavery (and the slave trade), in its treatment of Native Americans, and in its shamelessly acquisitive war on Mexico.[12] But he also makes it quite clear that his were not acts of legal disobedience that were undertaken by one committed to demonstrating his general fidelity to law or his continuing allegiance to his government. On the contrary, Thoreau argues that "his" government and law have no legitimate claim to his obedience or support at all. Far from being the civilly disobedient protester discussed in the literature spawned by Rawls's treatments,[13] Thoreau held a view of his legal disobedience that may in fact be closer to that of contemporary "philosophical anarchists" like Robert Paul Wolff.[14] While Rawls and those who use or engage his account are, of course, free to use the term "civil disobedience" as they choose, their discussion thus threatens to be irrelevant to any analysis of the arguments of those we think of as the paradigmatic practitioners of civil disobedience.

Thoreau's radicalism has usually been obscured in philosophical discussions of his thought. There are, I think, two natural—but in the end both at least incomplete—ways in which Thoreau's stance on civil disobedience has usually been read. First, we might suppose that Thoreau's view is that legal disobedience

[10] Rawls acknowledges that Thoreau's ("traditional") understanding of "civil disobedience" encompasses both what Rawls calls "civil disobedience" and what Rawls calls "conscientious refusal" (Rawls [1971], 368). I focus here on deeper disagreements between Thoreau and Rawls.

[11] The essay was originally published in 1849 under the title "Resistance to Civil Government" and only later renamed "Civil Disobedience"—by the editor of a posthumous collection of Thoreau's writings (who claimed, however, that Thoreau had himself renamed the essay before his death). The written essay was based on Thoreau's 1848 public lecture in Concord, which was titled "The Rights and Duties of the Individual in Relation to Government" and was designed to explain to his neighbors his reasons for refusing to pay his legally required poll tax (which had gone unpaid for six consecutive years at the time of his arrest). As a result of that refusal, Thoreau was arrested and spent one night in jail—a night which was, by his own account, a happy and interesting one. His edifying incarceration was cut disagreeably short when an "interfering" aunt paid his taxes for him.

[12] "Have [all these soldiers] been trained merely to rob Mexico and carry back fugitive slaves to their masters?" (Thoreau (2000), "Slavery in Massachusetts").

[13] See Rosenblum (1996), xxiv.

[14] On the possible forms of and justifying arguments for "philosophical anarchism," see Simmons (2001b).

is morally justified either where the laws disobeyed are themselves intolerably unjust or where obedience to law would (in some reasonably direct fashion) facilitate or support the state's unjust policies. Otherwise, however, legal obedience is morally required. Tax resistance like Thoreau's, on this reading, is permissible where those taxes can be reasonably expected to support injustice (as Thoreau believed to be true in his case); but it is impermissible where they cannot be. So this first reading has Thoreau accepting the idea that even in a society with some seriously or deeply unjust laws or policies, there is still a generic moral obligation to obey the law (where doing so does not give direct support to that injustice) and to help to uphold the state's just policies and laws.

The second, more radical (but equally natural) reading of Thoreau takes him to be arguing that the unjust policies and laws of the United States had exceeded morally tolerable limits and that the state had, in enforcing and pursuing such laws and policies, simply rendered itself morally illegitimate. In doing so, the state had deprived itself of the moral authority to impose on its citizens any obligations of obedience or support whatsoever, leaving them all (morally speaking) to their own devices. When a state's injustices exceed reasonable limits, the argument would go (sounding now rather like one of Locke's arguments), governments forfeit the rights with which they were entrusted and no longer have any moral standing beyond that of a powerful bully. This second reading (correctly, in my view) presents Thoreau as denying not just the moral authority of particular American laws, but the moral authority of his government itself. But, I will suggest, even this more radical reading of Thoreau is still insufficiently radical to do full justice to Thoreau's critique of his state and his defense of his legal disobedience.

Because the second reading of Thoreau presents his views as more radical than his popular reputation suggests, the first reading has been more common. For instance, I think the first reading probably lies behind Hugo Bedau's treatment of Thoreau in a well-known article on civil disobedience. Bedau focuses in his discussion of Thoreau on what he calls "Thoreau's principle," that is, on Thoreau's insistence that "what I have to do is to see that I do not lend myself to the wrong which I condemn."[15] Thoreau's refusal to pay his taxes was, Bedau argues, a refusal to participate in the state's injustices against third parties (since Thoreau knew that his tax money would be used by his government to carry out unjust policies), and so constituted a strategy for avoiding partial responsibility for those wrongs. This, Bedau argues, is a justification for the use of "indirect" civil disobedience that offers a plausible defense of such practices—that is, a plausible defense against those who maintain that only "direct" civil

[15] Thoreau (1996), 9 ("Civil Disobedience"); Bedau (1991), 53.

disobedience (which violates only the actual unjust law that is being protested), and never indirect disobedience, can be morally justified.

While Bedau has no doubt identified one of Thoreau's concerns about paying taxes to an unjust government, Thoreau's position was more complicated than Bedau's observations suggest. Bedau, for instance, goes on to worry that tax resistance of this sort is in fact an undesirably "blunt" instrument to properly sever the links of our responsibility for unjust government policies, since it also unfairly severs our ties to the *just* policies and practices of our government.[16] But Bedau's concern on that point clearly misses Thoreau's aim, which was precisely to deny the authority of United States over him and to deny any duty of allegiance to its government. Thoreau was arguing that he should be understood to have abandoned all ties between him and "his" country, in consequence of which he can be held to bear no responsibility for any of its actions or policies, unjust *or* just.

This, of course, seems to characterize Thoreau's position in a way that is more consistent with the second, more radical, reading suggested above. But that reading is still not, as I have said, radical enough. According to the second reading, it is the state's unjust laws and policies that have delegitimated it. To maintain (or regain) its moral authority, that state need only avoid (or rectify) such injustice, leaving its moral standing "in its own hands," as it were. But Thoreau's arguments include suggestions that the state's legitimacy or authority depends less on what the state itself does than on the wills or the independent obligations of the state's subjects. Thoreau makes two such claims, both of which would make his argument more radical than and clearly logically distinct from any argument that simply ties the state's moral authority to the presence or absence of intolerable injustice.

The first of these claims makes the state's authority and the subject's political obligations a function of individual *consent*. Thoreau insists that *his* political obligations and the authority of the state over *him* can derive only from his own personal consent, a consent which he may never have given in the first place or which may have been withdrawn because of his perception of, or voided by the fact of, severe governmental injustice: "The authority of government, . . . to be strictly just, . . . must have the sanction and consent of the governed. It can have no pure right over my person and property but what I concede to it."[17] Given that the injustice of politically sanctioned human slavery (along with the abuse of Native Americans) not only predated Thoreau's birth but is repeatedly mentioned by him as the source of his refusal of consent ("I cannot for an instant recognize the political organization as *my* government which is the

[16] Bedau (1991), 65–6.

[17] Thoreau (1996), 20 ("Civil Disobedience"): "I, Henry Thoreau, do not wish to be regarded as a member of any incorporated society which I have never joined" (13).

slave's government also"[18]), it may be that Thoreau took himself *never* to have consented to the authority of his government over him. Or perhaps he takes himself to have given and then legitimately withdrawn that consent (or to have given only a conditional consent, whose conditions were exceeded by severe societal injustice).[19]

In any event, Thoreau presumably regards the same consent-style argument as applicable to the positions of all of his fellow citizens (the individuals who constitute the "higher and independent power" from which all of the state's "own power and authority are derived"[20]), which might imply governmental illegitimacy with respect to either many or all of those citizens.

Whether or not Thoreau believed that his fellow citizens had never really consented at all, he was well known for believing at least that his neighbors should withdraw their consent and, when appropriate, disobey as he had done: recall the oft-quoted (but probably apocryphal) exchange between a distressed Emerson and an untroubled Thoreau in the Concord jail: "Henry, why are you here?"; "Waldo, why are you *not* here?" It is less clear (as we will see) where Thoreau stood on the question of whether all United States citizens should withdraw their consent if their doing so would result in the collapse of the United States, rather than merely in its reform.

The second, still more radical, claim made by Thoreau is that political allegiance and state authority conflict with our more fundamental moral obligation to act rightly—that is, to act in accordance with our own, not our society's (or the majority's), judgment of where the right lies: "I think that we should be men first, and subjects afterward. It is not desirable to cultivate a respect for the law, so much as for the right. The only obligation which I have a right to assume, is to do at any time what I think right."[21] On this point, Thoreau stands on familiar *anarchist* ground, denying that the state's demand for *obedience* could ever be legitimate.[22]

[18] Ibid., 4. Of the governor of his state, Thoreau writes "He was no Governor of mine. He did not govern me" (Thoreau [2000], 699 ["Slavery in Massachusetts"]).

[19] "Let each inhabitant of the State dissolve his union with her, as long as she delays to do her duty" (Thoreau [2000)], 709 ["Slavery in Massachusetts"]).

[20] Thoreau (1996), 21 ("Civil Disobedience").

[21] Ibid., 2. "I would remind my countrymen that they are to be men first, and Americans only at a late and convenient hour" (Thoreau [2000], 707 ["Slavery in Massachusetts"]). "What right have *you* to enter into a compact with yourself that you *will* do thus or so, against the light within you? Is it for *you* to *make up* your mind . . . and not accept the convictions that are forced upon you . . .?" (Thoreau [1996], 156 ["A Plea for Captain John Brown"]).

[22] Thoreau's relationship to anarchism is a subject of some controversy. He is often mentioned as one of the American fathers of "individualist anarchism" (along with the so-called Boston anarchists, including Tucker and Spooner). But it is just as frequently denied that Thoreau was any sort of anarchist: see, e.g., Rosenblum (1996), xix; and Simon (1984). In the opening paragraphs of "Civil Disobedience," Thoreau is plainly distancing himself from *one sort* of anarchism—namely,

He anticipates Robert Wolff's virtually identical assertion of an "absolute obligation" of personal "autonomy,"[23] discussed in chapter 1, and he echoes William Godwin's related concern that any duty of political allegiance would conflict with our fundamental moral duty to promote utility and with each individual's right to privately judge the actions mandated by the utilitarian calculus. Here the idea is that any sort of generic, content-independent obligation to obey the law—including an obligation to obey all *just* laws, or to obey all laws that are simply within a tolerable distance from the just—is inconsistent with our more fundamental moral obligations.[24] So such an obligation of legal obedience simply cannot exist, however hard we might try to undertake or impose it. Laws *must* be complied with only where the acts (or omissions) they require are independently morally obligatory, and they *may* be complied with only where they require acts that are independently morally permissible. But *obedience* to law, where "obedience" is strictly construed, cannot be morally required at all. This line of argument not only constitutes a defense of anarchism, it makes the truth of anarchism knowable a priori. *No* state, no matter how just it might be, could claim genuine moral authority to impose on its subjects moral obligations of legal obedience.

Like a contemporary philosophical anarchist, Thoreau is not unwilling to acknowledge the obvious virtues of the United States,[25] nor does he deny that the state may be useful in various ways. Indeed, he intends to make good use of his state where doing so advances his purposes. Thoreau, rather dramatically,

the Christian anarchism of Garrison and his abolitionist followers, who were pacifist "non-resisters" (because of God's prohibitions on violence) and "no-government men" (rejecting the state because of the superiority of God's claims to control over man to those made by government). But Thoreau *is*, I believe, defending another, more "philosophical" sort of anarchism—one that acknowledges the potential usefulness of the state ("government is at best but an expedient" [Thoreau {1996}, 1]) and that denies any moral imperative to do away with states ("I ask for, not at once no government, but *at once* a better government" [2]), but that maintains nonetheless the moral *illegitimacy* of the state's demand for obedience (as I argue in the text below). We may not yet be ready to live without government. But: " 'That government is best which governs not at all'; and when men are prepared for it, that will be the kind of government which they will have" (1).

[23] Wolff (1998). Wolff says, as we saw in chapter 1, that "the primary obligation of man is autonomy" (18), which obligation he characterizes in terms of "taking responsibility for one's actions," refusing "to be subject to the will of another," and never neglecting the task "of attempting to ascertain what is right" (13–14). Compare Thoreau: "What is it to be born free and not to live free? What is the value of any political freedom, but as a means to moral freedom?" (Thoreau [1996], 117 ["Life without Principle"]).

[24] And these obligations are ubiquitous: "Our whole life is startlingly moral" (Thoreau [2000], 206). "It is not for a man to put himself in such an attitude to society, but to maintain himself in whatever attitude he find himself through obedience to the laws of his being" (302).

[25] "The Constitution, with all its faults, is very good; the law and the courts are very respectable; even this State and this American government are, in many respects, very admirable and rare things, to be thankful for . . ." (Thoreau [1996], 18 ["Civil Disobedience"]).

claims "I quietly declare war with the State, after my fashion, though I will make what use and get what advantage of her I can, as is usual in such cases."[26] He is principally concerned to deny only that the United States has legitimate authority with respect to him and that it may justifiably demand his obedience.[27] He thus declares his intention "to refuse allegiance to the State, to withdraw and stand aloof from it effectually."[28] Thoreau will comply with law only in a selective fashion, as the right permits, confident that he can discharge his moral obligations as a person (as well as his duties as a neighbor) without accepting either membership in the political society or its demanded obligations of compliance and support.

Thoreau's declaring his willingness to quietly "use" the state that illegitimately coerces him, rather than his advocating for or engaging in revolutionary activity against the state, highlights the principal respect in which Thoreau's is a more "philosophical" brand of anarchism (in contrast with the familiar caricature of anarchists as "bomb-throwers"[29]). Thoreau seems to allow both (a) that his obligations to his fellow humans and his duties to his neighbors set limits on permissible strategies of disobedience, and (b) that the state's illegitimacy with respect to him does not require him (or anyone else) to actively oppose or attempt to do away with that state. Less plausibly, perhaps, he also seems to take his obligations and duties to be at least primarily negative—that is, to be requirements only to refrain from directly harming others or from participating in activities that do harm to them. Not only does he not take himself to be obligated to actively oppose the state that illegitimately coerces him, he appears not to take himself to be bound even to try to actively oppose the injustices that led him to withdraw his consent to his government's political authority over him: "It is not a man's duty, as a matter of course, to devote himself to the eradication of any, even the most enormous wrong; he may still properly have other concerns to engage him; but it is his duty, at least, to wash his hands of it, and . . . not to give it practically his support."[30] Thoreau was, of course, raised in an abolitionist household (that served as a refuge for fugitive slaves), and he became himself increasingly active in the abolitionist movement in New England in his later years. But he seemed never to regard such positive involvement as each person's moral duty. At the

[26] Ibid., 17.

[27] In *Walden*, Thoreau says that he was arrested because he "did not . . . recognize the authority of . . . the state which buys and sells men, women, and children, like cattle at the door of its senate-house" (Thoreau [2000], 162).

[28] Thoreau (1996), 17 ("Civil Disobedience").

[29] Of his jailing and his possible responses to it, Thoreau says "It is true, I might have resisted forcibly with more or less effect, might have run 'amok' against society; but I preferred that society should run 'amok' against me, it being the desperate party" (Thoreau [2000], 162).

[30] Thoreau (1996), 7 ("Civil Disobedience").

very least, though, we should take Thoreau to be subscribing to the Rawlsian view that our natural duty of justice is limited by a cost-qualifier, that we need not "further just arrangements" beyond that point where we can do so "without too much cost to ourselves."[31]

There is one final respect in which the civil disobedience defended and practiced by Thoreau was plainly unlike the kind of civil disobedience discussed by Rawls (and his interlocutors). While Thoreau was, of course, concerned that his conduct toward his neighbors should be suitably "neighborly," it is unlikely that the "civil" in Thoreau's term "civil disobedience" was intended by him to refer to forms of obedience that were appropriately neighborly, peaceful, or otherwise characterized by any special kind of "civility." Our inclination to regard Thoreau as so motivated seems less a matter of our reading his texts than one of our reading back into those texts the commitments to pacifism and nonviolence with which many of the more recent campaigns of civil disobedience (such as those of Gandhi and King) have been associated. Thoreau's first title for the published essay was simply "Resistance to Civil Government," in which the "civil" clearly refers to the sort of institution at which the disobedience was directed, not the kind of disobedience employed. Though Thoreau disobeyed peacefully and went quite contentedly to jail for it, he was by no means obviously committed, at least as any matter of principle, to nonviolence in protesting or combating injustice.[32] Indeed, he strongly praised the "noble" (and, of course, quite violent) actions of John Brown, which in Thoreau's view "earned immortality" for Brown and finally cast their shared abolitionist cause "in the clearest light that shines on this land."[33]

Nonideal Theory and Principles for Individuals

Rawls's discussion of civil disobedience (and conscientious refusal) in *A Theory of Justice* stands out from the bulk of that work—as well as from Rawls's entire body of philosophical writings—in two ways. First, most of Rawls's work concerns the principles of justice for the basic structure of society, those principles that should shape society's fundamental political, legal, and economic institutions. These are principles that are not directly applicable to the conduct of

[31] Rawls (1971), 115.

[32] "Show me a free state, and a court truly of justice, and I will fight for them, if need be" (Thoreau [2000)], 711 ["Slavery in Massachusetts"]); "I do not wish to kill nor be killed, but I can foresee circumstances in which both these things would be by me unavoidable" (Thoreau [2000)], 153 ["A Plea for Captain John Brown"]).

[33] Thoreau (1996), 169 ("The Last Days of John Brown").

private individuals, including conduct involving individual disobedience to law. Rawls's treatment of civil disobedience, by contrast, is said by him to be part of his explication of what he calls "principles for individuals."[34] Second, where Rawls's philosophical work concentrated throughout on the "ideal theory" of justice, his discussion of civil disobedience was (until *The Law of Peoples*) Rawls's only serious foray into what he called the "nonideal theory" of justice. As Rawls gradually recast the arguments of *A Theory of Justice*, first to shape them into a more straightforwardly "political conception" of justice and then to extend them to the domain of international relations, the nature of the distinction between ideal and nonideal theory, I think, grew clearer. At the same time, however, the role of the "principles for individuals" in Rawls's theory of justice grew progressively more obscure.

Rawls introduced the distinction between ideal and nonideal theory in order to structure his ideas about the relationships between philosophical theory and political practice.[35] Like so many of the distinctions he first drew, this one is now widely employed, with the language of ideal and nonideal theory now a commonplace in moral and political philosophy. The basic distinction seems simple and uncontroversial: Rawls proposes to "split the theory of justice into two parts."[36] The first—ideal—part of the theory identifies and defends the principles of justice according to which a perfectly just society would be ordered. Assuming "strict compliance" with the principles (but otherwise taking full account of the most intractable features of humans' moral and psychological characters and the facts about the ways in which social institutions must accommodate them), we ask which principles of justice ought to guide the design and operation of the basic structure of a society. This "ideal part presents a conception of a just society that we are to achieve if we can. Existing institutions are to be judged in the light of this conception."[37] Ideal theory thus specifies the institutional shape of what Rawls later came to call "a realistic utopia."[38]

Nonideal theory, taking this ideal of social justice as its long-term goal or target, then identifies and defends the principles that should guide our actions

[34] Rawls (1971), 333.

[35] Some of the following summarizes the much more detailed treatment of Rawls's ideal and nonideal theories in Simmons (2010), 5–36. I should note that I there (and in this book) accept and defend Rawls's view of the basic nature of and the relationship between ideal and nonideal theory in political philosophy. It is only with the specific content or substance of Rawls's ideal and nonideal theories that I quarrel here. I argue later (in parts II and III) for a Lockean version of ideal and nonideal theory, but it is a version that accepts both Rawls's "target" characterization of ideal theory and his "transitional" version of nonideal theory (which are explained below).

[36] Rawls (1971), 245.

[37] Ibid., 246.

[38] Rawls (1999a), 7.

and policies in our discharging of our "natural duty of justice"—that is, our duty "to support and to comply with just institutions that exist and apply to us" and "to further just arrangements not yet established."[39] Nonideal theory "looks for courses of action that are morally permissible and politically possible as well as likely to be effective"[40] in advancing us toward a perfectly just social arrangement. Like ideal theory, nonideal theory will thus require both normative and empirical input, including specific empirical facts about the society under consideration as well as more generally applicable social-scientific data. Wherever "here" happens to be, nonideal theory provides philosophical guidance concerning how various agents ought to try to get from "here" to the target ideal of social justice. Nonideal theory is thus a *transitional* theory, consisting of principles to guide the transition from here to there. And because Rawls takes civil disobedience to have as its goal the improvement of near-just social institutions, nonideal theory will include the principles that should guide the actions of civil disobedients. But because societies are not always (or even commonly) nearly just, nonideal theory must also include principles governing actions aimed at more radical or revolutionary social change.

The ideal theory of *A Theory of Justice* is actually more complex than suggested above, for it appears to be divided into three parts, only the first of which is discussed at length in the book. Rawls divides "the concept of right" into three kinds of principles (each set of principles being, in "justice as fairness," the subject of a separate choice for original position contractors): the principles for "social systems and institutions," those for "individuals," and those for "the law of nations."[41] The two principles of justice, explained and defended at great length by Rawls in *A Theory of Justice*, are the principles for the first ("social systems and institutions") part of ideal theory. And the principles for the law of nations are eventually described and defended by Rawls (as the choice that would be made in a second kind of original position) in *The Law of Peoples*. But by the time we get to *The Law of Peoples*, we find Rawls saying that ideal theory has only "*two* parts":[42] the principles for the basic structure of a perfectly just liberal society and the principles for a just international "society of peoples." The "principles for individuals"—including those that apparently formed the basis for Rawls's earlier account of justified civil disobedience and conscientious refusal—seem to have been lost somewhere in the transition.

In *A Theory of Justice*, Rawls describes the principles for individuals as consisting of "the principle of fairness" (under which fall all "obligations"—that is,

[39] Rawls (1971), 115.

[40] Ibid., 89.

[41] Ibid., 109.

[42] Rawls (1999a), 4–5 (my emphasis).

all voluntarily assumed moral requirements arising from special relationships or transactions)[43] and the various principles that define our "natural duties." These duties importantly include the natural duty of justice (which underlies Rawls's defense of civil disobedience), but include as well our duties not to injure the innocent and to give mutual aid and respect.[44] What became of this portion of Rawls's ideal theory? I think the likeliest explanation is that as Rawls developed justice as fairness into a purely "political conception of justice," he came to think of these principles for individuals as part of the kind of "comprehensive conception" that he wished to reject. The political conception of justice as fairness treats its principles as parts of an autonomous domain of moral philosophy, distinct from and in no way derived from more general moral principles that would be applicable to individuals' private lives. But the "natural" duties to aid and to refrain from injuring others have the look of parts of a moral theory of "natural law" (or of some other kind—perhaps a Kantian kind or a religious kind—of comprehensive moral theory), a theory applicable to persons both in and out of political society, in both their private and their public lives.

Once Rawls had elected (in the papers leading up to *Political Liberalism*) to defend the principles for society's basic structure as only "reasonable" (for a liberal society with a shared liberal political culture), rather than as parts of a "true" comprehensive moral theory, it may have seemed to him that the principles for individuals—and especially the natural duties—ought to be jettisoned as now-unnecessary parts of his abandoned comprehensive moral theory of "rightness as fairness."[45] Thus, by the time of *The Law of Peoples*, the principles for individuals are nowhere in evidence. They do make a kind of brief reappearance in a new guise in *Justice as Fairness: A Restatement*, where Rawls again describes "three levels of justice": "first, local justice (principles applying directly to institutions and associations); second, domestic justice (principles applying to the basic structure of society); and finally, global justice (principles applying to international law)."[46] While Rawls is not entirely clear about what he means by "local justice," he appears to be thinking of special principles of justice that govern our "substructural level" voluntary arrangements and associations. While local associations are, as Rawls explains, constrained and limited by the broader principles of domestic justice—so that we may not associate in ways prohibited by just institutions of the basic structure—there are additional moral constraints (of justice) on how local associations may operate (without which there would, of course, *be* no "third level" of justice, no third group of principles, at all).

[43] Rawls (1971), 111.

[44] Ibid., 109.

[45] Ibid., 17.

[46] Rawls (2001), 11.

Rawls does not tell us what principles of "local justice" might look like, but a natural conjecture is that a central principle would be something like the principle of fairness—the principle that specifies that we must honor our agreements[47] and do our fair shares within cooperative schemes (that is, within voluntary local associations and institutions).[48] If so, then one part of Rawls's earlier "principles for individuals" has reemerged, but only under a heading that appears designed to distance the principle of fairness from any more general (or comprehensive) moral theory that might be taken to apply as well to our more private lives. Rawls now has his theory of justice require fairness only in our more "institutional" interactions with others. Oddly, this way of reintroducing the principles for individuals again appears to commit Rawls to abandoning his efforts to offer theoretical guidance to practitioners of civil disobedience and conscientious refusal. For those activities plainly need not be undertaken through anything that qualifies as a local "association" or "institution," meaning that they will not necessarily fall within the domain of "local justice," as Rawls describes it.

Even more oddly, this entire strategy of avoidance in the "progress" of Rawls's theory of justice seems to me entirely unnecessary. For we can surely accept (though I, myself, do not) Rawls's insistence on the autonomy of political philosophy—accept his insistence that we sharply separate the theory of social justice from the principles of interpersonal morality[49]—without abandoning the idea of principles for individuals as a (third) part of the ideal theory of justice. All that is necessary is that we construe the principles for individuals not as moral principles for individuals *qua* persons, but only as principles requiring just conduct by individuals in their roles as citizens of just societies. The original position contractors will presumably be interested (just as Rawls argued in *A Theory of Justice*) not only in the ways in which their basic institutions are structured, but also in the ways that individuals behave in their institutional roles or in their public roles as citizens. And the principles for individuals originally defended by

[47] In *A Theory of Justice*, Rawls argues that "the principle of fidelity [which requires the keeping of promises] is but a special case of the principle of fairness applied to the social practice of promising" (Rawls [1971], 344).

[48] The kinds of local institutions or associations Rawls has in mind would presumably have to be voluntary ones, since justified use of coercion is the special province of the political or legal institutions at the level of the basic structure.

[49] This separation is, of course, a result of Rawls's worries that a defensible conception of justice must be *stable* (and "stable for the right reasons"). If we defend justice as fairness as a *true* conception of justice, derived from more comprehensive true moral principles (say, principles defining the natural rights of persons), those who embrace competing comprehensive principles (say, utilitarian ones or those of some religious ethic) must reject justice as fairness. That conception cannot then serve as a *public* conception of justice which we can expect to be endorsed and supported by all reasonable members of the society. It can at best generate its own support as the subject of a shared *modus vivendi*, rather than being regarded by all as the *best* conception of justice for their society.

Rawls seem a particularly likely expression of this latter interest. A just society requires that its citizens acknowledge both special, voluntarily assumed obligations of certain kinds (including those created by the oaths of office of those citizens who become public officials) and various nonvoluntary ("natural") duties (including the duty to support and comply with the state's just institutions). Nothing in the acceptance of such principles of justice for individuals seems (to me, at least) in any way at odds with the "political turn" in Rawls's thought. If so, then we should expect that even a "fully developed" (i.e., "political, not metaphysical") Rawlsian theory will indeed include the kinds of moral principles that Rawls claims are directly at issue in the justifications of various kinds of legal disobedience.

Because Rawls's ideal theory of justice contains multiple parts (either two or, as I have argued, three), so must his nonideal theory, which governs our responses to failures to live up to the relevant ideal principles. The ideal theory of domestic (basic structural) justice, then, will define the "target" for the nonideal theory of domestic justice, the ideal theory of international justice will define the target for nonideal international theory, and so on. That much seems clear. When Rawls initially tries to explain further the structure and content of nonideal theory in *A Theory of Justice*, however, his few remarks are confusing: he tells us that nonideal theory (focusing here, it seems, only on *domestic* nonideal theory) has "two rather different subparts," the first consisting of principles for addressing "natural limitations and historical contingencies" and the second of "principles for meeting injustice."[50] Since nonideal theory in its entirety was originally characterized as telling us how we ought to respond to injustice—that is, to failures to satisfy the ideal principles of justice—having only one of these "subparts" of nonideal theory concern "meeting injustice" remains somewhat mysterious in *A Theory of Justice*. The point of the distinction eventually becomes clearer, however, when Rawls addresses (twenty-eight years later) nonideal theory for *international* relations.[51]

In *The Law of Peoples*, remember, Rawls again describes a two-part nonideal theory, the parts similarly concerned, respectively, with "unfavorable conditions" and "noncompliance." But in the international theory, the "cases" covered in the two parts are two kinds of societies or "peoples." The "unfavorable conditions" cases are what Rawls calls "burdened societies," while the "noncompliance" cases are the so-called outlaw states. Burdened societies are ones that should be helped (to become well ordered); outlaw states should be pressured to change their ways, and their wrongs (both internal and external) should be opposed

[50] Rawls (1971), 246.

[51] Most of the following interpretive points in this section are argued for in much more detail and at much greater length in Simmons (2010), 12–18.

(by force, if necessary).[52] This makes it clear, I think, that Rawls's real intention (in his divisions of nonideal theory) is to distinguish between the nonideal principles governing our dealings with merely unfortunate (or nonblameworthy) failures to comply with ideal principles and the nonideal principles governing our responses to deliberate (or blameworthy) failures. And, of course, Rawls seems correct that the ways we should address those two kinds of failures might be quite different; a morally permissible (and effective) response, for instance, to societal poverty or cultural obstacles to full justice would likely be rather different from the response we ought to make to deliberate human rights violations or international aggression.

Bearing in mind this two-part division of nonideal theory—while recalling that ideal theory itself has multiple parts, each with its own corresponding branch of nonideal theory—we are left with a more complicated picture of the structure of Rawlsian nonideal theory than might have been anticipated. In fact, there would seem to be six separate parts of nonideal theory, comprising, respectively, the principles for dealing with:

(1) deliberate noncompliance with ideal principles for the basic structure;
(2) unfortunate noncompliance with ideal principles for the basic structure;
(3) deliberate noncompliance with ideal principles for international society;
(4) unfortunate noncompliance with ideal principles for international society;
(5) deliberate noncompliance with ideal principles for individuals;
(6) unfortunate noncompliance with ideal principles for individuals.

As we have seen, the principles of part 3 (covering responses to outlaw states) will specify the occasions for and permissible (or obligatory) forms of international intervention and just war. The principles of part 4 (for burdened societies) will cover the requirements of international aid.

Further, Rawls appears to suggest in *A Theory of Justice* that the principles of nonideal theory for *individuals* will divide into those flowing, on the one hand, from the principle of paternalism—for the treatment of unfortunate noncompliance with the principles for individuals (my part 6), as in cases of immaturity or insanity[53]—and, on the other, from principles of retributive and compensatory justice, which will dictate appropriate responses to crimes and other (deliberate or blameworthy) wrongs (in part 5). Finally, nonideal theory for noncompliance with the two principles of justice (the ideal theory for basic structures)—the part of nonideal theory with which Rawls concerned himself in *A Theory of*

[52] Rawls (1999a), 5.
[53] Rawls (1971), 244, 249.

Justice—divides into (a) "temporary adjustments," guided by "the general conception of justice" and aimed at eventual full compliance, in order to deal with unfortunate societal poverty or historical or cultural limitations (in part 2);[54] and (b) the principles of civil disobedience, conscientious refusal, and noncivil resistance, understood now as responses to deliberate or blameworthy domestic injustice (in part 1).

Rawls's theory of civil disobedience (and conscientious refusal), then, is part of nonideal theory for the basic structure, because civil disobedience, properly understood, is motivated by and aimed at repairing injustice in the institutions of society's basic structure. Rawls's account of civil disobedience is *not*, as I understand it (and contrary to at least the appearance of some of Rawls's claims about it), a part of the nonideal theory that deals with failures to comply with the principles for individuals.[55] The theory of civil disobedience is connected to Rawls's "principles for individuals" only in the following sense: the ideal principles of justice for individuals specify the obligations and duties of citizens in just or near-just societies, some of which must be overridden in order to justify legal disobedience, and some of which directly require that we respond to societal injustice. In particular, the individual citizen's natural duty of justice both requires general compliance with the institutional rules of a just basic structure (a duty that must be overridden in order for legal disobedience to be justified) and requires that we further just arrangements where they do not exist (which imposes a duty to try to remedy injustices in our basic institutions).

Possible Objects of Disobedience

Rawls's nonideal theory of justified legal disobedience by individuals thus identifies as the object of that disobedience repairing injustice in society's basic structure. If that injustice is limited or anomalous, so that we have a near-just institutional structure, then any justified disobedience must be *civil*. If injustice is more widespread and intransigent, then noncivil forms of disobedience may be justified (which might aim at repairing the injustice by radically changing or

[54] Ibid., 152, 62.

[55] Each of the three general categories of nonideal theory will specify secondary principles for addressing noncompliance with the primary principles of its corresponding part of ideal theory. And the agents bound by the principles of nonideal theory need not be of only one kind. So, for instance, for noncompliance by the institutions of society's basic structure, nonideal theory may specify different principles to direct the actions of individual citizens, of government officials, of foreign nationals, and so on. Rawls's theory of civil disobedience is (part of) the content of nonideal theory for the basic structure; but it is the part addressed to ordinary citizens of the particular society whose basic structure has failed the test of ideal justice.

even by removing the infected institutions). Recall, however, that Thoreau's civil disobedience was a response not only to injustice in his society's core institutions. Thoreau also took his disobedience to be justified by the fact that he owed no obligations of allegiance at all to his state or government. The presence of such obligations establishes (at least) a strong moral presumption in favor of obedience to law. But Thoreau saw no moral presumption at all in favor of legal obedience, no presumption which needed to be overcome or outweighed in order to justify his disobedience. How might a position like Thoreau's be reconciled with the structure of Rawlsian nonideal theory?

We can for current purposes set to one side Thoreau's anarchist pronouncements; Rawls obviously cannot endorse any argument aiming to show that even a perfectly just state would still be morally illegitimate with respect to all of its subjects (because, according to Thoreau, their accepting its authority would be inconsistent with their fundamental obligations to personally decide and do what is right). And Rawls clearly supposes that he has good grounds for rejecting Thoreau's *personal consent-based* standards for governmental legitimacy,[56] so that Thoreau could not reasonably insist that *he himself*, simply in virtue of his personal withdrawal of (or failure to) consent, was freed of duties of allegiance. What cannot be so blithely dismissed by Rawls (or by Rawlsians or Kantians), however, is the more general line of argument suggested by Thoreau's remarks: namely, that *structural* injustice is not the only defensible object of legal disobedience, that *historical* illegitimacy can also poison the state's claims to allegiance and can justify disobedience as a response to (or in order to repair) that wrong.

By "structural injustice," of course, I mean injustice in the institutional rules of society's basic structure. But by "historical illegitimacy" I mean wrongful conduct in the history of the state's subjection of persons or territories to its coercive powers.[57] Thoreau's critique of his United States, I think, involved charging it with *both* of these kinds of defects. Now it might seem that one cannot charge a state with historical illegitimacy except *in consequence* of its great structural injustices, so that while perhaps Thoreau's critique was defensible in his day, it might not have been in a better, more just day. In the kind of near-just state discussed by Rawls there could only be justified complaints about the remaining

[56] On Rawls's objections to consent theory and my replies to them), see Simmons (2005), 345–6.

[57] My subsequent focus in this chapter (and later in this book) on questions of historical legitimacy should not be taken to indicate that I think state legitimacy is the only important dimension of the moral assessments of states (and their conduct). But I do think that it is a dimension importantly distinct from those factors that bear on states' *justifications*. My remarks here should be read in light of the distinction between state legitimacy and the justification of the state, as I present it in "Justification and Legitimacy" (Simmons [2001a]).

imperfections in the basic structure—but no warranted complaints about historical illegitimacy.

But any such appearance is clearly mistaken. Societies may have nearly, or even perfectly, just basic structures in Rawls's sense while still wrongly imposing those structures on persons, in consequence of historical "wrongs of subjection." Justice for Rawls is perfectly forward-looking; just institutions are simply those that satisfy Rawls's two principles of justice, neither of which in any way addresses the issue of *to which particular persons* those institutions' rules are legitimately applied. Consider again the charges Thoreau levels against "his" country. His state's institutions had *plainly* not been imposed in defensible ways on those who had been kidnaped and brought to his country in chains to live out short, miserable lives in bondage, or on the aboriginal peoples who had been decimated and forcibly relocated, and whose ways of life had been destroyed or deliberately corrupted. Nor were the territories (or their inhabitants) seized from (or "ceded" by) Mexico in a trumped-up war of acquisition subjected to the United States' institutional rules in a legitimate fashion. Nor (finally) is it in any way obvious that the United States somehow mysteriously acquired legitimate authority over those persons or territories—or over the children of those persons—simply through the passage of time.[58]

Rawls must say of Thoreau's United States that it was simply too unjust to be able to legitimate its coercive powers. But let us imaginatively strip Thoreau's United States of human slavery and its program of destroying its aboriginal peoples, alter its constitution and laws to protect the basic rights of its subjects, and deny it its expansionist propensities, and we would then have a state sufficiently just to legitimate its demands for support and compliance. Thoreau's refusal of allegiance would then be indefensible in Rawlsian terms, as would be similar refusals of allegiance by the remnants of and the children of slaughtered aboriginal peoples, by the suddenly freed African slaves and their children, or by newly anointed US citizens in former Mexican territories. The grim and bloody histories of political subjection and their enduring consequences would purportedly be laid to rest by simple institutional reform and modification.

But surely that is to ignore an extremely important dimension of the citizen-state relationship, a dimension regularly appealed to by (or on behalf of) those

[58] I address questions about the (alleged) gradual "supersession" of historical wrongs later in the book, principally in chapter 7. The passage of time can, of course, complicate questions about *membership* in illegitimately subjected groups (because of intermarriage, etc.), as Susanne Sreedhar observed in her comments on an early version of this chapter (Sreedhar [2010], 1836–7). Such complications, however, seem to me only complications, not in any way *nullifications* of the relevant moral facts. Those facts may be easiest to sort out—as they were in Thoreau's case—when they are addressed soon after the historical wrongs at issue.

who claim to have been (possibly because of having ancestors who were) wrongly subjected to states' claimed authority. It is a dimension that is quite distinct from the dimension of structural justice. To take an obvious contemporary example (but also a deeply complicated one, to only one aspect of which I attend here): consider the stated position of some Palestinians. Their principal charge is *not* that Israel's basic structure is in itself deeply unjust or that its government is (for that or for any other reason) illegitimate with respect to *all* who live in Israel's claimed territories. It is rather that the subjection specifically of Palestinians and their homeland to Israeli rule was historically (and in consequence continues to be) illegitimate.[59]

Many groups around the world that are seeking independence or greater autonomy make similar claims. The numerous suits by Native Americans tribes all around the United States aimed at recovering lands (or the value of lands) stolen or fraudulently acquired from them constitute similar appeals to the historical illegitimacy of state subjection, *not* appeals to any structural injustice.[60] When we assess the *plausibility* of such group demands for reparations or for political autonomy, I think the kinds of historical standards for legitimacy which we are discussing are precisely the ones we are normally inclined to employ. Whether or not persons are legitimately subject to political power—whether or not a government has morally justified political authority over them—is a question most naturally addressed by considering whether or not they were (or have since become) *willingly* subjected. Whether or not a geographical territory is legitimately subject to state control is a question most naturally addressed by considering whether or not that land has been lived on or used by the state's willing subjects and whether or not those subjects wrongly forced others from the land.[61]

My point here is only that many of the objects of legal disobedience in actual political affairs concern neither some simple structural injustice nor some particularly deep structural injustice that is thought to have delegitimated the state with respect to all of its claimed subjects (or territories). Rather, the claim is often one of *partial* state illegitimacy with respect to certain wronged peoples, and the object of their disobedience is precisely to defy or to repair that wrong.

[59] Such claims, of course, are meant to deny or trump similar historical claims to this same territory by Israeli citizens. That is just one of the many complexities of the case that I do not even begin to address here.

[60] This is not to say, of course, that the relative *urgency* of demands for reparation would not be likely to be reduced by instead simply moving closer to or bringing about full structural justice. It is to say, rather, that Rawls's theory seems unable to account for a significant moral "vector" in our commonsense analysis of such cases.

[61] These are, of course, precisely the central standards of the Lockean theory of territorial rights that I will defend in parts II and III of the present work.

Rawls's theory of domestic justice appears to have no place for such complaints of *partial* illegitimacy, for considering the moral positions of *subsets* of the society's members who have been wrongfully subjected to state power.[62] Rawls begins with the idea of domestic societies or nations ("peoples") as having fixed sets of members and fixed geographical boundaries. The moral question for Rawls is simply whether the basic structure of the society is sufficiently just that its coercive powers can be justified to all reasonable persons within its claimed (or acknowledged) boundaries.

There is, then, no place in Rawls's theory of *domestic* justice where it can acknowledge the legitimate grievances of—and the special moral justifications for legal disobedience by—persons who have been wrongfully subjected to state coercion, except in cases where *all* subjects can be so described. States, for Rawls, are either sufficiently just that all of their claimed subjects are legitimately subject to their authority (with all being equally entitled only to limited forms of disobedience to particular unjust laws)—because the states' basic structures could be expected to be endorsed by all reasonable persons and are thus fully legitimate[63]—or they are sufficiently unjust that they have no authority whatsoever, leaving all of their claimed subjects morally at liberty (that is, bound only by whatever morality they are subject to simply as persons). Rawls's nonideal theory is not, then, inadequate merely because its account of civil disobedience fails to apply to the paradigm practitioners of civil disobedience (like Thoreau). It is more deeply inadequate in precluding without argument even the possible justifiability of legal disobedience for the sorts of reasons (and with the sorts of objects) that characterize not only some of Thoreau's concerns, but those of many others, both historical and contemporary.

Now it might seem that the place to look for Rawls's acknowledgment of the justifiability of disobedience on grounds of "partial illegitimacy" or "wrongful subjection" is not in his theory of *domestic* justice at all, but rather in his theory of *international* justice. The principles of "the law of peoples," after all, include

[62] Rawls does, of course, allow that the duty to obey unjust laws is limited or absent in the case of minorities that have been disproportionately disadvantaged by such laws. But such minorities are still taken by Rawls to be legitimately subject to the (near-just) state's authority (e.g., in the case of just law). I in fact subscribe to the kind of philosophical anarchism to which some of Thoreau's remarks point. On that view, of course, the "partial state legitimacy" to which I refer here is actually pretty complete. Most of us are illegitimately subjected to state coercion. My purpose here is to *grant* Rawls his denial of the anarchist view to see whether his position could *then* yield a plausible account of justified legal disobedience. My argument here is that the answer to that question is "no."

[63] "Our exercise of political power is fully proper only when it is exercised in accordance with a constitution the essentials of which all citizens as free and equal may reasonably be expected to endorse in the light of principles and ideals acceptable to their common human reason. This is the liberal principle of legitimacy" (Rawls [1993], 137).

the prohibition of aggressive war and require that human rights be honored;[64] so wrongful subjection of persons (though perhaps not always of territories) might appear to be prohibited by Rawls's ideal "law of nations." But notice that the law of peoples requires these things only *going forward*. None of the principles of the law of peoples require that *past* wrongs be corrected or rectified, even if those past wrongs are identical in all but temporal location to wrongs that would *now* justify intervention or defensive war with the objective of restoring the status quo ante.[65] Rawls's reasoning about the law of peoples, like his reasoning about domestic justice, simply presumes the current legitimacy of generally recognized territories and claimed subject groups.

Rawls does comment (very) briefly in passing on the fact that societies' boundaries may be viewed as "historically arbitrary":

> It does not follow from the fact that boundaries are historically arbitrary that their role in the Law of Peoples cannot be justified. On the contrary, to fix on their arbitrariness is to fix on the wrong thing. In the absence of a world-state, there *must* be boundaries of some kind, which when viewed in isolation will seem arbitrary, and depend to some degree on historical circumstances.[66]

But, of course, the kind of complaint about "historical illegitimacy" with which I am here concerned is not just the complaint that a society's boundaries (and thus the individual [and groups of] persons and useful resources that are subject to its coercive control) are "arbitrary" in the sense that they could easily have been otherwise, given different historical events—that they could just as easily have been drawn there as here, or that there was no obvious moral barrier to drawing them there rather than here. The problem is that the boundaries have been and continue to be drawn and redrawn in ways that involve straightforward moral wrongs by states and their agents to innocent individuals and groups (a fact that many who join Rawls in defending broadly Kantian views appear to regard as morally uninteresting[67]). And these are wrongs not only according

[64] Rawls (1999a), 37.

[65] Nor would violations of the principles of the law of peoples justify responses by individuals or substate groups who were victims of such wrongs. Nonideal international theory for Rawls governs the justified responses by *peoples* or *nations* (or "societies") to violations by other societies of the ideal principles for "international society" (ibid., 5). The justified responses to injustice by individuals or substate groups appear to be thought by Rawls to be the province of the theory of *domestic* justice. But, as we have seen, they are in fact not adequately addressed there either.

[66] Ibid., 39.

[67] For instance: "in many cases these common worlds were forged by the use of force and fraud. But however one thinks of how these common worlds are formed, the fact of a common world is a morally relevant fact now. Arbitrariness of origins does not imply the moral unimportance of the

to widely shared understandings of the basic moral rights of those who are illegitimately subjected to political coercion, but also according to the very same conventional and legal rules that purport to establish the authority of states over their other, less controversially claimed subjects.

As far as I can see, Rawls's only argument for disregarding such wrongs (and for taking "presently accepted" boundaries as morally "fixed") is the following:

> An important role of a people's government, however arbitrary a society's boundaries may appear from a historical point of view, is to be the representative and effective agent of a people as they take responsibility for their territory and its environmental integrity, as well as for the size of their population. . . . [U]nless a definite agent is given responsibility for maintaining an asset and bears the loss for not doing so, that asset tends to deteriorate. In this case the asset is the people's territory and its capacity to support them *in perpetuity* . . .[68]

But this kind of "stewardship argument" (and the potential for "commons tragedies" to which it refers)—even if we were to accept it without qualification—cannot help Rawls deal with the problem of "partial illegitimacy" to which Thoreau's arguments have pointed us. At most this argument shows that *some state or other* should control useful land and material assets (and the people who depend on them), not that any *particular* state should control any particular assets—and certainly not that all "currently established" boundaries (according to whatever "consensus" the "community of nations" might have managed to achieve) are morally unchallengeable.[69] For Rawls to think otherwise seems to

phenomenon that has been formed" (Christiano [2008], 83). This apparent attempt to dismiss the problem of historical illegitimacy is puzzling. We can certainly allow with Christiano that force and fraud can create situations in which new obligations arise for the wronged parties. That I was purchased as a slave to care for the master's children may, of course, put me in a situation where it would be wrong for me to abandon the children (for instance, when doing so would put them in great danger). But it surely does not follow from that that I should not be freed from slavery (and compensated for the wrongs done me); the master (and his agents) can acquire no moral authority over me by forcibly "intertwining" my interests with those of the master's children. Annie Stilz similarly claimed "one thing a liberal theory of citizenship cannot do, however, is tell us why we should have separate states in the world at all, or why borders happen to fall where they do. . .. But in my view this is in no way problematic" (Stilz [2009a], 211). Stilz's more recent work, as we will see in chapter 6, suggests that her views on this point may have changed.

68 Rawls (1999a), 38–9.

69 I also do not believe that Rawls's points actually show (or even argue for) political control of *all* of the world's (or the solar system's, or the universe's) usable assets. As I will argue later, the value of self-government seems to me to argue (in the opposite direction) for leaving (or making) some usable territory and resources available to those individuals and groups who seek political independence or new forms of political association.

me to amount to his committing himself to one or the other of two indefensible views: (a) that wrongs that occurred *yesterday* are in principle morally different from the same kinds of wrongs occurring tomorrow; or (b) that all cases of "historical illegitimacy"—that is, all past wrongful subjections by states of persons and territories—are in principle irremediable and so morally uninteresting. Both views seem to me to be self-evidently false. And non-Rawlsian explanations for such moral conservatism about "historically arbitrary" boundaries—such as utilitarian worries about the transition costs of territorial adjustments—seem to me also inadequate to justify that conservatism. While we may indeed need to "start somewhere" in political philosophy, the particular place where we find ourselves now need not be that place.

The focus in Rawls's theory of *domestic* justice is on the structural features of just political, legal, or economic institutions (just as the focus of his theory of *international* justice is on the structural features of a just society of peoples, and of its participating liberal [and other "decent"] peoples). But *structurally* just arrangements, no matter how admirable they may be in themselves, may not be justifiably imposed on all and sundry, without regard for whether this imposition is defensible *as a process*. Simply in virtue of (let us say, *arguendo*) the near-justice of the basic structure of the United States, the United States surely could not be *justified* in annexing a portion of Mexico and coercively imposing US law on Mexican citizens (even if that were accompanied by the granting of US *rights*)—as we tried to do, after a fashion, with a portion of Mexico in Thoreau's day.

And if we cannot do this now, then we may not reasonably assume that all existing states' currently accepted *claims* with regard to subject populations or geographical territories are simply to be given a free pass, subjected to no moral scrutiny—*regardless* of how fine or just those states' legal, political, and economic institutions may have been (or have become). The legitimacy of state coercion requires more than its being in accordance with near-just institutions. It requires that those institutions be (and have been) imposed on persons and territories in morally defensible ways.[70] These points highlight inadequacies not only in Rawls's particular political philosophy. As we will see in the next chapter, much of contemporary, broadly Kantian, democratic theory suffers from the same problems. In trying to explain "democratic authority," philosophers

[70] Rawls's only reference to more historical—or "pedigree-based"—standards for legitimacy concerns simply the nonmoral, *internal* (primarily legal) criteria for governmental legitimacy (or for the legitimacy of specific rulers or specific laws) within a *structurally* just or legitimate state. Rawls does not consider the sorts of *nonstructural*, historical moral standards for the legitimate subjection of persons or territories to state coercion with which we are here concerned. On such internal "pedigree" requirements for legitimacy, see Rawls (1995), 175.

often proceed as if the problem of legitimate subjection for democratic states has already been resolved. Our only concern need be, then, how to explain the peculiar authority of the resolutions of disagreements accomplished by democratic institutions in action. But democratic decision procedures could plausibly be thought to be authoritative with respect to all members of a group of persons only if all of those persons had been *previously* determined to be legitimately subject to *one and the same* collective decision procedure. And that determination requires consideration of *historical,* not merely (democratic) *structural,* factors. It requires that we *assess,* not that we *accept,* the claims of even democratic states to authority over particular persons and territories.

In my view, then, nonideal theory for political philosophy must take as its target not simple structural or functional justice—that is, not simply achieving an institutional structure that effectively administers justice going forward—but rather full, including historical, legitimacy with respect to the uses of political coercion in controlling subjects and territories. Legal disobedience may be justified either simply in response to historically illegitimate subjection (by demonstrating the absence of political authority) or by showing how disobedience can justifiably advance the cause of full political legitimacy—which we can here take to include full structural justice. Nonideal theory will then recommend the most effective and feasible, morally permissible path to that end. And determinations of moral permissibility will in part involve balancing the progress that legal disobedience can stimulate against any harms done to others and their associations by acts of legal disobedience, along with any negative effects that disobedience might have on the provision of goods that even bad states often accomplish (such as the deterrence and disabling of ordinary criminals). Whether and when legal disobedience must be *civil* (in Rawls's sense of that term) will be determined by this same set of factors.

In the end then, I think, Thoreau is correct in stressing the importance of historical considerations in the analysis of state authority and legitimacy—in implying that an account like Rawls's is importantly truncated, that true moral legitimacy requires more of political societies than that they produce adequately just institutions while wearing forward-looking blinders. It requires options and rectifications for those indefensibly subjected to societies' coercive powers.[71]

[71] Societies owe rectifications to those they have illegitimately subjected to their political and legal institutions. In my view, this group includes not only the obvious cases of subjugated peoples, but most of the rest of us as well. May we then justifiably disobey the law with the object of doing away with the state altogether? Because many innocent people rely on and want to preserve their states, legal disobedience may in practice now be justified in pursuing only quite gradualist aims, with the achievement of structural justice within the familiar sovereign state as its most imperative "short-term" goal. Thoreau's dream of free political association—and free political disassociation—may be an ideal that can only defensibly be approached very slowly.

Perhaps it requires even that states eventually become the kind of state that Thoreau "pleases himself" to imagine: "a State at last which can afford to be just to all men, and to treat the individual with respect as a neighbor; which even would not think it inconsistent with its own repose, if a few were to live aloof from it, not meddling with it, nor embraced by it, who fulfilled all the duties of neighbors and fellow men."[72]

[72] Thoreau (1996), 21 ("Civil Disobedience").

3

Kantian Functionalism and the Boundary Problem

Structure and History

In chapter 2, I argued that there is a kind of blindness to history at work in Rawls's political philosophy. Rawls's single-minded focus on the structural aspects of domestic and international justice leaves his political philosophy systematically insensitive to a whole class of morally compelling claims about political authority: namely, that the authority of (even near-just) contemporary states may be limited by past incidents of "wrongful subjection," that such past wrongs by states may leave them (partially or completely) illegitimate with respect to groups or individuals. In this chapter, my aim is to broaden this critique in two ways. First, the critique will be expanded to more explicitly include concerns about the wrongful establishment of territorial claims, not just concerns about the wrongful subjection of persons. I will call this broader issue "the boundary problem."[1] Second, this chapter will maintain that the problems we saw in Rawls's political philosophy have not been—and cannot be—corrected using the resources available to the various contemporary versions of "Kantian functionalism." I will argue that neither Kant's own theory nor any of the new brands of Kantian political philosophy that have developed under the influence of Rawls's work—which are arguably the most popular and fully developed of any approaches in recent political philosophy or theory—is able to advance beyond Rawls's inadequate "structuralist" arguments in any way that will make discernible progress toward solving this fundamental boundary problem.

[1] The version of "the boundary problem" that is already familiar in democratic theory—namely, that of determining the "boundaries of the *demos*"—is, as I will show, only part of the problem that concerns me here. The familiar version is also a problem that is more about authority over persons than it is about authority over land and resources.

Critiques of "structuralist" theories, of course, are already quite familiar in contemporary political philosophy, but they have thus far occurred primarily within debates about distributive justice. In defending his historical entitlement theory of "justice in holdings," for instance, Robert Nozick wrote that "most persons do not accept current time-slice [i.e., "structural"] principles as constituting the whole story about distributive shares. They think it relevant in assessing the justice of a situation to consider not only the distribution it embodies, but also how that distribution came about."[2] Many of us reacted to that claim, I suspect, by saying (or thinking) that most persons *also* do not think that *historical* considerations constitute the whole story about justice (as Nozick in fact ends up insisting that they do). *Both* historical *and* structural factors seem to most of us relevant to determining what counts as a just distribution of, say, property. That someone labored to produce a good (or had it given to her by another who produced it) seems relevant to assessing her claim to it, as does the fact that she has far more than she needs while others in her society struggle to survive. Nozick, we might say, overreacted to Rawls's apparent privileging of structural factors in his theory of justice by just as mistakenly privileging the historical.

But theories of political authority, as we've seen in the last two chapters, can similarly locate the source of states' (or governments') rights in either structural features of states—for instance, in the justice of their right-creating or distributive institutions or in their democratic constitutions—or in historical facts about how they acquired their control over persons and territories. Here again, I suspect, many people think that both structural and historical considerations are relevant to a proper understanding of the authority of states. Whether a state acquired its control through bloody conquest or willing participation seems important to the extent of its legitimate territorial claims, just as does the structure of the institutions through which it exercises that control. It is this kind of *pluralism* in our evaluations of states that I think is resisted by the Kantian tradition in political philosophy (just as it was resisted by Nozick, with his unrelenting historicism). Kantian theories generally, not merely Rawls's theory, appear to aspire to being purely "functionalist" or "structuralist" in nature—that is, they aspire to ground the state's political authority solely in its successful performance of its morally mandated functions (through its creating and/or sustaining an appropriate structure of political/legal institutions). I do not believe that we can give a plausible account of the proper *boundaries* of the political and legal authority of the state in so monistic a fashion.

This version of the "boundary problem" is actually one aspect of a more general problem for theories of political authority. Its nature becomes clear when we explore the implications of what, in my first work on these topics,

[2] Nozick (1974), 154.

I dubbed the *particularity requirement.*[3] The particularity requirement states that theories of political obligation (with their correlative theories of political authority) must, to be successful, explain why a person's political obligations are owed specially to one particular political society (or government or body of citizens) over all others—namely, to that society naturally identified as the person's "own."[4] A theory that instead explains our obligations to our own society only in a way that implies that we are equally (or more imperatively) bound to other societies, as well as our own, fails to capture that connection between political obligation and the special allegiances we associate with membership or citizenship. (And so the theory fails in the sense of failing to show that there are political obligations, as these obligations are normally conceived.) Thus, an act-utilitarian account of our political obligations, while perhaps explaining why we are sometimes or even often bound to compliance with domestic law or to support domestic political institutions, cannot explain this in a way that does not at the same time show that we may often be equally (or more imperatively) required to comply with or otherwise support foreign political societies. We must (as Godwin argued[5]) follow the utilitarian calculus where it points us, whether it points to legal obedience or disobedience, to action locally or abroad. Domestic utility is not to be preferred to foreign utility, except for purely circumstantial reasons.

I have employed the particularity requirement in my work on political obligation primarily in my efforts to show why theories that attempt to ground political obligations in general moral duties to promote impartial goods—goods such as utility or justice—yield accounts that are *under*-inclusive. That is, I have argued that such theories cannot explain why all of those persons naturally identified as the members or subjects of some political society are in fact specially bound to that society, above all others. But there are other facets of the particularity requirement. One, of course, is that states are naturally associated not only with particular sets of members or subjects, but also with particular geographical *territories*—with particular portions of the earth's land, air, sea, and resources. And a version of the particularity requirement can thus be employed

[3] Simmons (1979), 31–5.

[4] As Dorota Mokrosinska points out (and as I conceded from the start), the particularity requirement, taken strictly, "does not exclude the possibility that we might have political obligations to more states than just one" (Mokrosinska [2007], 172). We might have special, particularized relationships with multiple states, just as we can have special moral relationships with multiple persons or more than one "home." So there might be more than one state that was naturally identified as a person's "own." But unless we accept the possibility of conflicting moral obligations, we could not have obligations of full allegiance (which would include requirements to "serve when called" and otherwise fully participate in and specially support a particular state) that were owed to multiple states.

[5] Godwin (1976), 238–48 ([bk.] 3, [chap.] 4).

in discussing justifications for states' territorial jurisdiction, not just in discussing political authority over persons.

Further, the particularity requirement can also generate a potential problem of *over*inclusiveness for theories of political authority and territorial jurisdiction.[6] If a theory explains, for instance, the special obligations of those who are naturally identified as members only in a way that also implies political obligations for persons who are plainly *not* bound by members' obligations, that theory fails through overinclusiveness (as it would, for instance, if the theory entailed that the citizens of British Columbia owed special political obligations exclusively to the United States). A theory of political obligation and authority should explain why all and only those naturally identified as a political society's members are specially bound to that particular political society. The boundary problem is the problem faced by such a theory of providing an argument that draws the "boundaries" of political obligation, political authority, and territorial sovereignty in the correct places.

The boundary problem is a special difficulty for theories of political authority and obligation that participate in the Kantian tradition of thought on these subjects. And it is a special difficulty precisely because the theories in that tradition attempt to solve the boundary problem without recourse to the kinds of historical considerations that are routinely employed to identify the legitimate moral boundaries of political authority and obligation. When asked why I should regard as having legitimate authority over me this particular political society in which I was simply born and raised—that is, why I should accept the "conservative conclusion" about political authority—the standard Kantian answer is simply that justice requires it. Following Rawls, the Kantian may say that I have a natural duty of justice to support and comply with that just institutional structure that applies to me. Or, following Kant more directly, the Kantian may say that in order to avoid being unjust threats to those around us, in order for all to enjoy nonprovisional rights, we must accept the authority of the justice-administering institutions at work where we happen to find ourselves. Either way, structural or functional factors—the justice (or justice-administering functionality) of the political institutions in our countries of residence—are left to (try to) do all of the labor in Kantian theories of political authority and obligation. That labor is more naturally and intuitively shared, I suggest, with moral assessments based in the actual histories of states and persons.

In speaking here of the Kantian tradition in political philosophy, of course, I intend to speak loosely, meaning to include not only Kant's own theory (and the theories of those who follow Kant's quite closely), but also those of

[6] I discuss these two aspects of the particularity requirement more fully in Simmons (2007), 19.

contemporary Kantians like Rawls and the many who work on defending and developing Rawlsian political philosophy. And, speaking perhaps even more loosely still, I want to include and focus here on what can, I think, be fairly identified as the most recent wave of Kantian theories of political authority and obligation: the theories of democratic political authority defended by Dave Estlund,[7] Tom Christiano,[8] Scott Shapiro,[9] Annie Stilz,[10] Jeremy Waldron,[11] and others.[12] These collectively constitute, I think, a kind of Kantian backlash against the skepticism about political authority that was for a time an increasingly common feature of the recent literature on the subject.

Contemporary Kantians have, of course, advanced positions in political philosophy which Kant himself never endorsed (and not all of them, I'm sure, would even identify themselves as "Kantians"). Rawls's strongly egalitarian conception of justice, for instance, goes far beyond the relatively modest redistribution (in order to provide relief for the poor) called for in Kant's own theory of justice. And, while Kant defended some of the features of political society that we today associate with modern democratic states—such as the separation of powers and formal equality of opportunity—he was plainly not defending the sort of democratic decision making that is said by many contemporary theorists (again including Rawls) to give government and law their moral authority. This "democratic Kantianism" obviously narrows the application of the Kantian arguments, since they now can justify the political authority only of states with a very particular institutional structure. But the new Kantianism shares with the old a determination to justify political authority and territorial jurisdiction solely by appeal to structural or functional features of states. They are thus far more strongly united by that shared approach—the one that I criticize here—than they are divided by their differences in emphasis.

[7] Estlund (2008).

[8] Christiano (2008).

[9] Shapiro (2002).

[10] Stilz (2009a).

[11] Waldron (1999a), esp. chap. 5.

[12] Allen Buchanan, for instance, presents arguments for "democratic authority" that are very similar to those defended by the other Kantian political philosophers I've mentioned; but, unlike the others, he insists that "democratic theory . . . does not provide an account of political authority." It provides only "an account of the conditions under which citizens can have an obligation *to one another* to take compliance with the laws seriously" (Buchanan [2004], 253). I believe that Buchanan's theory, however we describe it, is still vulnerable to a variant of the same criticisms I level against the other theories of democratic authority discussed here. Henry Richardson also may belong in this group (in Richardson [2011]). (I say that Richardson "may" belong in this group because he appears to regard the boundary problem that I describe here as part of a prior issue of political "legitimacy," with Estlund-style accounts of democratic authority defended as compelling only within states already determined to be legitimate. That view could, in fact, be consistent with my own, depending on precisely how the relevant standards of legitimacy are characterized.)

Proximity and Necessity

Suppose there are two clusters[13] of people living at a considerable distance from one another "in a condition of mere nature." All of the people have settled where they are willingly; and the members of each cluster have little or no contact with those of the other, but are inevitably brought into regular contact with those of their own cluster. Neither cluster, of course, constitutes a political society, lacking shared government or laws. The situation of the persons located within each cluster will probably be at least "inconvenient" (to use Locke's language), and possibly intolerable (as Hobbes believed) or morally wrongful (i.e., unjust, as Kant thought). The absence of government and law makes life difficult (because of inadequate power to enforce morality against aggressors and predictable disagreements even among nonaggressors about what morality requires), perhaps so difficult that life is solitary, poor, nasty, and so on.

A solution to these problems of intracluster life seems socially and morally necessary. And there is, of course, a "natural" solution. The members of each cluster could create a system for the mutual enforcement of their rights—for doing justice—that will operate only within, rather than between, their clusters. Such systems would be able to clarify what their rights are (within that cluster) in an impartial fashion and muster enough force to coercively impose this clarification (through threats, punishments, required reparations, etc.). Such a solution in effect permits the de facto "districting" accomplished by the arbitrary (but not unwilling) gathering of persons into two clusters to be transformed into the de jure districting of two distinct systems for administering justice.

Now imagine that as populations increase the two clusters gradually grow together, so that people in the two clusters begin inevitably to interact with one another. Where disagreements and conflicts arise, the people involved in them find themselves hung between two—perhaps two inconsistent—systems for administering justice. As such problems become frequent, the two administrations may reach some agreement as to how the "intercluster" problems will be addressed. Or perhaps the more natural solution will be to combine the two districts into one, creating a single new districted cluster that is governed by a new (internally consistent) single system of justice.

Now, finally, suppose that all of the clusters everywhere expand and grow together, so that population becomes more or less continuous across the face of the earth. People's new proximity to one another (along, we may add, with

[13] I use the perhaps unhappy language of "clusters" here to convey the mere proximity of individuals to one another, and thus to avoid any suggestion of voluntary incorporation into groups or shared, cooperative activities of a structured sort—which might be thought to have brought about a voluntary departure from a state of nature.

improved interactive technologies) makes intercluster interaction and conflict a regular feature of their lives. Once again, perhaps intercluster treaty can solve the new problems (though we all know by now, of course, how effectively new technologies can defeat such interstate efforts at treaty solutions). Or, once again, perhaps the more natural solution is to unite the various clusters under the authority of one, internally consistent system for administering justice—which would be, of course, the rough equivalent of a world-state. Kant himself famously resisted this last step, as does virtually every contemporary Kantian political philosopher with whose work I'm familiar.[14] They almost unanimously favor something like our actual world's multistate solution, a solution featuring a plurality of (roughly) "sovereign"[15] administrations for dealing with justice locally. As Dave Estlund puts it, "the best solution is a districted one."[16] In order to create a "districted" solution in a world of more or less continuous population, however, boundary lines between districts will have to be drawn in more or less arbitrary ways—or, at least, in ways no longer guided simply by "natural" facts about who will inevitably interact with whom.

The actual history of districting and boundary drawing in the real political world, however, has been far worse than "merely arbitrary" in painfully obvious ways (as I stressed in chapter 2). While at some points in time at least some boundaries have been drawn according to "natural" divisions—taking advantage of the mere proximity that created clusters, or (more often) salient geographical features, the facts of shared linguistic, tribal, cultural, or ethnic characteristics in those clusters, and so on—most existing political boundaries no longer even remotely approximate such "natural" (and, one might perhaps imagine, morally respectable) solutions to the problem of districting the administration of justice. Opponents and minorities within "naturally occurring" clusters have been decimated, reeducated, and absorbed; territories and populations have been coercively expanded and contracted in bloody-handed quests for natural resources, geographical advantages (such as ports, navigable waterways, and defensible boundary features) and simple expansions of dominion (often accompanied by the slaughter of aboriginal peoples); and powerful administrations have been

[14] One contemporary Kantian who at least comes close to *not* resisting it is Lea Ypi, whose Kantian "permissive theory" makes states' claims to authority within their effective domains *conditional* on their efforts to organize international institutions that will constitute a rightful association of states. See Ypi (2014).

[15] As I suggested earlier, I use the term "sovereign" very cautiously here, given its historical associations with the idea of *absolute* authority or with the notion that internal political matters are morally immune from outside interference. But to the extent that the idea of sovereignty has plainly evolved beyond its original meaning(s), it seems fair to say that Kantians favor the division of the world into sovereign political entities.

[16] Estlund (2008), 150.

able to manipulate justice and in other ways subvert the systems of justice operating in the districts of the less powerful. Easy compromise has compromised the lives of many, and the accommodation of the powerful has left many powerless.

If existing political boundaries fail to reflect "morally respectable" solutions to the problem of the need for localized justice, why should we take the legitimate territorial jurisdictions or political authority of existing states or the genuine political obligations of their claimed subjects to be determined by such a morally tainted process? Notice that this way of framing the boundary problem for Kantian theory shows it to be a kind of "second-stage" question within the theory. The first stage of the theory is designed to establish "the moral necessity of the state" and its system of justice,[17] the moral duty on each person to leave the state of nature and submit to or to help create (and then submit to) some districted political authority and its omnilaterally authorized determination and enforcement of peoples' rights. The justification for this first-stage claim is taken by Kantians to lie in the necessity of persons' possessing secure, conclusive, enforceable rights conjoined with the impossibility of persons possessing such rights in a state of nature (that is, in the absence of a body authorized by all to determine and enforce those rights). In a state of nature, rights over things cannot be acquired unilaterally, imposing obligations on others by one's own act of will, even where things are morally available for appropriation. Nor can rights once established legitimately be enforced, since people have no obligation to refrain from interfering with others when they lack the assurance that others will refrain from interfering with them. Nor can rights in a state of nature even be characterized in an objective, determinate form that allows for their application to particular subjects.[18] Since no person is any more entitled than any other to determine the terms of their interactions, all must remain free to act on their own judgments of right in the absence of some body entitled to judge for all.[19] But this puts all in a wrongful condition with respect to others, making the creation or authorization of a state to do such judging morally mandatory for all.

While I am myself convinced that this ("first stage") argument fails at multiple points, I propose to accept it here *arguendo*.[20] I shall concentrate instead

[17] Christiano (2008), 237–9.

[18] See Arthur Ripstein's discussion of Kant's argument concerning the "three defects in the state of nature" in Ripstein (2009), 145–81. See also Mokrosinska (2007), 152–4.

[19] See Stilz (2009a), 47–53.

[20] One of my doubts (among others) about the first-stage Kantian argument is this: suppose we grant (as I in fact do not) that we normally wrong others by attempting to unilaterally enforce our (perceived) natural rights. Still, there is one "innate" right—the right to maximal freedom—of which (on the standard Kantian position) this is not true. Both parties to a dispute over their rights have a right to force the other to submit to an *omnilateral* (political or legal) determination of right. But the parties can also reasonably disagree about the existence or nature of *that* right (i.e., the alleged right

on the required second stage of the argument. Once it is established that each has a moral obligation to enter a state and accept its legitimate authority—thus leaving the wrongful condition in which moral right is indeterminate, unenforceable, and insecure—it must still be explained *which* state one is obligated to enter. Must we accept the dominion of whatever state *claims* our allegiance or is conventionally or legally determined to have authority over us? If so, which feature of the first-stage argument secures that conservative conclusion? While conventional or legal claims to allegiance do, of course, *purport* to appropriately particularize the relevant obligations, it is precisely their moral respectability—hence, their ability to *legitimately* particularize obligations—that is at issue here. Instead of accepting the dominion of our "home" states, may we permissibly opt to enter some other state, or even join with others to create a preferred new state of our own design? If not, this presumably cannot be because in doing so we would fail to leave the wrongful condition of the state of nature. Insofar as multiple sovereign states are to be a permissible Kantian option, one state looks to be as good as another for first-stage purposes (within obvious limits); what is called for by the first-stage argument is only membership in a state (with a certain acceptable structure), not membership in any *particular* established state.

Notice that the most salient improvements contemporary Kantians have made to the first-stage argument do not really help us address this second-stage boundary problem. When Rawls improves on Kant's argument by insisting that our natural duty to comply with and to help establish institutions to administer justice refers only to distributively just (hence broadly egalitarian) political institutions, this does not help us to understand *which* just political authority we must accept. Rawls, of course, does insist that our natural duty of justice binds us specifically to comply with those just institutions that "exist and apply to us."[21] But this is mere assertion, not argument, and it simply begs the question in favor of the most conservative possible solution to the boundary problem.[22] Similarly, when "democratic Kantians" (including Rawls) improve Kant's argument by

to compel omnilateral judgment), given the "burdens" of philosophical judgment in such matters. Why, then, is it acceptable to unilaterally enforce *that* disputed right, but not the others? Is it because, in the enforcing, one actually ends the state of nature, in which disputes about the relevant rights are a problem? But, of course, one only gets out of the state of nature if one's enforcement efforts actually *succeed* in creating a state. So is it morally acceptable to try to force others into political society only when one is certain to succeed in one's efforts? If so, at least that much might be plausibly said about *unilateral* enforcement of *other* rights, as well—as when such enforcement creates salient, widely accepted, but nonpolitical or nonlegal solutions to disagreements about property claims.

[21] Rawls (1971), 334.

[22] I return below to consider Rawlsian arguments that might be thought to support the conservative solution. On the apparent question-begging character of Rawls's formulation of the natural duty of justice, see my discussion in Simmons and Wellman (2005), 162–4.

adding to the requirements necessary to realizing equality (or our "equal freedom") the insistence that "a legitimate authority must always be democratic,"[23] heft is perhaps added to the first-stage argument. But we are not helped to see why entering or creating a democracy distinct from that one democracy that claims (and is generally thought to be entitled to) your allegiance is not a permissible option (in these Kantian terms). Kantians thus owe us an explanation of why the current conventional or legal division of the world into states with specific territories and subject populations should be thought to be the division that fixes mandatory moral boundaries of political authority and obligation, that sets mandatory targets for what seemed (according to the terms of the first-stage argument) to be merely duties to subject ourselves to *some* political authority or other.[24]

One of the best-known (of the few) attempts by a Kantian political philosopher to specifically address the boundary problem is the argument of Jeremy Waldron's paper "Special Ties and Natural Duties."[25] Waldron directly targets what he calls "the 'special allegiance' objection" and "the 'application' objection" to Rawlsian/Kantian natural duty arguments (which taken together constitute my objection from "particularity," outlined above), and he takes one element of Kant's own arguments to indicate the proper line of response. Waldron, of course, reiterates the first-stage Kantian arguments we've been considering; but he emphasizes as well a potential second-stage argument that relies on (what he later calls) Kant's "Proximity Principle":[26] it is when we are "unavoidably side by side with others" that we must enter *with them* (that is, with specifically those with whom we are side by side) into a civil condition.[27] What appeared at first to be a general duty merely to leave the state of nature (so that conclusive rights for yourself and others could be established, as morality requires) now appears to

[23] Stilz (2009a), 84.

[24] Stilz's *Liberal Loyalty* nicely illustrates the required two-stage structure to which I refer here, with the arguments of parts 1 and 2 of her book dividing the labor of the two stages. Her second-stage case (the heart of which is chap. 7 of the book) relies on the arguments from proximity and social emergency that I discuss below. Most of Stilz's chap. 7 is in fact a reply to cosmopolitan critics, arguing that we can "justify our allegiance to" our own states. This, of course, would not constitute a solution to the boundary problem—which concerns the identification of those who are *required to* support (not merely *justified in* supporting) the particular states that claim their allegiance. The arguments that *do* bear on the boundary problem are those that close Stilz's book (Stilz [2009a], 195–204). These are discussed below.

[25] Waldron (1993).

[26] "People have a natural duty to enter into society with those with whom they find themselves in a condition of unavoidable coexistence" (Waldron [2002], 137–8).

[27] Waldron (1993), 14. See also Waldron (1999a), 110; (1999b), 57; Stilz (2009a), 198–200; Mokrosinska (2007), 75, 162.

be "localized" by the fact that "those with whom I come into conflict will in the first instance be my near neighbors."[28] It is my neighbors to whom I am a special threat. And since the systems attempting to administer justice to groups of us who are "side by side" are precisely those existing polities that currently claim our allegiance, a Kantian moral justification for the "conservative solution" to the boundary problem appears to have been identified.

But we must, I think, be careful in assessing this plausible-looking argument to (what will surely be for most theorists) an agreeable conclusion. For the claim that we are *special* threats to those with whom we are side by side—which, remember, is what is supposed to direct us to cooperate specifically with one set of persons, to enter and obey one particular state—is a straightforwardly *factual* claim and must be evaluated as such. It is not a *formal* claim, as the premises of the first-stage Kantian argument might be taken to be.[29] And the special-threat premise seems to me plainly false as a matter of fact.[30] Who is a special threat to whom depends on far more than simple physical proximity. It plainly depends on the personal characters and moral commitments of the persons involved; it depends on the offensive and defensive capabilities of the persons involved; it depends on the available technologies for delivering harm to distant others (which may actually make it *easier* to harm people at a distance than those who are physically nearby); and so on.

Would we do better to take the "threat" (that near neighbors are to one another) to be just the more limited threat of falling "into confusion and conflict over the boundaries of their many adjacent property rights"?[31] If so, the "threat" at issue seems to me a bit thin to motivate the momentous moral requirement to subject oneself to (or to help create from the ground up) the coercive institutions of the state. So long as there is broad agreement among near neighbors on ownership of the "core" property being actively used in the lives of each—as Locke thinks (and I agree) there is likely to be, even in a state of nature—disagreements about the precise boundaries of neighbors' properties (which Locke allows need "settling" in civil society) seem unlikely to have a severe impact on their lives. It is, instead, likely to be the more distant (less neighborly) and ill-motivated others who constitute serious threats.

But even were the truth of this initial premise not an issue, the argument could *still* not be plausibly characterized as offering us a convincing path to the conservative conclusion (that is, to the conclusion that each has an obligation

[28] Waldron (1993), 15.

[29] Ripstein (2009), 170.

[30] Simmons and Wellman (2005), 173–7.

[31] This is the version of the Kantian proximity argument supported by Cara Nine (Nine [2012], 36).

to enter and obey that particular state whose claims [to authority over her, as a subject] are generally accepted). In the first place, so long as boundaries need to be drawn somewhere in a world in which population is virtually continuous over the face of the earth, there are indefinitely many ways to draw such boundaries that will respect the command to district people with those with whom they are side by side. Inevitably, many people who are in fact side by side will find themselves in separate districts. In short, respecting physical proximity in boundary drawing (as Waldron's Kantian argument requires) in no way determines that the only acceptable result will be the one at which convention and law have in fact arrived. Further, of course, the actual state boundaries that are the result of historical process were neither intended to be guided by nor have otherwise conformed to the requirements of the Kantian argument. Residents of Honolulu are neither side by side with nor special threats to the residents of New York, while the residents of Beausoleil and those of Monte Carlo would almost certainly be selected for the same district were we to divide persons with the Kantian criteria in mind.

Waldron does, of course, sometimes write as if it is not these criteria that should guide contemporary districting, but rather only the more modest standard indicated by attending to which justice-administering institutions have in fact been framed to deal with the claims of which persons.[32] While adhering to this more modest standard will obviously bring the conservative conclusion more within reach, the standard itself seems a nonstarter in an attempt to solve the boundary problem. The mere fact that an institutional structure *names* persons as subject to its authority (or is framed with the purpose of dealing with the claims of a particular group of persons) is not a morally interesting feature of the relation between persons and institutions. Legislative or judicial intent alone cannot give authority or ground obligation. Germany cannot acquire authority over the French simply by framing institutions designed to settle the claims of residents of both countries.

To be fair, of course, Waldron insists as well that authority is possessed only by justice-administering institutional structures that are "effective" in performing that task.[33] Presumably, however, we would still object to German justice for the French even if Germany somehow managed to administer justice "effectively" in some or all of France. But our objections would then be historical rather than structural; they would refer centrally to the illegitimate seizure of "authority,"

[32] "A person is an insider in relation to an institution if and only if it is part of the point of that institution to do justice to some claim of his among all the claims with which it deals" (Waldron [1993], 16).

[33] Or, as Estlund puts it, "their significance stems from their availability and effectiveness" (Estlund [2008], 149).

not (necessarily) to the fashion in which justice was administered by Germany. And we should remember in this context that states' institutional structures have regularly been framed with the intention of "dealing with" the claims of groups that have been seriously wronged in the first place by even being subjected to the authority of those states—as when the US Bureau of Indian Affairs was created in part to deal with the claims made by the shattered remnants of the Native American tribes so shamelessly slaughtered and subdued by that same US government. Regardless of the bureau's effectiveness (and the lack of competition with it to do the task in question), its authority should surely be questioned because of how it came to be the sole and effective justice-administering institution in this case. (We can for these purposes leave to one side any objections to its authority based on the regularly corrupt fashion in which the bureau actually did its job.)

But if the general line suggested by Waldron fails in this way, where are we to turn in the Kantian argument for help in understanding the moral (as opposed to the legal or conventional) boundaries of a state's authority over subjects? It may seem that the answer for the Kantian has been obvious all along, ever since we conceded the Kantian's first-stage argument.[34] If all persons have a moral obligation to enter *some* state—and if each person has a moral right that all others do so—then this rules out (as permissible options) both individuals living separately as self-governing agents and multiple individuals living together in any kind of *non*state group. Further, if existing states, through exercises of their coercive powers, make it physically impossible for any of their claimed subjects to secede and create new states that will be located within the old states' claimed territories—as existing states in fact do—and if existing states also coercively enforce their claims to dominion over all of the earth's usable surface—as they in fact do—then only two permissible options for persons living within existing states appear to remain: they must either consent to membership in the state that claims them as subjects, or they must leave the territories of that state and sign on as members in some other existing state.

This is not quite the conservative conclusion the Kantian wanted, of course, for it still has disjunctive form: we must either sign up as members of the states that claim our allegiance or leave those states for some other. But that may seem a good enough conclusion for the Kantian's purposes, especially when we remember that existing states could simply choose to use their coercive powers to *stop* their claimed subjects from leaving (or prevent new subjects from joining by closing their borders to immigrants). In that case, the only actual option for persons that would appear to be morally permissible would be for persons to accept membership in that particular existing state that claims authority over

[34] The following objection was suggested to me by Bas Van Der Vossen.

them. And that is precisely the conservative conclusion that the Kantian argument was trying to establish.

It is important to see, however, the ways in which this proposed solution to the boundary problem actually relies on premises that are no part of the first-stage Kantian argument and that are not implied by the Kantian conception of what makes states legitimate. From our general obligation to submit ourselves to the administration of some state (and from others' right that we do so) nothing at all follows about the rights of *existing* states to use coercion to limit the ways in which we may discharge this obligation—for instance, by making impossible the creation of new states or preventing transfers between existing states. The first-stage Kantian argument establishes neither the right of states to restrict movement by persons nor a collective right of states to control access to all usable portions of the earth. The state's legitimate purpose, according to the Kantian, is to make possible real, nonprovisional justice. Using coercion to limit the freedom of the unwilling is obviously authorized by that task only where exercises of individual freedom threaten that purpose—as migration between states or the creation of additional states do not. If the existence of *multiple* sovereign states is consistent with our obligation to submit ourselves to some state, as the Kantian allows, then so would be the creation of additional, new sovereign states and the redistribution of members between available states.

State coercion requires moral justification as much on the Kantian view as on alternative views. And the first-stage Kantian argument provides us with no reason to believe that states are entitled to solve the boundary problem by simple coercive fiat. The most natural solution to that problem, I've suggested, is to allow it to be resolved (at least in part) by facts about the actual history of the state in question, taking as that state's legitimate subjects those who have in fact been legitimately subjected to authority. But such historical facts are taken by Kantians to be irrelevant to understanding the limits of political authority. It is a state's structural or functional features, and in particular those features related to its current administration of justice to a group of persons, that determines the scope of its authority. And we have not yet seen an independently plausible argument for limiting our inquiry to such structural features.[35] Rather, the arguments

[35] Stilz and Mokrosinska both appear to appeal to broadly associativist considerations in order to try to more fully particularize the (natural duty-based) political obligations they describe, appealing to the many other ways in which people "act together" (Stilz [2009a], 175–91) and to the internal normativity of analogous relationships like friendship (Mokrosinska [2007], 146, 160, 231–2). But it is unclear how associative ties can aid the Kantian argument on this point. In any real political society, appeals to associative connections among members will inevitably be either underinclusive (if strong psychological connections between persons are taken to be necessary for associative bonds

thus far suggest the need for at least some non-Kantian pluralism—through the addition of an historical dimension—in our account of political authority and territorial jurisdiction.

Democratic Authority

So let us ask now whether contemporary theories of democratic authority can help Kantian political philosophy address the boundary problem. Now our question becomes the more limited one of how we can identify the precise boundaries of the group or territory over which specifically democratic political authority can be legitimately exercised? While this seems to me the most basic problem facing a theory of democratic authority, it seems also to be a question that is rarely raised by democratic theorists.[36] Great argumentative ingenuity has been employed in explaining why democratic solutions to disagreements within some group are to be preferred to alternative solutions. But there is little attention focused on explaining why any particular grouping of persons counts as one to which *any* single conflict-resolution procedure, democratic or not, may be legitimately applied. When theorists *have* addressed the problems involved in determining the proper boundaries of "the demos," they have concerned themselves primarily with possible reasons to *expand* those boundaries beyond the "uncontroversial" cores of the native citizenry of democratic nation-states—perhaps by extending the franchise to all whose interests are affected by democratic decisions or to all who are coerced by the state.[37] My concern here, however, is with the prior, and I think more fundamental, question of how even persons and territories in that "uncontroversial" core can be taken to be legitimately subject to the authority of the states that claim them. The worry here is not just about who should be legally granted the franchise, but rather also about

between them—as they clearly are for friendships or for playing music together, say) or overinclusive in the ways described below (if they are not). If *feeling* or *acknowledging* that one is engaged in a common enterprise is necessary for one to count as *being* so engaged, then the many divisions (between classes, parties, ethnic groups, etc.) within contemporary nation-states will suffice as well to define normative divisions. If, however, it is enough for associative normativity that *others* in society "start to act" as if there is a common enterprise (Mokrosinska [2007], 154), this seems consistent with the overinclusiveness (due to the entailed acceptance of clearly illegitimate political subjection) with which I charge Kantian political philosophy in the following sections.

[36] For instance, Christiano's *The Constitution of Equality* includes chapters on "The Authority of Democracy" and "The Limits to Democratic Authority"; but neither chapter includes any discussion of the boundary problem. That problem is dismissed earlier in the book with a three-sentence argument (which I discuss below).

[37] See, e.g., Goodin (2007), Miller (2009), and Whelan (1983).

why even those who *are* granted the right to vote are subsequently bound to comply with democratically authored decisions.

The nature of the problem for democratic theory is clear. Democratic solutions to conflicts of interest (or preference) are plainly not naturally authoritative. This remains true even if we accept all that has been written about the superiority of democratic procedures—superiority either in intrinsic terms (i.e., as the procedures that realize or most fully respect, say, human autonomy or equality) or in instrumental terms (i.e., as the procedures that most reliably yield the best [e.g., social happiness maximizing or substantively just] results). That the students in my classes uniformly outnumber me—and so are capable of outvoting me on questions of class requirements—does not make their expressed preference for a lighter workload in my class in any way authoritative. Nor would it do so if they set up a formal procedure for voting on that question or for elected representatives to do their voting for them. What they lack, of course, is the prior authority to impose on the class *any* procedure—democratic or not—for resolving disagreements in the group which consists of them plus me. Similarly, my club may not legitimately kidnap an outsider, confer membership and voting rights on him, and then simply impose on him the restrictions authorized by the majority of the club's members. The nature of the group—and how one comes to be a part of the group—makes all the difference in whether or not *any* conflict-resolution procedure can be authoritative for the group (that is, can yield results that bind to compliance all persons within the group). The superiority of the conflict-resolution procedure in question, however this should be determined, is straightforwardly irrelevant to that conclusion.

The fact that democratic procedures are not naturally authoritative is, of course, what produces the boundary problem for theories of democratic authority. For precisely which collections of individuals do particular democratic procedures yield authoritative outcomes? If this question cannot be answered by appeal to the structural superiority of democratic institutions to their rivals, how can it be answered within democratic theory. The universally desired answer, of course, is that the democratic procedures of a nation are authoritative with respect to precisely that collection of persons that is legally or conventionally identified as the group subject to the democratic institutions in place in the nation in question. This, as we have seen, is the conservative answer, and one that is necessarily insensitive to the historical events that produced the legal or conventional sorting of individuals into groups of political subjects. It is also an answer that requires *justification*. And it is once again difficult to see what kind of justification might be constructed simply from the resources of democratic theory.

Appeals to the need to rectify quite ancient historic wrongs done in the political districting of persons may, of course, seem to some excessive or excessively moralizing; and, as a result, the conservative conclusion may seem less disturbing or misguided than my discussion thus far has suggested. Some philosophers (including Waldron), for instance, argue that while such historic wrongs may indeed once have generated rights to rectification for the wronged parties, those rights may "fade with time" (and with the deaths of the wronged parties), and the original injustice may be "superseded."[38] While I believe that "supersession" of historic injustice is far less common and simple than do such critics of historical rights claims, we can concede their position for present purposes. (I will not argue for my position on this subject until chapter 7, where I will try to give a fuller account of the problem of rights supersession than is common in discussions of these problems.) So let us think less about the bloody past history of our states (and less about the kinds of imaginary, state-of-nature scenarios discussed above) and instead concentrate on our states' present capabilities for and possible extensions of their districted administrations of justice.

Remembering our example from chapter 2, imagine that (perhaps citing concerns about national security) the United States somehow manages to move its southern border barriers further south by several miles, declaring the newly enclosed territory to now be part of the United States. The United States commences then to effectively and fairly administer justice in this new territory and extends full US citizenship rights to all of the (former Mexican) residents of the territory. Mexico, of course, vigorously objects but is unable to do more than that; and after the prescribed period of international protests and hand wringing, this attempted expansion of territorial jurisdiction begins to look successful.

How should we understand the moral position of these newly minted US citizens?[39] Are they bound to support and comply with the basic institutions of the United States, just as we take native-born US citizens to be—at least if we suppose (as I shall, for the sake of argument) that the basic legal, political, and economic structure of the United States is reasonably just, that its government and laws have been settled on in an acceptably democratic fashion, and so on? And how should we understand US rights with respect to its new territories? The question now is not one of historic wrongs done by a state long ago in subjecting its claimed subjects and territories to state power, wrongs that might be said to have faded away and to have no moral relevance now. Rather, the question concerns a wrongful political subjection inflicted last week (let us say) on thousands

[38] Waldron (1992), 27, 24.

[39] I am supposing, for purposes of this example, that both states are sufficiently just (or possess whatever other legitimating properties are necessary) for the relevant Kantian or functionalist view to count both states as having started (prior to the imagined seizure) with legitimate territorial rights over their claimed territories.

of innocent persons (and over the geographical territory within which they reside). And if *last week's* wrongs are said to by *today* have faded away and been superseded (which Waldron, of course, does *not* say[40]), something has plainly gone deeply wrong. To affirm that would not be to show morally appropriate sensitivity to changing circumstances; it would rather be to affirm, in effect, that there simply are no moral rights or duties against unprovoked aggression.

Some of the new US citizens may, of course, welcome their new status, since life prospects north of the border are significantly better than those south of it. Others may feel wronged by the change, perhaps still feeling allegiance to their former state and preferring to be districted with more like-minded folks, or perhaps anticipating discrimination from their new compatriots on the basis of language or ethnicity or religion, or fearing that relationships with relatives and friends and culture still further south will now be difficult to maintain. But regardless of the new citizens' feelings about the matter, the unilateral, coercive seizure by the United States of the acknowledged territory and subjects of another sovereign state surely constitutes a clear wrong against Mexico and a clear wrong against those forcibly subjected citizens. And, importantly, it constitutes a clear wrong according to the very same conventional or legal standards that purport to make it acceptable for the United States to subject its other, native-born citizens to its coercive authority. Whatever we may think of those standards, forcible subjection still looks like a palpable moral wrong even independent of the standards, a wrong that simply can't result in the wronged parties having exactly the same obligations toward the state which has wronged them as do the native-born citizens to whom (we can allow here) no such wrong has been done.

Is the appropriate response that this imagined aggression against Mexico would render the United States' government or laws—or render the United States itself—unjust, and so owed no duties of support and compliance by any of its citizens? Or is it rendered unjust, but only with respect to those newly shanghaied citizens in former Mexican territory? Neither can be true if justice is a purely functional or structural, nonhistorical matter. Nothing about the basic structure or the core functions of the United States is necessarily altered simply by indefensible acts of state aggression. Its distributive tax and transfer system can remain unaltered, as can the domestic liberties guaranteed in its constitution and its democratic political institutions. That the new citizens' "wills" are not reflected in the representatives or the laws to whose authority they are now suddenly subjected does not distinguish them from any native-born citizen who reaches adulthood in the state. What distinguishes them (if anything does), of course, is the clear wrong that has been done to the new citizens in forcibly

[40] Waldron (2002), 146–7.

including them in the group to by governed by a particular government and legal system.

I submit that the natural moral conclusion to reach about this case is that coercively subjected citizens are not bound by the democratically produced laws of their new country, any more than the kidnapped "member" of my club is bound by the democratically produced rules of my club. If anything seems clear here, it is that wrongs of illegitimate subjection must at the very least limit the obligations that wrongdoing states can unilaterally impose on those they've wronged. Surely the fact that I have been wronged by others—and especially when they have wronged me in their efforts to forcibly impose the very obligations at issue—must leave me less fully obligated to them than I would be had I not been so wronged. This is simply the same kind of rule to which we appeal when we insist on serious differences between the moral (and legal) consequences of contracts made under duress and those made freely.

Historical considerations matter to the nature and extent of our obligations as citizens and to the nature and extent of the authority of our states. Mere institutional structure—including the institutions of democratic conflict-resolution—cannot do all the work that needs doing in explaining political obligation and political authority. Kantian theories, including Kantian theories of democratic authority, that offer us purely structural or functional accounts of state authority and territorial jurisdiction thus suffer from the problem of "overinclusiveness" described above.[41] The forcibly incorporated former citizens of Mexico in my example are not among those who would be naturally or intuitively identified as morally bound members of the political community that constitutes the United States.

The peculiar feature of my criticism, of course, is that virtually all Kantians would certainly be prepared to *agree* that such forcible incorporation of innocents (and territory) through state coercion is a clear moral wrong against them (and against their home states). But the pure Kantian position cannot consistently regard this as the kind of moral wrong which has as a consequence the forfeiture or the limitation of claims to political authority by aggressor states. For to concede that would be to concede that historical considerations are, after all, relevant to determining the extent—the legitimate boundaries—of the political authority of existing states. And once that point is conceded, of course, the

[41] Notice that when Kantians who acknowledge the particularity problem claim that their accounts have solved it, they tend to have in mind only the *under*inclusiveness problem—that is, they believe they have explained why the focus of duties of justice must be local, so that those who are clearly members of some polity turn out to be bound specially to their own states. See, e.g., Christiano (2008), 250n; Stilz (2009a), 20–22. The problem of *over*inclusiveness being stressed here cannot be addressed in that way.

Kantian can no longer insist that the mere "application" to persons of just (or justice-administering) institutions is *sufficient* to ground their political obligations or the legitimate authority over them of those institutions. That would deprive Kantians of their simple, sweeping answer to questions about why the native-born are legitimately subject to the authority of states they never chose. *Refusing* to concede that point, however, leaves the Kantian with the extremely counterintuitive view that apparently illegitimate subjection makes no moral difference to the obligations of those so subjected to state power or to the territorial authority of aggressive states.[42]

Now it may well be that contemporary Kantians will want in the end to insist that their apparently structuralist or functionalist conceptions of justice are actually intended to *include* (or be sensitive to) the kinds of issues of historical justice or legitimacy that I am here emphasizing, so that a state cannot in fact *count* as ("structurally" or "functionally") just unless it satisfactorily rectifies its wrongs of illegitimate subjection (of persons and territories). In that case, however, Kantians would do well to acknowledge this fact more explicitly, rather than writing as if such historical considerations are simply irrelevant to questions about the authority of contemporary states. And Kantians will have to refrain as well from suggesting that the mere "application" to persons of effective, justice-administering institutions fully determines the boundaries of authority and obligation. Determining where those boundaries lie will have to be a far more complicated matter than the simple Kantian formulae suggest, and the political philosophy at work will have to be far more pluralistic than a simple Kantian/Rawlsian functionalism. And, of course, the desired conservative outcomes (with respect to currently just states) will no longer be so obviously within reach.

This point that I'm trying to make against the pure Kantian position might also be enlarged by being employed as the small point of a large wedge, opening the structuralist/functionalist door to a host of historical claims by other possible victims of illegitimate subjection to state authority—claims that would then have to be individually analyzed and resolved, not swept away en masse by appeal to an exclusively structural or functional theory of authority. In my view, for instance, the arguments against more distant historical bases for claims to rectification are in many cases unconvincing, calling for closer examination of claims made by, for example, the descendants of slaves or members of decimated aboriginal peoples that they too have been illegitimately subjected to state authority. These are claims that might justify the

[42] In her most recent work, Stilz appears to accept this point, defending a more pluralistic—hence, less purely Kantian—account of these matters. I discuss her developed view in some detail below in chapter 6.

conclusion not only that reparations are owed but that the political obligations of such subjects are (at least) much more limited than those of other citizens, that the boundaries of political authority must be drawn with such subjects (at least) partially outside.

These same principles apply in the case of many nations' suppression of or resistance to secessionist or autonomy movements by groups claiming to have been illegitimately subjected to their states' power.[43] The claims in many of these cases, as we saw in chapter 2, are not principally claims of structural injustice in their states. The claim is often rather that their group was wrongfully made subject to that state in the first place (in the near or more distant past), with continuing consequences for their wellbeing, for their culture, and for their very identities. To respond to such complaints with offers of full democratic citizenship in a just state would appear to simply miss the point. The object of such movements is not just to secure the institutional rights guaranteed to other citizens of their states. It is instead to right the wrongs done them in the past, to be permitted the autonomy of which they were wrongly robbed and to be compensated for those wrongs and their continuing effects.[44] Are those involved in movements of this sort, often at serious risk to their lives and wellbeing, simply confused in supposing that legitimate claims to autonomy or liberation might derive from historical wrongs of illegitimate subjection? From what we have seen thus far, it would appear that Kantian political philosophy has no choice but to either implausibly answer in the affirmative or admit the need for a more pluralistic approach to questions about political authority and territorial jurisdiction.

[43] Presumably Waldron would not include all of these movements in the category of "things like separatism, ethnic cleansing, and the sort of fastidious abhorrence of one another . . . that might impede political cooperation"—"strategies" which he describes as "wrong in themselves" (Waldron [2002], 140).

[44] To be clear, the issue here is not how well-off or badly off the wronged groups are *now*. The most poignant actual cases, of course, involve wrongs that produced profound and intergenerational suffering (as in the cases of many aboriginal peoples). But such ongoing suffering is not *necessary* for those who have been wronged to be owed restitution and compensation (from the wrongdoers or the beneficiaries of their wrongs)—any more than a thief's victim has to be poor in order to be owed restitution and/or compensation by the thief. The degree of poverty or suffering produced by historical wrongs is not directly relevant to the moral issues that concern me here. Those who are badly off may, of course, have a different kind of claim of justice against their societies, largely regardless of how their plight was produced. But the *illegitimately subjected*, by contrast, are owed a return of what was wrongly taken from them (subject to the constraints discussed in chapter 7) and compensation for the negative impact of the wrong (even if those negative consequences were subsequently overcome by the wronged parties). There are owed a return of their stolen land (again, within certain limits) and their stolen autonomy, along with compensation for their loss of family, property, society, and lifestyle.

Arrogance and Urgency

How might a Kantian functionalist theory of democratic authority try to respond to this charge: the charge that it lacks the resources to resolve what seems to be a very basic problem for any theory of political authority and territorial rights? The solution to which democratic theory of course aspires is that the boundaries of the state's political authority will be defined simply in terms of the persons to whom the resources of democratic government (including both rights of participation and rights of equal standing) are in fact made available. Because democratic participation has a "consensual look" to it, this might be mistaken for an appeal to a consent theory of political obligation and authority, with boundaries drawn voluntaristically (and historically) by the free choices of the participants in democratic political practices. That would be a confusion, of course, since democratic theory does not typically allow that those who scrupulously *refrain* from participating in the democratic life of the community are thereby freed from the state's political authority. (And democratic participation can successfully retain its "consensual look" only if participation actually alters the moral position of those who participate, relative to the position of those who decline to do so.) The actual argument must be rather that persons are subject to the political authority of a democratic state when their *rights* of participation (etc.) are appropriately acknowledged and enforced by the state. But such acknowledgment and enforcement is perfectly consistent with great wrongs by democratic states in their subjection of persons and groups to state authority (provided only that democratic rights are genuinely conferred after this wrongful subjection). So democratic theory needs to offer us more of an argument in order to deal with the boundary problem.

But most of the other arguments on offer in recent democratic theory—that is, most of the arguments from that quarter that are designed to embarrass skeptics about political authority—in fact appear to have no traction on the problem sketched here. Scott Shapiro, for instance, argues that "one who disagrees with the outcomes of a socially necessary, empowering, and fair procedure, and thus disregards it, acts, we might say, like a dictator: he unilaterally 'dictates' the terms of social interaction to others and thereby exercises inappropriate control over the lives of his fellow citizens." Societies have the right to impose fair decision procedures, provided this is done under "conditions of meaningful freedom" (including rights for all of political franchise and free expression). So "disobedience to the democratic will, at least under certain conditions, amounts to an unreasonable arrogation of power."[45] Tom Christiano, similarly, argues

[45] Shapiro (2002), 437. I assume that the "arrogant," "unreasonable," and "dictatorial" conduct described is supposed by Shapiro to be not merely unpleasant but morally wrong.

that people who "refuse to go along and disrupt the democratically chosen arrangements" are "assuming the positions of dictators in relation to others."[46] Such people, in effect, treat their compatriots as of inferior standing to their own, "affirming a superior right to that of others in determining how the shared aspects of social life ought to be arranged."[47]

Now it is easy enough to imagine contexts in which my insistence that collective judgments have no force for me does indeed look unreasonable or arrogant (or perhaps even dictatorial). If my club operates according to well-established procedures for resolving disagreements among its members, and if the outcome I favor is rejected in a fair application of those procedures, then it surely would look unreasonable or arrogant to insist nonetheless on the outcome that I favored in advance. This would be especially true (and might then even appear to be "dictatorial") if my unilateral intransigence undermined the outcome that was chosen by following the club's procedures and forced others to do things my way instead.

But the problem for democratic (and other) theories of authority that I have been emphasizing here is not one that can be effectively addressed by accusing noncompliers of arrogance or dictatorial conduct. For the problem at issue here is not one of justifying exercises of collective authority to those who are plainly legitimately included in the collective. It is rather the *prior* problem of determining who is legitimately included in the collective in the first place, and so who is legitimately subject to whatever conflict-resolution procedure is utilized by the collective. It is the problem of determining who does and does not have a moral status analogous to that of my imagined *kidnapped* "member" of my club. And there is plainly nothing selfish or arrogant or dictatorial about the kidnapped party's insistence that the club's decisions have no authority over him, that he is not to be thought of as a legitimate member of the club at all. That insistence is only the quite correct insistence that the value of his autonomy, the force of his rights to liberty, must have some weight in the determination of his moral obligations. So the question is not Christiano's question of "how to structure their shared world together";[48] it is the question whether, morally speaking, they *have*

[46] Christiano (2013). It is not clear from this passage whether or not Christiano is equating "refusing to go along" with "disrupting" the arrangements in question. It seems plain that one can, at least in many circumstances, do the former without doing the latter. And given the enormous coercive power of the state, it seems almost certain that most individuals who "refuse to go along" with enacted state policies will not find themselves in a position to interestingly "disrupt" the instituted arrangements or to "dictate" to society the terms of the social arrangements they prefer. They typically can be no more than nuisances; and they need not even be that. The claims by Shapiro and Christiano that refusal to comply with democratically produced authority constitutes "dictatorial" behavior thus seem to be (deliberate?) exaggerations.

[47] Christiano (2004), 286; (2008), 250.

[48] Christiano (2013).

a "shared world."[49] "The establishment of justice," Christiano argues, "creates a common world shared by all members of the society and in which the interests of all members are deeply intertwined."[50] But where political and legal structures (including internally *just*, functionally effective structures) are imposed on people in morally illegitimate ways, the resulting "deep intertwining" of their interests with those of their oppressors is something calling for moral remedy, not something that simply creates the very same obligations of submission and compliance for wronged persons that we think would bind those who had been legitimately incorporated into "a common world."

Grant that democratic decision making is a fair procedure for resolving disagreement. Grant even that it is the fairest possible procedure, or that it is, among the various fair procedures, the one that is most likely to generate good or correct results.[51] It is not "unreasonable" or "arrogant" or "dictatorial" to refuse to accept even *fair* terms of cooperation from those whose subjection of you to *any* terms at all is morally wrong. To deny this is to deny that individual liberty has any moral value worth considering. One might try to respond, of course, by claiming "that personal liberty has value only when schemes of social cooperation are already in place."[52] While that claim seems to me false, it is certainly possible to overstate the importance of many kinds of personal liberty (as we saw in chapter 1, in the case of Wolff's arguments for philosophical anarchism). But it hardly overstates the value of individual liberty to insist that it is possible for wrongs of subjection to be done *within* or *by* active "schemes of social cooperation," that authority can be wrongly claimed and illegitimately imposed on innocents by those who represent cooperative political schemes. No reasonable person, I think, could deny *this*.

A more promising strategy would appear to be to return our focus to the apparently predistricted nature of the problems that exercises of political authority are designed to solve. Political authorities are tasked to solve distinctive kinds of coordination problems and prevent catastrophic social chaos, and these problems (their "urgent tasks"), while global, must be solved locally. Estlund, for example, asks us to imagine (as an illustration of his "normative consent theory") a case in which a flight attendant, in her efforts "to help the injured after a crash," begins telling the people around her how they should assist her in this task. Because it would be "morally wrong not to agree to do as she says,"

[49] Christiano does mention in passing that "external limits to democratic authority arise in cases where the democratic authority makes decisions about how to treat persons who are not part of the society over which the assembly has a right to rule" (Christiano [2008], 262). But he plainly has in mind by "society" here only the idea of a legally or conventionally drawn society, not the kind of case I focus on here.

[50] Christiano (2008), 79.

[51] Estlund (2008), 8, 12.

[52] Shapiro (2002), 437.

someone who declines to agree "is under [her] authority even without having consented."[53] In this case, "non-consent to authority is null."[54] The catastrophe in question is districted, just as are the social problems political authorities must address. So where there is "normative consent" to just, democratic political authority—that is, where consent has been "wrongfully withheld" from that authority—"authority can simply befall us." Hence, Estlund argues, "existing democratic arrangements" can have political authority "over each citizen just as if they had established its authority by actual consent."[55]

"Political authority is [thus] no more problematic than humanitarian duties." Like poverty, "juridical anarchy" is a humanitarian problem, and it is one that cannot "be solved until there is a justice system that is generally complied with."[56] Each of us has a duty to contribute to that solution, primarily through obedience to the authorities that administer the local justice system. Where we fail to do so, we contribute instead to what Estlund has called (in the same spirit as Shapiro and Christiano) "the tyranny of non-consent."[57] In a similar vein,[58] Kit Wellman tries to deal with the particularity problem by emphasizing the territorial nature of the social problem to which political authority is the unique solution: "political instability is a coordination problem that must be solved territorially." And because the relevant territories have distinct populations, "there is something about those in the relevant territory that singles them out as special."[59] While Wellman's version of state-of-nature theory (like Estlund's) actually looks more Hobbesian than Kantian—and while the moral principle appealed to establish the obligation to accept political authority is one of obligatory "samaritanism" rather than a duty of justice or of "normative consent"—the boundary problem presents itself to his account (at its "second stage") in the same way that it does for Kantian political philosophy.[60] And he attempts a similar sort of solution to

[53] Most often, I believe, what seems wrong with "nonconsent" (when it does in fact seem wrong) is either that consent is in some way owed to others—e.g., on the grounds that it is unfair to others to benefit without doing one's part—or that one cannot discharge some freestanding moral duty (e.g., of justice, charity, rescue) without consenting to cooperate with others.

[54] Estlund (2008), 124.

[55] Ibid., 117, 157.

[56] Ibid., 145, 146.

[57] Estlund (2005).

[58] Estlund, of course, denies that "localized duties" of obedience are to be thought of (à la Wellman) "on the model of duties of rescue" (Estlund [2008], 150). He instead favors a "range-limited" analysis of the sort defended by Waldron (and criticized above).

[59] Simmons and Wellman (2005), 39.

[60] Indeed, once the first stage of the argument is completed, the same boundary problem arises for a variety of related theories of political authority, including simple necessity theories of the sort developed by Anscombe and Honore. See my discussion of these theories in Simmons and Wellman (2005), 127–42.

the problem (as does, for example, Stilz[61]). Obedience to the authorities that actually administer justice in our "district" is required in order to rescue others there from the constant state of emergency that characterizes life in a state of nature.

One obvious, awkward feature of this kind of analysis is that we already have at hand a relatively clear conception of the emergency powers of states. These consist of temporary powers beyond the normal limits of states' authority, powers that override the normal rights of citizens in dealing with short-term crises—after which those normal rights are to be restored. Emergency powers are thus standardly defined *in contrast to* the normal-case, standing, or ongoing authority of states. The arguments under consideration require that we think of our social condition as (and of political authority as a response to) a continuous emergency, since we cannot explain any ordinary notion of ongoing political authority without the state's emergency powers also being ongoing. While I'm not sure that the idea of a "continuous emergency" makes clear sense ("emergencies" being, as they are, essentially nonroutine), suppose that we do try to think of political life in something like these terms.

An initial response is that the analysis in question is simply descriptively inaccurate: in most established, stable political societies, the social condition to which political authority is the alleged solution is not one of continuous crisis. If we are asked why one individual or a small group of individuals must accept the authority of the state and comply with its commands, the answer cannot be that their failure to do so will create a crisis requiring the state to exercise emergency powers. Individuals and small groups in stable societies cannot bring about instability by their mere refusal to comply or to accept the state's dictates as authoritative. Unless they resort to conduct that is not only disobedient but deeply wrong on other grounds (such as terrorist acts against innocents), disobedience by individuals and small groups simply cannot "arrogantly or tyrannically dictate" to the society how things will go. Wellman (like Estlund), recognizing the fact that the wrong done by individual disobedience cannot be its unilateral creation of a (new, or newly severe) social emergency, introduces a fairness argument (again like Estlund's) to explain why disobedience by individuals is nonetheless wrong: disobedience to law treats unfairly other members of the society, who freely and cooperatively refrain from unilateral consumption of the good of discretionary disobedience.[62] But such a response is simply a non sequitur. One cannot be obligated to do one's fair share in a cooperative enterprise unless one legitimately counts as a member of the cooperating group in the first place. And

[61] Stilz's localized duties of allegiance are also modeled on moral duties of rescue (Stilz [2009a], 195–8).

[62] In Simmons and Wellman (2005), 40–45; Estlund (2008), 146.

that is precisely the "districting" question that the "social emergency" argument was introduced to solve. The argument is not entitled to simply presume the truth of the conservative solution to the problem.

Even forgetting about this first (and, I think, fatal) problem with the argument, it also fails to explain why we should think of familiar coordination problems and social emergencies as actually being subject to "natural districting" in conditions (like those in most of the real world) where population is more or less continuous. In such conditions, any districting that is done will inevitably result from "big sticks" simply declaring that some of the people who might naturally be called on to cooperate in meeting the emergency in zone A will instead by allocated to meeting a similar emergency in zone B. Instead of Estlund's single plane crash, surrounded by a conveniently discrete group of possible helpers, we must imagine a tightly packed nightmare of multiple plane crashes in the midst of a continuous population. Which flight attendant is then entitled to demand cooperation from which members of the surrounding undifferentiated population—or which persons are required to sacrifice in order to make possible which rescue (to put it Wellman's way)—is a question with no obvious answer. If we are talking about moral authority and not just about grim political reality, it is at least not obvious that the answer must be: whatever the agencies with the most physical power declare the answer to be.

Perhaps the best answer is that people are morally permitted to pitch in and help where they choose to, with people being turned away or recruited only when too many or too few cooks are already engaged. But—and this is the point that matters—the "ongoing emergency" (or "coordinated rescue") analysis of our political condition requires a very different answer. Its answer must be that *states* are permitted to answer the moral question by coercive *fiat,* even when doing so involves plain wrongs against those "recruited" for the local good cause. *Of course* coordinated emergency aid requires that *this particular* group pitch in, once that group has been sorted or "united" by a state's coercive districting of individuals and groups, once the borders between "groups" are locked down by states. But it is the legitimacy of such coercive districting that is here at issue and that constitutes a moral problem that is logically prior to any possible claims of "naturalness" in assignments of local duties.

No doubt there are certain kinds of genuine social emergencies in response to which the best policy is indeed to ignore such wrongs of subjection by the state and to simply treat those so subjected as if they had actually been incorporated into the body politic by legitimate means. But this does not mean that such wrongs do not call for eventual rectification. Nor is the threat to authority in ordinary political life—at least for most of the people who will read these words—accurately described as such a "genuine social emergency." Nor, finally, is it plausible to characterize a state's right to wrong people in the name of meeting social emergencies as an enduring political *authority*, at least as we normally understand the idea of "authority." Thinking of political authority in terms of emergency powers, then, in my view fails to satisfactorily resolve the boundary problem for Kantian theories of democratic authority (and related views).

The problem here for Kantian theories—and for all functionalist or structuralist approaches—is that the focus of their justificatory arguments is purely inward, taking the political units being analyzed as already given, the (prima facie) legitimate territorial boundaries and subject populations as established prior to the beginning of the argument—as if there were only one state, one territory, one body of persons to consider. This approach is quite explicitly adopted by Rawls, as we have seen, who begins *A Theory of Justice* by asking us to think of the society whose justice he will discuss "as a closed system isolated from other societies."[63] It is only after his theory of domestic justice is complete—along with its companion theory of political authority and duties of compliance—that Rawls moves on to consider a world of multiple states and the "law of peoples" that is to govern relations *between* societies. And the reasoning leading to the law of peoples then proceeds as if the units of persons and territories available for evaluation were already determined, and as if only current structural or functional shortcomings in those units could disqualify them from initial legitimacy.

Rawls's international theory does, of course (and as we saw in the last chapter), forbid the kinds of unwarranted state aggression I've discussed here. Rawls, like any reasonable person, regards state aggression against innocents as morally wrong. But he cannot regard it as the kind of wrong that requires for its remedy any redrawing of or limitations on the political authority exercised within existing state boundaries. Existing states with their claimed territories and subjects are the starting point of the theory. No part of the law of peoples requires that states acknowledge or rectify their past wrongs of illegitimate subjection, even those wrongs that took place yesterday. If, however, we believe that states cannot gain legitimate political authority over persons and lands simply by having committed great enough wrongs, then our theory of political authority and political obligation *must* have an historical dimension. We do, of course, "have to start somewhere" in political philosophy, as Rawls insists. But that surely does not entail that the place we have to start must be one that gives a moral free pass to states for the past wrongs they have done.

If I am correct in my basic claims here, one simply cannot defend a plausible theory of domestic justice and legitimacy without first identifying the persons and territories that count as rightfully inside and rightfully outside a state's boundaries of authority. And this task requires that we have in hand an account of the moral boundaries between states and between states and possible

[63] Rawls (1971), 8.

nonsubject groups, an account that will not be plausible without being in some way sensitive to the wrongs that can be done in establishing territorial claims and subject populations. In short, the "inward-looking" approach to issues of state legitimacy and territoriality cannot succeed without incorporating "outward-looking" principles; and *both* aspects of the theory need to have historical, not purely structuralist or functionalist dimensions.

Others have, of course, argued that a theory of domestic justice cannot, in the Rawlsian fashion, be developed prior to an international moral and political philosophy, that the two must be developed in concert. This kind of argument is a commonplace claim among cosmopolitan theorists, who see the claims of outsiders as imposing serious limits on what even domestically perfect states may do within their boundaries. Cosmopolitans, however, have primarily focused on different aspects of states' territorial claims than those I question here, leaving states' claims to domestic authority and territorial jurisdiction largely untouched: for instance, they have argued that even otherwise excellent states are not entitled to exclusive control over the natural resources that good fortune happens to have located in their territories; and they have argued that states are not entitled to defend "hard" territorial boundaries, but are instead obligated to open or soften their borders. The boundary problem does, of course, bear as well on states' claims to resource and border control (as we will see in part III). Here, however, I have tried to show that the problem runs even deeper for Kantian theories, affecting the plausibility of their views even in the case of the most basic kinds of claims that states make about territories and subjects: their core claims to territorial jurisdiction.

Is it Really Nonideal Theory?

One possible diagnosis of the difficulties we've been discussing for Kantian theories of political authority is that Kantian theorists are unwittingly aiming at (and are producing theories that would be more defensible if they were understood as) *nonideal* theories of political authority—that is, theories about the best demands to make of existing states and their subjects in real-world conditions of injustice and illegitimacy. This may initially seem an odd diagnosis, given that it was Rawls, contemporary Kantian, who (as we've seen) brought the distinction between ideal and nonideal theories onto center stage in contemporary political philosophy. And Rawls, of course, took himself to be very much engaged in the enterprise of doing *ideal* theory, with only brief (and decidedly secondary) forays into nonideal theory.

Rawls, remember, characterized the political ideal which should be the object of ideal theory as a "realistic utopia," in order to distinguish defensible utopianism in political philosophy from idle utopianism (which advances an ideal that could be realized, for instance, only if people were very different than they are now). So he explained the concept of a realistic utopia for ideal theory by quoting Rousseau, who proposed to proceed in his own theorizing by "taking men as they are and laws as they might be."[64] The idea seems to be, then, that, holding constant the relatively intractable features (psychological, physical, and moral) of human nature, the nature of social institutions and their operations, and the nature of relations between persons and between persons and social institutions, ideal theory should tell us what is necessary in order to perfect (as far as these limits permit) the "rightfulness" of our political condition.

Now there is, of course, a clear sense in which Rawls did in fact take laws and states "as they might be," not as they are, since his ideal of justice plainly requires all existing states to make substantial changes in their domestic institutional structures (in order to satisfy the demands of his two principles of justice). But there is another clear sense in which Rawls stopped far short of imagining states as they might be. For he chose to take as his starting point—and so to grant prima facie legitimacy to—the existing conventional or legal sorting of persons and territories into the districts controlled by the various sovereign states, focusing his attention instead on the justice (or injustice) of domestic, structural features of states "as they might be." But states might, of course, be quite different than they now are in far more dramatic ways than can be accomplished simply by alterations to their domestic basic structures. And these more dramatic differences could yield (what seem to me) obvious increases in the extent to which the system of multiple sovereign states constitutes a rightful condition. The extent of states' recognized sovereignty over both persons and territories (including especially the natural resources located in those territories) might be decreased to good moral effect, and states might be viewed as obligated to make more than feeble symbolic gestures to illegitimately subjected persons and the victims of past wrongs *by* states.

If we are to "take laws as they might be" all the way down (as it were), we must not stop without full justification at the level of merely internal, structural requirements for justice. We must rather question also both the presumed extent of and the very *boundaries* of existing states' authority and ask about the obligations that their histories impose on states. Might not a *full* political ideal require that states surrender or limit their control over wrongly acquired subjects and territories, repair the injuries they have done? To acknowledge this, of course, requires that we acknowledge in ideal theory both the structural *and* the historical dimensions of existing states' authority (and their lack thereof). But Kantian

[64] Rawls (1999a), 12–13 (quoting Rousseau [1997], 41 [bk. 1, para. 1]).

theory attempts to be structuralist or functionalist throughout. The theory presupposes that societies are already "districted"; the only question is whether the performances or the institutional structures of those districts meet muster. Rawls's international political philosophy is as purely structural and nonhistorical as his theory of domestic justice. It is focused only on the conditions that must be satisfied for societies *as they are districted now* to be members of "a reasonably just [international] society of well-ordered peoples."[65] None of the principles of the law of peoples (the rules that would be followed by members of such a society of peoples") requires that past wrongs by states be corrected or that states' claimed boundaries be subject to adjustment.

If, as I believe, both more limited state sovereignty and greater state responsibility for states' wrongful historical acts would make for a morally preferable political world—a more rightful condition—then such requirements should be incorporated into the target ideal of ideal theory in political philosophy. While requiring such reforms as sharing resources and granting partial or complete autonomy to those wronged by subjection to state power may be difficult pills for states to swallow, ideal theory should surely not be taken to be committed to specifying only easy political goals. There is, I recognize, a very real and reasonably contested question as to where to draw the line between idealism and utopianism—or, as Rawls might prefer, between realistic utopianism and unrealistic or idle utopianism. But I am confident that the correct place to draw this line cannot be between an ideal that takes seriously only domestic structural features of states and a competing ideal that insists on also taking seriously the history of states' actions in the world. It is neither idle nor unrealistic to believe that both our domestic and our international political ideals should include a commitment to acknowledging and righting significant wrongs, so far as doing so is within our power.[66]

We saw in chapter 2 that the arguments Rawls actually offers cannot constitute moral justifications for accepting the extant, but "historically arbitrary," national boundaries in the world. However, a better justification (than the one Rawls offers) for taking states' existing boundaries as (for now) fixed in our political philosophizing is, perhaps, available. It involves, though, reinterpreting the basic arguments of Kantian (and recent "democratic Kantian") theory as parts of a comprehensive *nonideal* theory. Within such a theory it could be argued that achieving structural justice should have priority (over responding to past wrongs of subjection). One could argue, for instance, that while nonideal

[65] Ibid., 17.

[66] Risse dismisses "anarchism and views of the world order that dismantle the state system in favor of other structures" as demanding change that is "too radical" for a "realistic utopia" (Risse [2012], 323). The ideal I suggest here calls only for changes that are far less "radical."

theory should aim at the eventual achievement of a political ideal that includes both full structural and full historical political rightness, the most imperative of the permissible and feasible steps on the path toward that ideal is structural change in the domestic institutions of states. Such changes are imperative to alleviate human suffering and to realize respect for the equal humanity of all. Such changes would also, of course, give those who have been illegitimately subjected to political power a genuine opportunity to freely choose a good political option—namely, membership in a just state.

Perhaps it could be argued that nonideal theory should, at our point in history, treat as secondary goals (in both urgency and feasibility) the potentially destabilizing transitions that would be required in order to rectify the wrongs done by states in acquiring their current districts and subjects.[67] Domestic egalitarian reform may conceivably be easier to accomplish in the current political climate than trying to get fiercely independent states to institute humiliating rectifications of past wrongs, accept possible losses in territories and subjects, modify their unilateral control over resources in their territories, and so on. Since nonideal theory will most likely dictate only a relatively gradual transition to perfect justice (because of concerns about transitional fairness), perhaps the natural first step is to press for domestic structural reform that will produce more egalitarian, more democratic states. Such states might be more likely than those currently on offer to enter with one another into comprehensive treaties and federations that could gradually diminish states' commitments to full domestic sovereignty. At that point, it might finally become feasible to begin redressing past wrongs of subjection or to initiate a sharing of those resources that mere good fortune has located within the acknowledged territorial boundaries of this or that state.

Such arguments in nonideal theory would, of course, leave the boundary problem as a very real and substantial issue for ideal theory in political philosophy. But it would be an issue on which we should not now concentrate our attention in the nonideal theorizing that should govern practical politics. We might even, in that spirit, take ourselves to have theoretical warrant, for the time being at least, to speak of political authority and its justification in the ways that Kantian political philosophy and its democratic offspring have suggested. But we should only do so while understanding that as moral agents and social beings we have an eventual duty to do better.

[67] There are surely, however, strong arguments as well for other priorities within nonideal theory. Given the crushing and dehumanizing poverty of those who are unfortunate enough to live outside of the small group of the world's most prosperous states, the location and the accepted significance of state boundaries—for instance, their accepted significance in the assignment of states' control over local resources—seems an urgent object for change.

PART II

STATES' TERRITORIAL RIGHTS

4

Territorial Rights

Justificatory Strategies

Justifying Territorial Claims

Recall my earlier summary of the kinds of standard-case rights of control over particular geographical territories that modern states claim: (a) the right to coercively regulate the conduct of all within the territory by means of enforcing all legal rules and directives of the state; (b) the right to full control over the land and resources within the territory that are not privately owned; (c) the right to tax and regulate privately owned land and resources within the territory; (d) the right to control or prohibit movement across territorial boundaries; (e) the right to determine the standing of those within the territory (by, e.g., establishing rules governing residency, diplomatic status, or citizenship); and (f) the right to prohibit individual or group territorial secession or alienation of territory to nonmember persons or groups. These rights, remember, divide naturally into those that are primarily *jurisdictional*—in being claims primarily to regulate and *control* a particular territory—and those that are more *property-like*, exclusionary claims over a region: claims to choose who or what may pass over its boundaries and who may use (and how they may use) the land and resources located within those boundaries.[1]

[1] Others seem to prefer instead a threefold categorization of territorial rights, the categories being jurisdictional rights, resource rights, and rights to control movement over borders (or to control immigration) (e.g., Miller [2011], 92–3; Ypi [2013], 242; Van der Vossen [2014], 714 [online, 2]). I take rights to control movement across borders, like resource rights, to be closely analogous to the property rights claimed by individual landowners (see chapter 9). And rights to control immigration *combine* these property-like border control rights with various jurisdictional rights (involving, e.g., rights to determine the legal status of immigrants, to make and enforce laws governing those who cross borders illegally, etc.). This division that I make here—between states' jurisdictional and property-like claims—is intended only as a clear *analytical* division. Many of the specific rights states name as their own are in fact best conceived as "composites" of the two kinds of claims. Part II of this

While we typically take for granted the legitimacy of established states' claims to these kinds of rights—at least where the claims are longstanding and unchallenged (or, at least, not widely or loudly challenged)—we mostly agree that at least *some* such claims by states surely cannot be morally justified. For instance, I write these words less than a year after the Crimean peninsula was annexed by Russia, in a political move regarded as legitimate by only a tiny handful of Russia's staunchest allies and condemned as indefensible by most of the world's nations. This annexation, of course, imposed Russian political authority over not only Crimean residents but (importantly, in terms of Russian motivation) over Crimean land and resources (including gas and oil reserves and strategic ports). But exactly what kind of *justification* for claims to territorial authority is it that we think Russia lacks (with respect to Crimea) but the United States enjoys (with respect to Hawaii, say)? That is the kind of justificatory question that I want to try to answer in the remainder of this work.

I should stress from the start, though, that this is only one kind of justificatory question that could be asked about states' territorial claims. This question concerns the *particular* claims made by *particular* states to *particular* territories. Another interesting question—that I will not systematically pursue here—asks what it is that could justify the *general* claims made by states together to the entire world (indeed, to the entire usable universe). How did states collectively acquire the right to divide among themselves all usable land and resources? It is surely on reflection a quite striking and remarkable feature of our political lives that the usable earth is entirely claimed by states, and that of the territory remaining in the usable universe that is claimed by no particular state (e.g., the high seas, Antarctica, the earth's moon, outer space[2]), nearly all is regarded in international law as *res communis* (i.e., as held in common by *all* states collectively). Virtually nothing usable is treated as *res nullius* and so as legally available for appropriation or settlement.[3]

But however little we may actually question such arrangements, it is unquestionable that they have profound effects on individual and group liberty—particularly where groups seek to establish new, autonomous polities on territories of their own, but find all land (within or without existing states) legally closed to them. Locke famously wrote that "any number of men may"

work will deal (primarily) with the jurisdictional aspects of states' claims to territory. Part III considers primarily the property-like claims that states make over particular geographical spaces.

[2] The latter two as per the international *Outer Space Treaty*. There is some disagreement about whether that 1967 treaty makes objects like asteroids *res communis* or *res nullius*.

[3] More precisely, international law recognizes four types of territory: that which is subject to the sovereignty of some state (or states); that which is not so subject, but which has its own legal status (e.g., trust territories); the *res communis*; and the *res nullius* (Brownlie [1998], 105).

join together in political society, but only because their doing so "injures not the freedom of the rest" (II, 95). Where the territorial claims made by political societies (on behalf of their willing members) *do* injure the freedom of other (less willing) individuals, are those territorial claims indefensible? Further, of course, Locke famously argued that *individuals* may legitimately appropriate unowned land only where there is "enough and as good left in common for others" (II, 27, 33). We may not by our appropriations deny others similar opportunities to appropriate. But are *states* immune from this Lockean proviso, free to take all usable territory as their own, without regard for actual or potential rival claimants? The Lockean theory of territory that I defend below implies, as we will see, that such practices by states cannot in fact be justified, and that what is not actively used, developed, or stewarded by the willing subjects of some legitimate polity (or by unincorporated individuals or groups) must be left unclaimed as *res nullius*.[4] But I will not pursue this issue in any systematic fashion.

And there are many other questions that touch on the territorial dimensions of the modern state that I will not try to answer here. For instance, it has been regularly argued both that certain kinds of groups of persons have by their natures a right to a territory on which to govern themselves—even when there is no particular piece of land to which they obviously have a valid claim—and that it is best in various ways for all or most of the land in the world to be controlled by states or societies, rather than to be simply open for all to use—even when there is no special reason why one state rather than another should control any particular portions of the earth. Groups' rights of self-determination might indeed imply rights to territory; and the need for societal stewardship, in the face of potential for "commons tragedies," might indeed show that the needs of all are best addressed by some system of state control over land and natural resources. But I set these arguments aside, to be addressed by others. My concern here, to repeat, will be with the possible justifications for particular states in the world to exercise exclusive control over those particular geographical domains they

[4] Harry Beran has argued that political societies need to set aside ungoverned "dissenters' territories" in order to create the genuine options that would make free consent fully possible for persons living within political societies (Beran [1987], 59, 67, 104, 125). The maintenance of *res nullius* territory of this sort seems to me unlikely by itself to solve any real problems for the consent theorist, since the high costs of relocation to such territory simply mirror the high costs of emigration generally, generating similar (and familiar) worries about the voluntariness of remaining (and consenting). But the rather different problem of *territorial* legitimacy that I am addressing in the text seems to me to push us by a different argumentative route toward practical recommendations similar to those made by Beran. The requirement that states leave enough and as good land for rival (i.e., nonstate or new-state) claimants may oblige states to downsize and make new spaces available for appropriation by individuals or groups.

claim as their territories.[5] And that issue cannot be adequately addressed simply by showing that *some* system of state control over land is morally required, that groups' rights of self-determination imply their rights to control *some* land or other, or that states cannot perform their core functions adequately without control over *some* territory.[6] It is only through exploring additional principles—principles that indicate *which* (of the many possible) systems and *which* (of the many possible) distributions of land and resources are morally favored—that we can evaluate the specific territorial claims made by actual states.

Neither will I raise any basic questions about justifications for the modern state's territorial form. The Lockean theory I defend implies that it is perfectly permissible for political societies to take territorial form. But quite independent of that theory, of course, it is not especially difficult to think of good reasons, both explanatory and justificatory, for the evolution of political societies into territorial entities of the modern sort. States are in the business of delivering certain goods to their members, and their ability to do so more efficiently (than individuals can secure those goods for themselves) is an important part of the justification for *having* states. The most important of the goods states deliver are *public* goods, such as security (from domestic and foreign aggression), a monetary system, or clean air and water. And it is far more efficient to deliver such benefits to a discrete geographical area—and so to all members of the state within it—than it would be to deliver them to a set of members who were geographically dispersed or who were interspersed with nonmembers. More generally, one simply can't beat territorial concentration for administrative convenience.[7]

[5] I take this to be the harder of the two sorts of questions. It is (relatively) easy, I think, to show that state stewardship of land and resources is likely to better serve long-term human interests than would the use of land and resources by large numbers of private individuals. It is (comparatively) harder to show why any particular state should get to control any particular chunk of the world. By analogy, we can also (relatively) easily explain why *individuals* ought to have personal *property*: without enduring control over external goods it is far more difficult for persons to secure essential interests and exercise self-government. But it has proved (comparatively) far more difficult for theorists to explain how individuals can be justified in claiming *particular* external goods as their property.

[6] E.g., "If we consider the range of functions that modern states perform, it quickly becomes obvious that these functions cannot be carried out effectively unless the state has authority over a determinate territory" (Miller [2007], 214). In Chaim Gans's nationalist theory of territorial rights, the distinction I make here—between what might ground a general right to territory and what could justify a *particular* territorial claim—is identified as the distinction between "the right to territorial sovereignty" and "the location of territorial sovereignty" (Gans [2003], 103).

[7] Political scientists have offered a variety of reasons why the bounded territorial state triumphed over its competitors and became the norm in political life. One interesting one is that bounded states, in acknowledging *limits* to their claims over land, were less threatening to their neighbors and so were the objects of fewer preemptive wars launched against them (e.g., Spruyt [1994], 169–70). For the importance of cartography in the emergence of the territorial state, see Branch (2014).

Here, though, I focus on (what I take to be) the most basic *normative* question we can ask about states' territorial claims: namely, what kinds of moral justifications are available for particular states' claims to their particular claimed portions of the universe. We can make a start on exploring this issue by remembering (from the introduction) that states actually claim three different kinds of rights, of which territorial rights might at first appear to be but one. States claim not only rights to control specific geographical territories, but also rights with respect to both particular subject populations and alien persons and groups. Against their subject populations, states claim rights to coercively enforce legal requirements and rights to corresponding obedience from those subjects. And against aliens, states claim rights of nonaggression and noninterference (in their "domestic affairs"). But these three kinds of claimed rights, as we saw, overlap in various ways. The rights states claim over subjects are largely rights of *territorial* jurisdiction—that is, rights to make and enforce law for all those who are physically within the claimed territory; and the rights states claim against aliens are largely rights not to be harmed or interfered with in exercising their *territorial* control. So it seems extremely unlikely that the best justifications for the three kinds of rights claimed by states will turn out to be independent of one another. The obvious first question, then, is: how are they related, and which elements (if any) have justificatory priority?

Those writing about territorial rights uniformly proceed, either explicitly or implicitly, as if the primary moral relationship at issue in political philosophy is that of state to subject, with the contours of the other two relationships (i.e., of state to aliens and state to territory) having a derivative status. This seems to me correct. What gives each legitimate state its rights against aliens (rights to "external sovereignty") seems clearly to be its need to limit interference by others in the assigned task of domestic governing, a task taken to be legitimated by the rightful association of the subjects that state comprises or represents. And what gives each legitimate state its rights to territorial control seems clearly to be the fact that the territory in question is either rightfully tied to the state's subjects in some way or needs to be controlled in order for the state to perform its rightfully assigned tasks. The accounts of states' territorial rights that will be discussed here all proceed on this understanding of the justificatory priority of the state-subject relationship, as will I.

We can call such accounts "hierarchical," insofar as they regard one of the three categories of states' claimed rights as primary or basic, with the others being derivative. But we could, in principle, defend an hierarchical account of territorial rights that did not, in this way, regard the state's rights over its subjects as primary. We could, for instance, try to portray the state's claims to territory as its most basic right and attempt to justify that kind of claim independently. We could then try to derive the state's rights over subjects and the state's rights against aliens by arguing that these are rights that are necessary to the state's free exercise of its more fundamental (and already justified) rights over territory. But such an account would be forced to regard the state as an independent agent, prior in moral standing to the citizens it serves, with claims to the earth that are more basic than those of individuals or nonpolitical groups. It is difficult (for me, at least) to see how the state's claim to territory could be justified *except* through appealing to the claims or needs of the persons it rules, making it essential to begin any derivation with the state's right to act on behalf of those subjects. So a "subject-based" hierarchical justification looks the most promising, a position confirmed by the structure of virtually all of the recent work (by philosophers and by political and legal theorists) on territorial rights.

But, of course, just as a theory of territorial rights *need not* be "subject-based" in its justificatory structure, it *need not* be hierarchical in any fashion at all. For instance, a utilitarian might try to justify the state's rights over territory by direct or indirect appeal to the effects of such state control on human (or animal) happiness.[8] But she could justify the state's rights over subjects and against aliens by precisely the same kind of direct appeal to utility, with none of the categories of right defended as primary and none derived from others regarded as more basic. How plausible one finds such suggestions will obviously depend on whether or not one believes that utilitarianism (or consequentialism more generally) is actually consistent with the defense of any theory of *rights*—either individual rights or state rights—as these rights are ordinarily understood. It is difficult on its face (for well-known reasons) to see how straightforwardly *act*-utilitarian reasoning could succeed in justifying much of anything in the way of enduring territorial rights for states. On such an approach, a state's particular territorial rights are to be determined at any moment by the extent to which those rights facilitate the promotion of ends like pleasure, happiness, or desire satisfaction (or, say, by the extent to which drawing the boundaries of the state in that particular place effectively internalizes externalities[9]). While there may, of course, be some tendency for such reasoning to yield as legitimate state territories those in fact currently effectively ruled by existing states—since utility tends to favor present settled possession (due to transaction costs)—it still seems likely that act-utilitarians will have to allow that state territories should change quite frequently, following the dramatic shifts in national or group needs produced by natural disasters, crop failures, droughts, exhaustion of natural resources, increases or decreases in population, and so on.[10] And this result will probably not match many people's

[8] As when Sidgwick vaguely gestures in this direction: "the main justification for the appropriation of territory to governments is that the prevention of mutual mischief among the human beings using it cannot otherwise be adequately secured" (Sidgwick [1897], 252 [15, 4]).

[9] Barry (1999a), 254.

[10] See, e.g., Moore (1998), 149.

intuitive sense of the morally justified territorial claims that states make—or, worse, it may strike us as failing to capture the idea of territorial *rights* at all.

Rule-centered consequentialist moral reasoning, of course, seems likely to come closer to justifying something like our intuitive view of enduring, stable states' rights over territories—due not only to the high transaction costs involved in less stable claims, but as well to the need for viable rules to both eliminate the necessity of complex calculation (so that the rules are relatively simple and memorable) and the need to look beyond utilities in the particular case to the general felicific tendencies of competing *policies*. But to defend such an approach, of course, we must first be prepared to defend some form of rule-consequentialism as our preferred moral theory—a genuinely daunting task in the opinion of most moral theorists. And even should we be prepared to go down that road, the results we reap might well turn out to be *more* conservative—with states' justified territorial rights turning out to be *more* stable and enduring—than we should be prepared to accept. For rule-consequentialist reasoning must be consistently influenced by the weight of frustrated expectations and desires, however unjustified these might otherwise seem to be, and by considerations of simple convenience, thus biasing the theory against those who have "lost out" in the relevant context and against claims on behalf of alternative forms of social organization that fail to be instantiated. As an illustration of the likely result of such reasoning, notice that the *deeply* conservative body of the *international law* of territory often appears to be guided precisely by such rule-consequentialist reasoning about preferable policies.[11]

[11] The international law of territory, while confusing at times, is unquestionably strongly biased in favor of settled possession and the power to defend a territorial claim—both of which strongly support the claims of the winners in the land game, regardless of the apparent moral merits of their claims: "It is a settled principle of the law of nations that a state of things which actually exists and has existed for a long time should be changed as little as possible" (Scott [1916], 121, 130). Many of the traditionally recognized bases for legitimate territorial acquisition (e.g., accretion, cession, occupation [of *terra nullius*], prescription) are still widely acknowledged. But in many cases the proper mode of application of these rules to contemporary circumstances is obscure, while in others the rules are either largely irrelevant (as in rules governing occupation) or clearly morally suspect (as in the rules of acquisitive prescription). Further, of course, actual rulings by international courts are muddied by their appeal to a huge variety of additional historical, cultural, economic, and geographical factors (e.g., contiguity, continuity, and geographical unity) that also tend to support settled possession. As a result, and as Martti Koskenniemi observes, "late modern practice of solving sovereignty disputes pays hardly more than lip-service to the traditional bases of territorial entitlement" (Koskenniemi [1999], 505). Finally, as previously noted, international acceptance and recognition confers eventual effective title on all manner of acquisitions; despite the law's contemporary condemnation of (e.g.) conquest as a source of territorial title, "conquest ripened by prescription" (as Sidgwick calls it [1897], 254 [15, 4]) will generally do the trick.

In any event, the real and most basic difficulty that I will stress here—that is, the real difficulty involved in defending any sort of consequentialist approach to the justification of states' territorial rights—will be that the unremittingly "functionalist" orientation of such an approach yields theoretical commitments that are deeply counterintuitive (and that even functionalists themselves, in their most perceptive moments at least, seem eager to avoid). Consequentialism is, in this regard at least, a strange bedfellow with the kind of Kantian functionalism I have been examining throughout this book. There are, however, also a number of clearly nonfunctionalist approaches to justifying states' territorial rights. I turn next to some broad organizational principles for discussing all of these approaches—and for discussing their responses to those who might be skeptical about the very possibility of justifying the kinds of territorial claims made by modern states.

Three Ways to Respond to the Skeptic

Plausible philosophical theories of states' territorial rights seem to me to divide naturally into three (very) broad types, each of which identifies a different sort of collective as being entitled to the status of territorial rightholder. I'll call these the "pure" types since, as we'll see, many actual theories of territorial rights mix elements of more than one type. (I discuss some of the more obviously pluralistic approaches in chapter 6.)

Voluntarist theories maintain that groups of persons that choose to be (and are capable of being) self-determining political societies in fact possess the moral right to be or to make themselves autonomous states. Those groups that make such a choice may have, in consequence, the right to be self-determining on the particular geographical territory that they occupy. Exercising (or having the right to exercise) jurisdictional and property-like rights over that territory, the argument goes, is necessary to their being genuinely self-determining. On "plebiscitary" or majoritarian versions of voluntarism, it is the majority (or, perhaps, a super-majority) of the persons living in some territory, acting on behalf of all residents, that is taken to be entitled to make this choice.[12] On Lockean-individualist versions of voluntarism (like the one I defend in chapter 5), the territorial rights of voluntarily incorporated groups derive not from the choices of the majority of residents in some territory, but only from the choices of individual persons to convey to their states certain of the rights they antecedently possessed over the specific land on which those individuals live and labor.

[12] See, e.g., Altman and Wellman (2009).

Second, *functionalist theories*[13] derive states' rights to territorial control from the fact that controlling territory is necessary to states' performances of their morally mandatory functions. Because those functions must be performed territorially, a state's right to perform them implies a right to exclusive control over the particular territories within which they are in fact performed. The moral mandates in question are generally derived from either broadly Kantian or broadly consequentialist moral theories. Kantians, as we have seen, take the morally mandatory function of states to be that of "doing justice"—that is, making it possible (as in Kant) for there to be determinate, enforceable individual rights ("especially property rights"[14]) or guaranteeing (as in Rawls) that all persons are subject to a just structure for the distribution of basic goods. Consequentialists take the morally mandatory task of the state to be that of maximizing overall good results, such as happiness or wellbeing.[15] In both cases, reasonably robust rights of control over the specific territories in which the state does its work are thought to be required for states to function effectively (or at all) in accomplishing what morality requires of them.

Finally, *nationalist theories*[16] hold that only groups that have certain additional characteristics, beyond mere willingness to be a polity or effectiveness in administering justice, possess the right of self-determination. These characteristics are generally taken to include features like a shared history, shared language, shared religion, shared customs or lifestyle, or (more generally) shared culture (perhaps along with a capacity for and shared interest in political self-determination, a shared sense of special associative obligations, etc.). And on many versions of nationalism, a further characteristic that is required for a right of self-determination is the group's attachment to a particular geographical territory on which the right to be self-determining may be exercised. The territory in question might be the group's "national homeland," or it might in some other way be specially tied to the group through the group's history, its productive labor, or

[13] See, e.g., Buchanan (2004), 370–71; Christiano (2006); Ypi (2014).

[14] Stilz (2011), 581–2. Stilz's basic position is Kantian (with a dose of Rousseau), with her central defense of legitimate states' territorial jurisdiction resting on the idea that a legitimate state is one that "effectively implements a system of law regulating property" and in which the "system of law rules 'in the name of the people'" (574) (see also Stilz [2009a]). But her final account of states' territorial rights, as we will see, is actually a more of a hybrid.

[15] As previously noted, the first defense of a utilitarian theory of territorial rights (that I've been able to discover) is in Sidgwick (1897), 252 (15, 4).

[16] See, e.g., Gans (2003), Miller (2007), Meisels (2009). Miller defines a "nation" as "a group of people who recognize one another as belonging to the same community, who acknowledge special obligations to one another, and who aspire to political autonomy—this by virtue of characteristics that they believe they share, typically a common history, attachment to a geographical space, and a public culture that differentiates them from their neighbors" (Miller [1998], 65).

locations that have acquired national symbolic value. But it is the specific, morally valuable relationship between a nation's history and identity and a particular portion of the earth that is thought to ground that nation's territorial rights.[17]

Thus, voluntarists argue that decent states' territorial rights derive from the moral importance of group or individual *choice*—controlling territory is necessary to the success of any choice to create or to continue as a political society. Functionalists say states' rights to control certain territories are required for them to perform the morally imperative tasks that only states can perform—without such territorial rights for states, for instance, there can be no *justice*. And nationalists justify states' territorial rights through appeal to the moral value of participation in cultural nationhood and to the ways in which control over a particular territory is centrally implicated in what it is to be one people, one nation.[18]

While these three approaches to justifying states' territorial rights disagree with one another in reasonably fundamental ways, their defenders have often cast their views as in even more basic opposition to a common opponent: the *cosmopolitan*.[19] Cosmopolitan critics of the international state system deny that the "robust" territorial rights conferred upon sovereign states by international law correspond to states' actual *moral* rights over their territories. States' boundaries, some cosmopolitans claim, ought to be "open" or very "soft" (with respect to immigrants and travelers, say), being legitimately subject to only quite limited control by states themselves. Similarly, most cosmopolitans have challenged states' claims over the natural resources within their territorial boundaries. Resource-rich countries, they argue, are morally required at least to share their good fortune with less fortunate states, and possibly to equalize access to or wealth deriving from their resources. Such arguments, of course, are primarily attacks on the *property-like* territorial rights claimed by states, leaving largely unchallenged states' claims to their particular *jurisdictional* authority. As a rule, even cosmopolitans have reservations about the possibility or the desirability of a world-state, leaving them relatively content with states separately performing their mundane jurisdictional tasks.[20]

[17] Territory forms "a principal aspect of national culture and consequently of individuals' cultural identity" (Meisels [2009], 5).

[18] Lea Ypi prefers a related division of theories of territorial rights, also dividing them into three classes—what she calls acquisition-based, attachment-based, and legitimacy-based theories (Ypi [2013], 242). That division seems to me to capture far less clearly the distinguishing orientations of the salient theories, since (e.g.) voluntarist theories, like functionalist ones, begin with a notion of "legitimacy," and Lockean theories, like nationalist ones, are oriented by a notion of "attachment."

[19] See, e.g., Pogge (1992, 1994). Left-libertarians are also generally skeptical about the territorial claims made by most actual states; but I will not here discuss their position (for summaries of a left-libertarian view of territorial rights, see Steiner [1996] and [2005], 34–6).

[20] Notice, however, that it is precisely this acceptance of the legitimacy of multiple sovereign states that necessitates the cosmopolitan skepticism about legitimate states' rights of border and

Importantly, this cosmopolitan skepticism about strong territorial rights is intended to apply not only to bad states, but to good ones. Justice requires of even (otherwise) perfectly just states that they exercise only quite nonrobust rights over the territories within which they have jurisdictional authority. It is also important to notice that each of the three approaches used to *justify* states' strong territorial rights might *instead* be employed to defend skepticism about states' claimed robust rights (a skepticism that would be similar to that associated with cosmopolitanism).[21] Voluntarists, functionalists, and nationalists might all defend a set of necessary and sufficient conditions for states to possess the de jure robust territorial rights that cosmopolitans think impossible, but then argue that no (or few) *existing* states in fact satisfy these conditions. The result would be a defense of a more *contingent* skepticism about the moral justifiability of states' territorial claims than the kind of skepticism typically expressed by cosmopolitans.[22] That, of course, is not the intent of the familiar versions of these theories, which aim to vindicate the territorial claims of reasonably just states. So our question in part will be: how convincingly can theories of states' territorial rights respond to such skepticism?[23]

resource control. If a world-state were the only legitimate political option, the resulting absence of any legitimate state borders and separate territories would eliminate these purported limits on the sovereignty of legitimate states.

[21] Some skepticism about robust territorial rights, of course, is much more "targeted" than this—for instance, maintaining that states lack the rights they claim in only one particular area (say, in the rights they claim to natural resources), while possessing them in the other salient areas.

[22] As an example, take my own (voluntarist) Lockean skepticism about actual states' territorial rights (as defended in chapter 5 below).

[23] It should be unsurprising—though it has not been much noted—that the three pure types of theories of territorial rights correspond to (what I have claimed are) the three principal kinds of theories of political obligation and authority. They, as it were, naturally fill out the more traditional theories of political obligation—theories that deal primarily with states' claimed rights over their subjects—by attempting to justify a different category of the rights that states claim. The fact that the theoretical projects concerning territorial rights so often take the form of "filling out" or "completing" a theory of political authority over persons reemphasizes the *normative priority* of claims to authority over persons that I stressed in Part I of this work. I have elsewhere divided theories of political obligation and authority into: transactional theories—that locate the source of political obligation and authority in specific "transactions" between persons and societies, such as contracts, consent, or the receipt or acceptance of benefits; natural duty theories—which locate this source in our more general moral duties to do or promote justice, or to advance other impartial goods (such as utility); and associative theories—which identify political obligation and authority with the kinds of duties and rights that are thought to arise within (and to partly constitute) relationships like families or friendships (see Simmons [2002]). The three types of accounts of states' territorial rights constitute natural extensions of these three approaches to political obligation and authority, with voluntarist approaches naturally "extending" transactional theories, functionalist approaches naturally extending natural duty theories, and nationalist approaches naturally extending associative accounts.

Many recent theories of states' territorial rights, of course, are not "pure" versions of any of these three types. Altman and Wellman's plebiscitary voluntarism, for instance, rides on a straightforwardly functionalist account of state legitimacy: what makes a polity legitimate is its willingness and ability to perform the essential functions of protecting and respecting human rights. But any group that is able to perform these functions can (within limits) *choose to make* itself the legitimate authority in its territory. Stilz, similarly, embraces Kantian functionalism but recognizes as well that the wrongs involved in plainly illegitimate expulsions and annexations "cannot be explained by purely functionalist considerations."[24] So she adds a number of historical principles that limit or exclude authority for even perfectly functional states, in effect producing a hybrid account of territorial rights. There are also theories of territorial rights that purport to be "Lockean" (such as Cara Nine's[25]) while incorporating significant functionalist elements, and theories that are clearly nationalist in basic orientation but that utilize certain aspects of a more Lockean-looking approach (such as those of Miller and Meisels[26]). So much in the literature on territorial rights is not as neat and clean as my division of theories into three distinct groups might suggest.

But while few actual attempts to justify states' territorial rights may thus fully exemplify one of the three pure forms identified above, it will still prove very useful, I think, to identify the virtues and limits of those forms. My treatment of them in the rest of this chapter will, admittedly, be brief and general, aimed primarily just at locating and assessing the argumentative "cores" of those approaches. My hope is that we will then be better able to see the directions in which the failures of the pure forms have pushed those attempts—and the directions in which those attempts may need to be further pushed in order to successfully justify strong territorial rights for actual states. It is to that task of briefly discussing the pure forms and their recent approximations that I turn next.

Nationalism

The most obvious strength of nationalist approaches to states' territorial rights is the ease with which they seem able to deal with the particularity of such rights. Because many nations have historical, cultural, and emotional ties to particular geographical territories, nationalists have a natural argumentative avenue for explaining why particular territories—and not just some territory

[24] Stilz (2011), 591. I discuss Stilz's theory in chapter 6.
[25] I consider Nine's approach more carefully below in chapter 6.
[26] Meisel's position is also examined in chapter 6.

or other—ought to be subject to the exclusive control of particular states. The "central case" used to motivate David Miller's account, for instance, is that of "a nation that over a long period occupies and transforms a piece of territory and continues to hold that territory in the present." That nation, he claims, has a "quasi-Lockean basis" for a right to "the enhanced value that the territory now has," both in the "economic sense" and in terms of "the symbolic significance" the national territory acquires.[27] Gans similarly takes the central roles that certain territories can play "in the formation of national identities" as an important determinant of the proper "location" for peoples to exercise their rights of self-determination.[28] The particular land and the particular people shape and transform one another, making them "belong" to one another.

An equally obvious first difficulty for such approaches, of course, is that even if we are persuaded of Miller's conclusion in the idealized "central case," "other cases may lack one or more of [these] features . . . so the strength of the claim to territorial rights may vary."[29] Nations may not have occupied their territory for very long, they may not have transformed it or enhanced its value significantly, or their identities may not have been shaped to their geographical locales in interesting ways. Worse, nations may not even be the current occupants of the territories to which they in fact have these sorts of connections. And still more important, most (if not all) of the states in the world that claim robust rights over particular territories are not single "nations" in any very strong sense, either because they are plainly multinational societies or because they simply lack the cultural cohesion or uniformity required for such an idealized notion of nationhood. These facts immediately suggest that nationalist accounts of what justifies territorial rights simply may not apply to many actual decent states, threatening to yield only skeptical conclusions, even should we embrace the argumentative paths nationalists advocate. And it gets worse.

Especially troubling are cases in which the state currently occupying (and claiming) the territory is not the one—or the only one—with the appropriate sorts of historical and cultural connections to the land to trigger nationalist-style reasoning about territorial rights. And, of course, even *more* troubling still are cases in which the current occupants took possession of the territory in question by plainly unjust or illegitimate means, but *do* (now) have these kinds of strong connections to "their" land. Such cases are unhappily commonplace, so any nationalist account that hopes to apply its arguments (nonskeptically) to the real world is obliged to address them. The standard argumentative move is to simply claim that the rights of innocent peoples (and persons) who are illegitimately

[27] Miller (2007), 217–18.
[28] Gans (2003), 116.
[29] Miller (2007), 219.

annexed, conquered, or expelled "fade out" with the passage of time, while new rights for those who have wrongly seized their territories (or for their descendants) "fade in." While it is, of course, hard to be very precise about this process, it is a process that is assumed by many (including nonnationalist) writers on the subject to reflect the moral facts. Miller, for instance, maintains that while wrongful conquest or expulsion does not "immediately" give the wrongdoer territorial rights over the land illegitimately seized—so that his position does not amount to "a charter for thieves"—the question of who eventually "has the better title will be a matter of judgement."[30] So while the wrongs states and groups do in achieving their territorial goals may initially call for restitution, for a restoration of the status quo ante, once those wrongs become older, the wrongs are "superseded" and there springs into being a new set of moral rights for a new set of people to control the unjustly acquired territory.[31]

Because virtually no modern states can make territorial claims that are not historically stained by such injustices, it may seem that a view like Miller's is a necessary feature of any adequate theory of territorial rights. We should note two points, however. First, the devil here is surely in the details. Exactly *when and why* rights go away and appear, how soon and for what reason victims lose their claims to restitution or reparation, and wrongdoers (or their heirs) gradually acquire claims to ill-gotten gains, is a matter of significant theoretical and practical importance and great theoretical difficulty. And most of those who centrally rely on claims about rights supersession do little more than gesture at the phenomenon. Second, we will be required to accept a very dramatic and suspiciously self-serving account of the supersession of our states' territorial wrongs only if we think a standard of adequacy for theories of territorial rights is that they not be interestingly *revisionist* in their implications—that is, that they be able to explain why stable, reasonably just states in the world actually have legitimate territorial jurisdiction over all of the territory that they claim as theirs. If we are prepared to accept instead the possibility that even reasonably just states may not be morally entitled to all they claim, we can defend a more plausible account of the moral significance of the many relatively recent wrongs done by states in their quests for territory.

It may seem, of course, that a liberal nationalist who was made uncomfortable by a commitment to the vague "fading" of historical rights could simply abandon

[30] Ibid., 220, 219. Elsewhere, Miller makes it clear that the claim to land made by (national) present possessors virtually always "trumps" the claim of any "rival group" (Miller [1998], 68), despite the fact that "this may sound uncomfortably like a version of 'might makes right'" (77).

[31] Miller (1998), 77. See also, e.g., Moore (2014), 127n22: "place-related rights . . . are subject to something like Waldron's . . . supersession thesis." She fills out her views on this subject in Moore (2015), chap. 7. I respond to such claims below in chapter 7.

that commitment,[32] accepting that the historical claims of wrongly conquered or expelled people in fact persist through time, in competition with the newer claims of current (national) possessors. Something like this, for instance, appears (at first, at least) to be the stance taken by Meisels in her hybrid nationalist position (discussed at length in chapter 6). But while such a move appears to make it easier to reach the desired liberal nationalist conclusions, it is not a move we should accept. Those who have been wrongly driven from or concentrated on (portions of) their lands have often also been decimated in the process, making it shamefully simple for the current possessors' claims to the land to appear to easily outnumber or outweigh those of the dispossessed (an appearance Meisels in fact seems to accept at face value). Worse, of course, it is not at all obvious why laboring to build a life, a society, or a nation on land that one fully knows (or ought to know) was wrongly taken from others should ground any moral rights at all to the land in question, any more than my waxing or building my life around the car I stole from you gives me any competing moral claim to the car. At most, we might well think, newcomers, settlers, or conquerors are entitled to access to only *some* fair share of land and resources sufficient to their needs, not to (all or even a share of) those *particular* lands and resources they have succeeded in stealing and holding onto. But I will not here further pursue this problem confronting nationalist accounts, but simply flag it for later consideration—call it "the problem of rights supersession"—since it is, I think, both a serious problem and a problem that (as we saw above and will see again below) also confronts virtually all of the prominent nonnationalist accounts of states' territorial rights. I devote chapter 7 to a careful exploration of the problem, and there I defend antisupersessionist conclusions that I believe call into question all of the theories of territorial rights discussed in this chapter.

Surely, though, the most severe hurdle faced by nationalist accounts of territorial rights is simply the absence of cultural or national uniformity within the marked boundaries of the political world.[33] Nationalists tend to locate the relevant territorial rights in the cultural or national *majorities* within pluralistic political units, leaving the preferences, interests, and goals of those not included in the majority national group disturbingly to one side. Miller acknowledges that one might complain that his position "seems to assume a homogeneous national culture in which all participants share the same goals." His response is that while all residents of a national territory may not share all of the same goals, they all

[32] Miller himself, however, "cannot see any reasonable alternative to the view" (Miller [1998], 77).

[33] Unless he is prepared to defend radically revisionist conclusions concerning territorial rights, the same kind of problem faces Avery Kolers's account of land rights held by "ethnogeographic" communities (Kolers [2009], 3–4). Indeed, I think the same problem of real-world nonuniformity faces other nonnationalist appeals to the rights of "peoples" (as in Nine and Moore).

do have "a common interest in being able to set those goals through democratic debate"—where, of course, "majority decisions" rule—and in belonging "to a community with a shared sense of national identity."[34]

But this response, using the idea of a shared "public political culture," seems only to push the relevant difficulty one step back. Minority groups and individuals may well have a version of the political interests described by Miller. But they might well have no interest at all in a shared setting of goals, engaging in democratic debate, and achieving a shared national identity in *the particular* political setting in which they find themselves—a setting in which they will be systematically outvoted on matters of central concern to them by the majority national group. Call this difficulty "the problem of trapped minorities."[35] It is again, however, as we will see, a difficulty shared by a variety of nonnationalist approaches. And as I show below (in my treatment of plebiscitary voluntarism), it is a problem that cannot be solved—as one might initially suppose—by simply appealing to a right of *secession* for trapped minorities.

Functionalism (Again, but This Time Briefly)

The strongest point of nationalist approaches—namely, their ability to explain and justify the particularity of territorial rights—seems a significant weakness of functionalist approaches. Legitimate states for the functionalist, remember, are simply functional political units: that is, institutionally structured collections of persons, of whatever size or location, that successfully perform their morally mandated functions (such as administering justice, establishing social equality, or adequately promoting social utility). The clearest strength of functionalist theories of territorial rights seems to me to lie in their plausible claims that states must advance important moral goods in order to legitimate their use of coercion, and that certain kinds of territorial control are essential for achieving those moral goals.

Why is particularity a special difficulty for functionalism? It is the institutional structure of the state—and the way that structure operates in the lives of its citizens—that matters from the functionalist viewpoint, not the location or

[34] Miller (2007), 224.

[35] Moore tries to address this problem—which she, tellingly, refers to as the problem of "the individual dissenter"—by suggesting that it is only a "libertarian or anarchist worry" and by stating that it "is a problem only if we believe that for a political authority to be justified it must achieve unanimous consent" (Moore [2015], 62). These claims seem false. Virtually all modern political societies contain not just isolated, cranky dissenting individuals, but also substantial associated groups of persons who do not share the same interests, identity, and aspirations as the "large majority" (35) that is collectively committed to (their own) political self-determination.

the history of the state. The fact that functional states happen to arise in one place or another need not reflect any special relationship between those states' citizens and the land they occupy. If those states could function effectively elsewhere or function effectively with altered boundaries, simple considerations of their morally mandated functions would present no principled bar to such changes. Without additional, nonfunctionalist principles in play, it is hard to see why our relocating, adding to, or subtracting from a legitimate state's territory would constitute a wrong. Further, of course, currently functional states can plainly rest on a sordid history of wrongdoing. What matters for the functionalist is that the state in question *here and now* successfully administers justice or successfully promotes social happiness.

This means, of course, that functionalist theories will not only have problems with the particularity of territorial claims, they will also face the same problems of trapped minorities and rights supersession that face nationalist theories. States can perform their morally required functions even with unwilling parties and groups subjected to political authority within their borders; and the functionalist, like the nationalist, owes us a convincing account of when and why the rights of wronged parties just fade away as they are opposed by the interests of established, adequately functioning states. These difficulties for functionalism add up to what I called in chapter 3 "the boundary problem." Pure functionalism simply cannot guarantee that the lands and persons counted by the theory as rightfully subject to the state's political authority do not include territory and people that have plainly been subjected illegitimately. Because functionalism grounds states' territorial rights in their current provision to areas of the services that states are morally required to provide, states can acquire justified territorial rights, according to the logic of the functionalist approach, simply by *making themselves* the provider to a territory of those services.

Remember our example from chapters 2 and 3: the United States one night secretly moves its southern border barriers a few miles further south into Mexico, claiming the newly enclosed Mexican territory and the surprised Mexican subjects living on it as its own. There would appear to be nothing wrong with this according to functionalist reasoning—provided only that the United States extended its effective administration of justice to this new territory as well. It is a state's effective administration of justice over a territory and people, not the *history* of the state's acquisition of territories and subjects, which functionalism identifies as the source of its legitimate territorial rights. My example in chapters 2 and 3, of course, was specifically targeting the Kantian version of functionalism. But many of these same points tell as well against consequentialist functionalism. Consequentialism is purely forward-looking, so the history of states' acquisitions of (claimed) territorial authority can matter only so far as it matters for its future consequential implications. And settled possession by states (as we have seen) will generally be sufficient, in consequentialist terms, to mandate continued state possession (along with the trapped minorities and automatic supersession of rights that this implies). Worse, even where settled possession is *not* in this way sufficient to dictate the conservative conclusion, the *reasons* why it is not seem potentially to be of dubious moral relevance—such as that some other group simply *wants* the territory more or could use it more efficiently than do its current residents.

These kinds of problems for functionalist theories of territorial rights are not faced (at least as immediately or directly) by the alternatives to functionalism. Nationalism, for instance, grounds states' territorial rights in national groups' historical "attachments" to particular territories. While national groups (and their territorial attachments) may, of course, extend across existing political boundaries, national groups at least cannot simply "make themselves" attached to some territory outside their current domain.[36] Similarly, political societies cannot, on the Lockean model, simply take control of—and on that basis purport to rule legitimately over—any land beyond that which is lived and labored on by those societies' willing members. Functionalism, however, seems unable to avoid licensing plainly illegitimate acquisitions of territorial jurisdiction. I consider at length in chapter 6 the question of whether a largely functionalist theory can plausibly address these problems through the addition of various nonfunctionalist principles. And I will consider more fully there as well both the general motivations for functionalist approaches to the problem of states' territorial rights and what I take to be the limits on hybrid, pluralistic approaches to this subject.

Voluntarism (Plebiscitary)

The majoritarian, plebiscitary version of voluntarism, though apparently designed to avoid them, can in fact be seen to share many of the same problems faced by the nationalist and functionalist approaches to territorial rights. Plebiscitary voluntarism, as we've seen, approaches territorial rights voluntaristically, but using a strongly functionalist account of state legitimacy. A state's legitimacy (that is, what justifies its use of coercive power) "rests on the ability

[36] Nationalist theories do not generally appear to take *mere* sentimental attachment to (or desire for) particular lands to be sufficient for the morally relevant "attachment" of nations to lands. There is, of course, no very obvious reason why nations could not form bizarre attachments to (or, indeed, build their national identities around) territories or landmarks with which they had little or no actual history of physical interaction. But most nationalist theorists insist on some history of productive use (of land by a nation) as a condition for national territorial rights.

and willingness of a state to protect the human rights of its constituents [i.e., to protect them from "'substantial and recurrent threats' to a decent human life"] and to respect the rights of all others."[37] A legitimate state, according to Altman and Wellman, for instance, is a "territorially based," "nonconsensual form of association" that enjoys a group "right of self-determination."[38] Any group that is "sufficiently large, wealthy, politically organized, and territorially contiguous so that it can secure for all individuals in the territory the essential benefits of political association," has the right to form or sustain its own state on (and exercise robust control over) the territory it occupies.[39]

Why even describe as "voluntarist" an account on which legitimate states are characterized as "nonconsensual associations"? This account makes legitimacy and territorial jurisdiction a matter of the *choice* of the relevant (politically capable) group to exercise the core functions of the state. But the "choice" at issue, of course, is the choice of the group conceived as a territorially organized whole. "States must be sufficiently territorially contiguous in order to perform their requisite functions, and achieving contiguity requires them to nonconsensually coerce all those within their territorial borders." While "individuals and legitimate states both have rights to self-determination," one cannot hold that the individual's right of self-determination takes "precedence over state sovereignty . . . without implicitly endorsing anarchism."[40] The structure of this position naturally suggests the question of whether it can plausibly solve "the problem of trapped minorities."

It may seem that the answer is obviously "yes," since "trapped minorities" can (according to Altman and Wellman's theory) escape their traps by opting for secession, choosing to create legitimate states of their own on their own territory. While this will be of no help to "trapped" individuals or to trapped small, dispersed, or disorganized groups,[41] any substantial, nonimpoverished group appears to have a reasonable route out from the trap of permanent minority status. Any group that is "willing and able" to perform as a legitimate state may do so (at least provided existing legitimate states are not disabled or unfairly impoverished by this choice). But consider for a moment what "willing and able" actually means here. "Willing," of course, refers to the will of the majority of residents. Suppose, however, that you are untroubled by how this simply pushes one level "downward" the problem of trapped minorities (for example

[37] Altman and Wellman (2009), 3–4.

[38] Ibid., 4–5.

[39] Ibid., 46–7.

[40] Ibid., 162, 176.

[41] All are free to exit, of course, but only by abandoning their lands and subjecting themselves to the dominion of whatever other society (if any) is willing to take them in.

the problem of Union sympathizers trapped in the seceding Confederate States of America). Focus instead on what it means for a group to be "able" to function as a legitimate state. As Altman and Wellman understand it, this means, first, that the group in question must be territorially concentrated. Second, it means that the group must be "sufficiently large, wealthy, and politically organized" to act as a state.

But notice that groups can be *made or kept* small, poor, politically disorganized, and territorially dispersed by the (wrongful?) coercive actions of *other parties* (such as other states or groups that oppose their political independence). The will to act as a legitimate state amounts to nothing if it is defeated by force at every point. So the "trap" in question will certainly look more dire and unavoidable if others can legitimately simply use coercion to guarantee that it will not be escaped. Indeed, even groups that *are* territorially concentrated, large, rich, and organized can still be *stopped* from acting as legitimate states if *other* states or groups are "willing and able" to forcibly intervene to *stop* them from doing so. Does a group fail to count as relevantly "able"—and so fail to have a right to self-determination as an autonomous state—if some other state will simply use force to prevent any attempt by the group to function as a state?[42]

Altman and Wellman, I assume, want to answer "no" to this question.[43] So suppose that we count as "able" to function as a legitimate state all those groups that could do so if others did not coercively intervene to prevent their doing so? Then, however, we must ask several questions: first, how far back in history is coercive intervention by others going to "count" in determining this? Consider a group that *could* have satisfied the requirements for being "willing and able" to act as a state, but that was forcibly expelled and dispersed by a militarily superior power—such as the Acadians expelled from Nova Scotia by Great Britain (during its conquest and resettlement of French Canada). Once they were dispersed (or fled) to Louisiana, France, and other parts of Canada, the Acadians were no longer a territorially concentrated or politically organized group. Indeed, they

[42] Margaret Moore, like Altman and Wellman, also requires that for groups to have territorial rights they must be territorially concentrated and have the capacity to "establish and sustain institutions of political self-determination" (Moore [2015], 35). But, again like them, she does not address the problem at issue here, beyond noting that incapacity to exercise jurisdictional authority should sometimes be addressed by assistance from other countries (50–52, 105). This response ignores those (quite common) cases in which territorial dispersal or lack of capacity are the results of outside coercion. (Nor does it even tell us how to deal with the equally common cases of deserving but impoverished peoples who do *not in fact receive* the [morally required] outside aid that would permit them to be self-determining.)

[43] They answer "no" to a similar question about whether a group loses its "right to political self-determination" if it is "unable to perform the requisite functions because its economic resources have been unjustly exploited or depleted by a foreign power" (Altman and Wellman [2009], 13).

lacked any territory at all, since their original territory was rapidly settled by others. Did the Acadians still possess the right to be a state? If so, on what territory did they have a right to establish their state? If they did not have a right, then Altman and Wellman's theory simply privileges the existing territorial concentrations of persons, for no good moral reason and regardless of how those concentrations were achieved.

But if such wrongs must be righted—and if the Acadians still possessed the right of self-determination at issue, even though "unable" to exercise it—when (if at all) did those wrongs and rights "fade away"? This, of course, is just "the problem of rights supersession" again, and Altman and Wellman must solve it before their position can be satisfactorily defended. The success or failure of a group to acquire the characteristics that give it the right to be a state and to control the territory it occupies (according to plebiscitary voluntarism) in each case has a *history*, and that history may be filled, even quite recently, with palpable wrongs. Unless the theory can convincingly address that fact, it will continue to appear simply without argument to privilege the status quo.

Indeed, the plebiscitary voluntarist theory builds into its basic logic an obvious privileging of the territorial status quo. If a territorially concentrated group derives its right to be self-determining on that territory from majoritarian voting within the group, the theory simply *must* be assuming that existing territorial concentrations of persons constitute prelegitimated groups.[44] Otherwise, there is no reason to suppose that the will of the majority has any right to determine the lives or constrain the choices available to all persons within that group. As we saw in chapter 3, majority voting within the group of six-foot-tall men, say—a group in which I happen to be included—surely (and happily) doesn't establish the right of the majority of six-footers in the world to impose their preferred arrangements on me. Neither can majority voting within the group consisting of me and my students legitimately establish the requirements for receiving a passing grade in my classes. Why, then, should we suppose, with the plebiscitary voluntarist, that the majority of persons who just happen to live in some arbitrarily defined geographical territory have the right to create a self-determining political society with territorial jurisdiction and political authority over the minority of residents? We should suppose this only if we believe that persons come presorted into prelegitimated groups, groups identified only by their members' geographical proximity to one another and bounded only by whatever arbitrary outer geographical boundaries we might choose to identify. But relying on that belief at the theory's foundations plainly just begs all of the important questions about what justifies states' claims to territory.

[44] See Nine (2012), 58. The same is again true of Moore's "self-determination" theory.

This result, of course, should be unsurprising in any theory that transforms so smoothly majority will into majority right. Wherever mere majority will is allowed to dominate the determination of state territorial boundaries, the manner of composition of the body of which that majority *is* the majority should be our primary moral concern. Just as my (populous) neighborhood may not legitimately incorporate the adjoining (less populous, less affluent, less organized) neighborhood without its consent and then control it by majority rule, political bodies may not legitimately subject to their authority all the unwilling people that they are able to surround and outvote. Nor should it matter that those so subjected were incapable of themselves functioning as a political society, especially if this incapacity is simply accepted as such without consideration of its causes. If a group's "inability" to function as a state is understood independently of the history and source of that inability, plebiscitary voluntarism will simply face the same kind of "boundary problem" that is faced by pure functionalism.

Altman and Wellman's only apparent attempt to counter such concerns occurs in their response to (what they call) the "regress argument." That argument maintains, against their view, that one can't use the principle of self-determination "to determine political boundaries, unless one first decides what the boundaries are within which voting is to take place. But the determination of the boundaries within which voting is to take place is itself a determination of political boundaries."[45] They consider this problem specifically in connection with the issue of secessionist movements; but I think the problem is one that confronts their view throughout. Unless we antecedently assume that existing occupations of territories by groups are legitimate and uncontroversial, how can we possibly proceed to argue that voting *within* those current "group boundaries"—that is, within the bounded territories simply *claimed* by or occupied by groups—will ground genuine moral rights to self-determination?

Altman and Wellman's response to the argument is that it is "possible to stop the regress in a nonarbitrary way . . . 'Let the separatist movement specify the area within which the plebiscite is to be held.'" In other words: how can groups desiring political autonomy complain if they are themselves permitted to identify the boundaries of the territory within which a vote on independence will be conducted? Altman and Wellman allow that "of course the precise contours of the territory picked out by the separatists is arbitrary in some respects."[46] But they appear to regard that problem as, relatively speaking, just a minor matter of detail.

[45] Altman and Wellman (2009), 49.

[46] Ibid.

This seems to me, however, a far deeper and more serious problem than their response acknowledges. Both the boundaries of the original states and the boundaries picked out by those forming new states may be morally arbitrary (or deeply illegitimate) in very important ways. For instance, "the separatists" discussed by Altman and Wellman might easily include in their "specified" territory not just the land occupied by their supporters, but also land occupied by others (who will be easily outvoted by those supporters), possibly because that land contains valuable resources or other desirable geographical features—just as the territory from which they desire to separate may itself have been formed by "trapping" unwilling minorities in various ways. Provided only that this "specification" does not incapacitate their original state (or take an unjust share of the state's resources, say), there appears to be no bar in the theory to such majority choices by secessionists.

While Altman and Wellman do condemn the annexation of less populous by more populous states,[47] they do so only where the less populous groups are already organized as states. Those people and groups who are "unable" to function as states (for whatever reason?) are simply left as grist for the statist mill.[48] Altman and Wellman seem primarily concerned to affirm that unwilling individuals, sprinkled here and there throughout an otherwise willing and territorially contiguous group, may be legitimately subjected to political authority without their consents. But the wrongs their position permits—both in terms of trapped minorities of significant sizes and rights superseded in an instant in the interest of the present possessor of territory—seem vastly more significant than those they seem principally concerned to deny. If a group's "inability" to function as a state is understood independently of the history and source of that inability, plebiscitary voluntarism will face the same kind of "boundary problem" faced by pure functionalism; and if it is not so understood, plebiscitary voluntarism will be pushed in the direction of a more fully voluntarist theory, an individualist voluntarism that is capable of greater sensitivity to historical wrongs against peoples and persons.

[47] Ibid., 52.

[48] Wellman does elsewhere insist that "willing and able" political groups "who occupy a territory enjoy jurisdictional rights over this land" only "other things being equal." But the only example he gives of a case where other things are *not* equal is again that of the forcible annexation of one state by another (Wellman and Cole [2011], 102–3).

5

A Lockean Voluntarist Account

The Theory and Its Limits

So the standard contemporary approaches to justifying states' territorial rights all seem to share a set of apparent problems: their justifications of territorial jurisdiction for reasonably just states permit those states to trap unwilling individuals and minorities within those jurisdictions, and they appear to deny persons and groups that are plainly wronged in the process of territorial acquisition and concentration any obvious just remedy for those wrongs. This appears to be true whether the theory attempts to derive territorial rights from the value of collective free choice and self-determination (as on the plebiscitary voluntarist view) or from the value of national orientation of a people on their land (as on the nationalist view) or from the value of justice or social happiness (as on the functionalist view).

Consider now a much older view of states' justified territorial rights that is distinctive precisely in virtue of its effectively avoiding *all* of these problems that are shared by its competitors. The Lockean view—an individualist version of voluntarism—rests on three compelling claims. First, that the only persons who are legitimately subject to a state's authority are those who are willingly subject to it. Second, that the only clear cases of rightful state claims to territorial rights (over particular geographical areas) are claims to what is lived on and labored on by that state's willing subjects. And third, that the rights of those persons who are wronged in states' territorial acquisitions do not simply fade away in the interest of the more powerful or the more numerous.

Locke himself, of course, argued (as we saw in chapter 1) that only those who have consented to membership in a political society are legitimately subject to its authority and have the obligations of citizens. And those who agree to be citizens, Locke claimed, must be understood to consent as well to submitting to the state's jurisdiction any land over which they have rights of occupancy or ownership. The heart of each legitimate state's rightful territory is thus constructed piecemeal from the free choices of persons to submit both themselves and the land on which they live and work to the state's authority. While agreements between legitimate states (and the collective or individual labors of states' subjects) may add to or subtract from states' legitimate territory, the heart and origin of that territory are its patchwork composition from the individual holdings of the state's members.[1] The Lockean view thus condemns both the political subjection of the unwilling and the exercise of territorial control by states over areas not legitimately employed in their willing subjects' lives.

Locke, remember, begins by imagining groups of loosely associated persons in a state of nature, many of whom possess property (or, at least, occupancy) rights in land, and attempts to describe how such persons might create a territorial state. All legitimate political societies originate for Locke in consent (or contract). But such consent, be it tacit or express, is typically vague or inexplicit, amounting to little more than an agreement to join together into one society. And this leaves us with the question of what subjects' consent is actually consent *to*. Locke argues that we should interpret inexplicit political consent as follows:[2]

> Whosoever therefore out of a state of nature unite into a community must be understood to give up all the power necessary to the ends for which they unite into society . . . And this is done by barely agreeing to unite into one political society, which is all the compact that is, or needs be, between the individuals that enter into or make up a commonwealth. (II, 99)

The principle of interpretation suggested here (and elsewhere) by Locke is this: consent should always be understood to be consent *to* all and only that

[1] An interesting alternative reading of Locke's views on territorial rights is defended in Van der Vossen (2014). While I (obviously) disagree with much of the textual analysis in Van der Vossen's interpretation of Locke (especially regarding the implications of the *First Treatise*), I agree with his insistence that "property is not necessary for territory" in Locke (4). States' authority over their coastal waters, like their authority over common land within their boundaries, is supposed by Locke to be a product not of (their members') prior property in them ("submitted" to the jurisdiction of the state by their consents), but rather a product of international consent (explicit or implied) (e.g., II, 45). Indeed, Locke's remarks on the origins of political society strongly suggest the possibility of states (communities, societies) acquiring jurisdiction ("political power") over *persons* independent of those states acquiring any *territorial* jurisdiction at all (a possibility that I noted earlier in the introduction). I will not argue here against Van der Vossen's alternative reading, observing only that it does Locke no favors, in my view; for it renders Locke's view an essentially functionalist one (with all of functionalism's problems): the right to govern a territory, according to this reading of Locke, is acquired "by governing effectively and justly within an area" (9).

[2] The discussion immediately below draws on my more detailed defense of this reading of Locke in Simmons (1998), esp. 168–70.

which is necessary to the purpose for which the consent is given, unless otherwise explicitly stated.

When people consent to make or join a political society, then, their consent should normally be understood as consent to whatever arrangements are necessary for a peaceful, stable society. This, Locke thinks, means consent to majority rule (or to some other rule for dispute resolution), to obedience to and support for law (within the limits set by natural law), to mutual defense, and so on. Most important for our purposes here, political consent is normally consent to incorporate one's rightful landholdings into that territory over which the society will have exclusive legal jurisdiction. It would, Locke thinks, be "a direct contradiction" for us to suppose that a person's "land . . . should be exempt from the jurisdiction of that government to which he himself, the proprietor of the land, is a subject" (II, 120). More generally, we might say, the state cannot effectively protect its subjects from domestic or alien aggression or usefully coordinate its subjects' actions if it cannot exercise certain distinctive kinds of control over (including enforcement of the law on) the territory where its subjects mostly reside and work. Importantly, though, this is no functionalist argument for political authority: it is only an argument concerning how best to understand the content of the political *consent* that grounds all such authority.

Further, stability in its advancement of the goals of societal security and coordination requires that the society's territories not be dismembered or perforated by the individual decisions of subjects, thus creating indefensible borders, allowing alien presences within established defenses, and so on. So a subject's consent should also be understood to be consent to the following arrangement: subjects will not bequeath, sell, or otherwise alienate land incorporated into the state's territories except on the condition that subsequent holders of that land will also be bound by the obligations of membership, including subjection of the land to state jurisdiction (II, 116–17, 120).[3] Thus, Locke argues, the consent that legitimates political society will normally legitimate as well that society's claims to jurisdiction and control over a particular (more or less) fixed and stable area of the earth's surface.[4]

[3] Nine criticizes the "individualistic Lockean" view of territory by mistakenly associating it (and mistakenly associating my own view) with Hillel Steiner's "Lockean" theory, according to which property owners permanently retain the "meta-jurisdictional" authority to unilaterally secede from their societies with their property (Nine [2008a] and [2008b]). Locke's actual position (and mine) holds that consent to membership in a legitimate society should normally be understood to include surrendering unilateral rights of secession, such rights being inconsistent with the point of creating a society that is intended to be stable, defensible, and enduring. As I detail below, the various incidents of natural property rights are distributed by political consent between citizen and state.

[4] Beitz summarizes Locke's argument as follows: "The founders restricted both the uses to which they (and their heirs and assigns) could put their land and created a limited power in the government to regulate its use. Since the territory of the commonwealth is like a quilt patched together

Territory can be legitimately *added* to the state, of course, as new subjects or subject settlers join new land to it, or as the state otherwise makes legitimate acquisitions (through purchase, say, or through collective labor by its subjects[5] or through seizures justified by prior alien aggression). The process that creates a state's territories thus needn't be an "all at once" contract, as Locke's remarks perhaps suggest. Neither should it be understood to (necessarily) be a "once and for all" settlement, contrary to what Locke's texts almost certainly imply. Because all plausible Lockean theories of property limit justified property rights to those that satisfy a robust Lockean proviso—requiring that we leave a fair share of the world for others to use or appropriate[6]—the extent of our justified holdings may diminish in changed circumstances, as the size of a "fair share" itself changes. (This kind of process will be examined in considerable detail in chapter 7.) But if the justified holdings of a political society's consenting members may diminish with changing circumstances, so may the justified territorial claims of their polities (which are tied to the sum of their members' legitimate holdings). If, then, we suppose that an adequate theory of territorial rights must justify only states' territorial rights that are necessarily *permanent*, we must of course reject the Lockean voluntarism that I defend here. But I see no reason to insist on such a standard of adequacy for a theory of territorial rights. Indeed, in a world plagued by poverty and overpopulation, but in which some nations have far more land and resources than they need, it is hard to see an insistence on the permanence of states' territorial rights as anything but (likely) self-serving moral blindness.

Still, for a Lockean account to end up justifying anything remotely like the territorial claims of actual modern states, it needs to explain why states should end up with legitimate *continuous* boundaries, not just how they can end up with legitimate jurisdiction over various chunks of land. Locke himself tries to do this, I think, by making two assumptions. The first is that members will tend to be clustered together on land adjacent to one another, with few "interior

from individual holdings in land, the system of covenants envisaged results in a uniform diminution of the ownership rights of the original owners and in the creation of a uniform set of rights in the government in respect of all the land in the commonwealth" (Beitz [1980], 493).

[5] Labor mixing can thus generate territory "indirectly"—through creating individual property that is later consensually incorporated into state territory—or "directly," through collective labor by consenting members. One need not choose between these two sources of territory, as Nine appears to suggest that we must (Nine [2012], 72). As Nine correctly observes (but without drawing the correct conclusion from it), "more than one set of entitlements . . . can be justified from Lockean property arguments" (83).

[6] Some, of course, are skeptical about the intelligibility of such provisos, due to the (alleged) unavailability of any uniquely best way of understanding the idea of a "fair" or "equal" share. See, e.g., Risse (2012), 122–3. While I believe we can do much better on this front than Risse suggests—and that Risse himself in fact needs to do better, especially in his account of intergenerational justice (184)—I will not pursue the matter further here.

dissenters"—that is, few landowning persons who decline membership but whose holdings are surrounded by those of consenting members.[7] The second is that *unowned* interior land (i.e., unowned land surrounded by the holdings of subjects) will, by international understanding, be accepted as the common property of all members of that political society within whose exterior boundaries it lies.[8]

Neither supposition, perhaps, seems very plausible on its face, but both can be made to seem more reasonable with further elaboration. States' territories can be expected to initially form by expanding outward from cores of adjacent, already associated persons with common goals. Interior dissenters are not very likely for a variety of reasons (at least where states do not illegitimately attempt, as modern states in fact routinely do, to subject all adjacent land to their jurisdictions). Dissenters who find themselves surrounded by consenters and consenters who find themselves separated by dissenters' lands from the core of members both have strong self-interested reasons to exchange land (or seek new holdings) in ways that will tend to create continuous boundaries for political societies (without any use of coercion). While being a dissenter surrounded by consenters might provide some attractive opportunities for riding free on the society's provision of public goods, the amounts of control over the lives of interior dissenters that Lockean states could still legitimately exercise (e.g., by controlling their movement and opportunities for productive interaction with others, by enforcing natural law against them, etc.) would in fact provide much stronger motivations for dissenters to either consent to membership or relocate to exterior spaces (supposing such spaces exist, as Locke does suppose). Similarly, members have strong incentives to offer favorable terms for movement to any interior dissenter, given the increased costs (in monitoring and defense) imposed on them by their polity's discontinuous boundaries.

[7] Jean Hampton objected to Locke's account precisely because the possibility (likelihood?) of such interior dissenters leaves as the only legitimate state "a patchwork state, which is so impractical as to be impossible" (Hampton [1997], 62). But Hampton did not consider the points noted below in the text concerning the unlikelihood of interior dissent. She also mistakenly supposed that *tacit* consenters in Locke would not count as having joined their land to the state, making discontinuous boundaries for the state seem virtually inevitable. This supposition is perhaps not unreasonable in light of the fact that Locke's principal example of tacit consent is that of enjoying land *already* under a state's jurisdiction (II, 119). But Locke plainly allows that tacit consent can be given in other ways; and tacit consent to join a political society given by those holding *unsubjected* land is clearly intended by Locke to involve incorporation of that land into the society's territories. See my defense of this reading of Locke in Simmons (1998), esp. 164–6, 168–70, 176.

[8] "And though it be common in respect of some men, it is not so to all mankind, but is the joint property of this country or this parish" (II, 35). The "several states and kingdoms" have "by common consent given up their pretenses to their natural common right, which originally they had to those countries" (II, 45). "By consent they came in time to set out the bounds of their distinct territories, and agree on limits between them and their neighbors" (II, 38).

The international "common consent" that Locke thinks creates "the commons" within states is, perhaps, an even more questionable assumption, for such consent would seem to bind neither independent persons (i.e., those who are subjects of no state) nor new states formed subsequent to such common consent, leaving both free to establish property in the allegedly common land. But the spirit of Locke's theory of property is, I think, consistent with allowing that *modest* common holdings of land can be legitimated by the exclusive use of the commons by society's members for gathering, recreation, or shared activities, *independent of* any "common consent" to this that other societies may have given. What the spirit of Locke's account *condemns*—rightly, I think—is the familiar practice of states declaring as the common property of their members (perhaps on the grounds of their "manifest destiny") vast and unused spaces, simply to facilitate defense or future settlement and expansion.

That, then, is the substance of Locke's theory—or, at least, of the Lockean voluntarist theory that I favor—of the grounds and limits of the territorial rights of states. Its basic principles strike me as more plausible and intuitive than any of the alternative theories on offer (in ways that I will explain in the remainder of this chapter). What is *not* plausible, however, is the practical use to which Locke himself put this theory. The *conjectural* history Locke offers (to explain the grounds and limits of states' territorial rights) clearly does not match (or even approximate) the *actual* history of any modern state. No modern state governs only consenting members, nor has any modern state's claimed territory been composed solely from the holdings of its consenting members. So Lockean voluntarism's *ideal theory*—its theory of when territorial claims by states are *perfectly rightful*—does not yield conclusions that straightforwardly confirm the actual territorial claims made by any modern state. Locke's conservative ambitions in *applying* his theory of territorial rights—that is, his desire to confirm the territorial claims of nontyrannical modern states, his own postrevolutionary England included[9]—were clearly unsupported by his theory, resting instead on a set of false factual assumptions. The power and plausibility of the Lockean theory lie rather in the principles of its ideal theory.[10]

[9] Locke's avowed purpose in the *Treatises* was "to make good [King William's] title, in the consent of the people" (*Two Treatises*, Preface).

[10] As we saw in chapter 2, ideal theory will in fact have three parts, dealing respectively with the moral principles for individuals, for domestic political societies, and for the world order. The Lockean moral principles for individuals require that we respect others' natural rights, that we honor and respect voluntary agreements between persons, that we do our fair share of helping those in dire need, that we appropriate no more than a fair share of the earth and its resources, and so on. I have already discussed in some detail, both in this chapter and elsewhere in this book, the Lockean domestic ideal of the legitimate state (as a voluntary association of a distinctive sort, typically with

And the primary virtues of these voluntarist principles, so understood, are plainly these: first, they explain the particularity of states' territorial claims in a natural and intuitive way, by identifying each state's territories with the particular areas in which its willing members live and labor. Second, the Lockean theory has a simple and persuasive answer to concerns about the supersession of rights and past injustices done by states. Lockean voluntarism rejects the idea of simple supersession of rights by seizure or mere passage of time (moral rights being, on this view, "imprescriptible").[11] It cannot be embarrassed by theoretical insensitivity to the plights of the expelled, the annexed, and the wrongly subjected—even when those unfortunates are mere individuals or when, as groups, they have never desired, been able, or been permitted to organize politically. The Lockean view is thus not vulnerable to charges of overeagerness to simply affirm the legitimacy of the territorial status quo. The rights of those maimed in the machinery of politics do not simply fade away for the convenience of the powerful or the numerous. Those whose rights have been violated in creating or reshaping states retain the right to rectification of those wrongs. Rights supersession is, according to the Lockean voluntarist position, normally just wishful thinking, typically done by those who most stand to benefit from it.

Third, Lockean voluntarism can address the problem of trapped minorities in a direct and appealing fashion. While it is possible (though, as we have seen, unlikely) that there will be minority individuals or groups who are *physically* "trapped" within the outer boundaries of a legitimate Lockean polity, Lockean voluntarism holds that there is simply no such thing as a person who is "trapped" in a stronger, de jure sense, as permitted by the rival theories of territorial rights (discussed above in chapter 4). The Lockean view is committed to the position that states may do no more to coerce or restrict the freedom of the unwilling located within their boundaries than private persons would be entitled to do to one another in a state of nature (since groups are entitled to politically incorporate in the first place only if in doing so they "injure not the freedom of the rest"

territorial rights of the sort described above). The global ideal of Lockean theory is simply that of a world of legitimate states, so described and limited, along with any individuals and groups that opt instead for nonpolitical conditions—all (including states, as corporate actors) obeying the rules of natural morality (as defined in the ideal principles for individuals) and respecting any (permissible) changes to their natural condition to which they have voluntarily agreed.

[11] Though, as we will see in chapter 7, this does not mean that the contents of those rights may not change as circumstances change (due to the operation of "the Lockean proviso")—nor does it mean either that rights may not sometimes simply "dissolve," or that they are absolute or indefeasible. Despite his reputation as a rights absolutist, Locke in fact allowed for the defeasibility of moral rights. Locke maintains that the legitimate claims to land (and other property) of a just conqueror may have to "give way to the pressing and preferable title of those who are in danger to perish without it" (II, 183). See also I, 42–3.

[II, 95]). Trapped minorities may not be subjected to political authority without their consent—though they may, of course, be watched and defended against—because they enjoy the same rights to live and choose freely[12] that each polity's members exercised in choosing to create or join a state. Just as such minorities may not undermine the rightful political arrangements of those around them, those whose arrangements they are may not interfere with the rightful activities of the unwilling. The complaint that states cannot run smoothly without uniformly subjecting all within the states' claimed boundaries to the same political authority is both normally factually false and, on the Lockean view, always morally beside the point.

Finally, intuition does, I think, typically identify closeness to satisfying Lockean standards for the legitimacy of states' claims to territorial rights with closeness to the *actual* legitimacy of states' territorial claims. Where states' territories have histories that approximate Locke's conjectural history—where persons have (relatively) innocently acquired or (relatively) exclusively used land that has been (relatively) freely subjected to state jurisdiction—we tend, I think, to be *least* skeptical about states' claims to territorial sovereignty and *most* skeptical about rival, alien claims to that territory. Where territories have been forcibly subjected, where "unimproved" lands have been claimed without use, or where claimed territories have been the subject of rival (especially prior) use or ownership claims, for instance, we tend to be most skeptical about states' claims. This suggests to me that the Lockean account of legitimate territorial rights is at the heart of our commonsense notion of rightful territorial sovereignty, with much of the remainder being mere accommodation to the (grim) realities of international political life. This should be unsurprising when we remember that the few early modern political philosophers who wrote anything at all about the state's territorial dimension—these being the serious philosophers who had the best historical perspective on the *rise* of the modern territorial state—seem to have agreed with Locke in taking legitimate state territory to be at least largely derived from that land that was rightfully used or owned by the state's willing subjects.[13] So perhaps the greatest strength of all of the Lockean voluntarist theory is the way in which it captures deeply entrenched and rationally supportable intuitions about what counts as a rightful territorial claim by a state.

[12] My Lockean theory's position on "freedom of movement" for nonmembers is discussed in chapter 9.

[13] As Baldwin ([1992], 213) correctly notes. For example, while neither Grotius nor Pufendorf had much to say on the subject, what they did say strongly suggests that both took the heart of each state's legitimate territory to be established in some way by adding together the original members' legitimate holdings. See, e.g., Pufendorf (1934), 958 (7, 1, 5), 994 (7, 2, 20), 1274–6 (8, 5, 1–2); Grotius (2005), 563, 669 ([bk.] 2, [chap.] 5, [sec.] 31; 2, 9, 4).

It may seem to some that I have condemned (in part I) the purely structural, antihistorical Kantian functionalist approach to territorial authority only to now embrace an equally one-sided, purely historical Lockean approach. The attractions of a seriously pluralistic approach to these questions, noted and praised in chapter 3, may appear now to have been forgotten. Such a reaction, though, would be an overreaction. In the first place, the Lockean theory of territorial rights is *itself* a pluralistic theory, limiting legitimate (historical) acquisitions and transfers of property and territory by their conformity with an egalitarian proviso, one that entitles all to access to a fair share of the earth and its resources. And in the second place, defense of a Lockean account of legitimate political authority over persons and land is perfectly consistent with defense of a non-Lockean theory of domestic justice. A state's legitimacy, I have argued at length elsewhere[14] (and noted above), is only one dimension in which a state may be morally evaluated. It may also be evaluated in terms of its possession of other virtues, such as justice (whether conceived in Rawlsian terms or others). A legitimate Lockean polity has the right to order its institutions as it chooses (provided that it violates no rights in doing so); but those societal choices are still subject to independent moral evaluation and criticism (in terms of their justice, say, or their efficiency or generosity). One of the central flaws of Kantian functionalism, in my view, is that it attempts to accomplish both of these kinds of moral evaluations of states with a theory that is in fact oriented toward only one of them.

The Standard Objections (and the Correct Responses to Them)

With all of these noteworthy virtues, why have political philosophers and political theorists not jumped at the opportunity to embrace the Lockean voluntarist theory? The answer is not, I think, that proponents of non-Lockean views simply reject the powerful intuitions on which the Lockean theory is built. For (as we will see in chapter 6) it is at precisely the point where concerns about historical wrongs are brought clearly into focus that rival theories are often motivated to take hybrid form, introducing historical principles in order to avoid the strongly counterintuitive implications of their core theories. I take, instead, the most persistent and fundamental objections to Lockean voluntarism to be three.[15]

[14] Simmons (2001a).

[15] I leave to one side an equally common basis for objection—namely, the defects in the arguments advanced by Locke himself. Stilz, for instance, appears to (mistakenly) reject the Lockean approach to territorial rights almost entirely because she (correctly) takes Locke's own arguments to be defective. As we have seen, Locke's conservative ambitions—to justify continuous, enduring rights over their full claimed territories for nontyrannical states—led him to undermine his own

The least troubling of these, despite its surprising resilience, is the common claim that the Lockean account confuses the idea of property with the quite different idea of jurisdiction or territory, in consequence of which the Lockean account of states' territorial rights must be equally confused.[16]

To identify the two would, of course, be confused. But state jurisdiction is plainly not, according to either Locke or Lockean voluntarism, *identical* to private property—since, among many other things, on the Lockean model individuals can still privately own land over which their state has legitimate jurisdiction. Rather, state jurisdiction is composed of some of the "incidents" (or component rights) of the fuller ownership of land that individuals can enjoy in the state of nature, along with some of the rights that individuals there possess over themselves. When persons subject themselves and their land to the state, they transfer to the state some of their rights over each. They then enjoy a less full property in their land (e.g., they can no longer accomplish unencumbered transfer of their land to others) and a less full freedom in their persons (e.g., they are now obligated to comply with valid law even on their own land).

State jurisdiction differs from individual property by including only some of the component rights of natural property in land (e.g., the rights to control borders and regulate uses) and by including some rights over persons which are *not* components of natural property in land (e.g., the right to make and coercively enforce law within the area). But the two are closely related, since property ownership clearly has a jurisdictional aspect, just as territorial jurisdiction has a property-like aspect (making it not at all confused to suppose that one might derive from the other).[17] Landowners have ("jurisdictional") rights to make certain kinds of rules to govern their lands, thus unilaterally restricting the liberty

foundational principles by making false factual assumptions, and thus to make some of the errors Stilz identifies (Stilz [2009b], 192–4). But a more genuinely voluntaristic (and less conservative, more revisionist) Lockean position than Locke's own, one that takes seriously each person's equal right to a fair share of the earth and its resources, is surely a better test of the Lockean approach to these issues—just as Kantians (like Stilz) often find their own positions more defensible when they depart from the letter of Kant's texts (198n8, 203). Similarly, many of the criticisms of Lockean theories of territorial rights noted by Meisels ([2009], esp. 24–6) appear to rest primarily on Locke's false empirical claims (e.g., about the actual histories of consent and incorporation).

[16] See, e.g., Buchanan (1991), 108–9, and (2003), 232–4; Brilmayer, (1989), 15–16; Morris (1998), 262–5; Nine (2012), 73–6.

[17] Indeed, even some of the great historical thinkers (like Grotius and Sidgwick) who strongly emphasized the differences between jurisdiction and property had to allow that state territorial jurisdiction (what Sidgwick misleadingly called "dominion") is strongly "analogous to private ownership from an international point of view" (Sidgwick [1897], 252 [15, 4]). See also Grotius (2005), 455–8 (2, 3, 4), who *identifies* territory and property, distinguishing both from jurisdiction. It is worth remembering in this context that the word "territory" derives from Latin roots that mean (roughly) "land that belongs to one"—covering *both* individual property *and* state territory.

of those who choose to (and are permitted to) enter on their land. Landowners who choose to submit their land to a state's authority give the state's rules priority on their lands, thus accounting for the state's consequent jurisdictional rights over those lands. They also agree to allow the state to regulate their land in other ways (which they were originally entitled to do themselves), including controlling those boundaries of it that will constitute parts of the state's territorial boundaries. The result is a kind of sharing between state and subject of the various incidents that comprise the fullest possible rights in land, and a concentration of some of those incidents (received from all subjects) in the hands of the state.[18] This latter concentration, I think, is an accurate representation of our normal conception of states' rights over their territories, not any kind of confusion of territorial jurisdiction with property. There is, then, nothing particularly mysterious about our ordinary conception of states' rights over territory that cannot in this way be accounted for "by subtraction" from individual natural rights over land and over their persons.

Often this first objection to Lockean accounts of territorial rights is combined with a second, in whose light the first becomes more intelligible. If rights in land are necessarily created through legal or institutional rule, then it plainly makes no sense to claim that individual rights in land serve as the justifying foundation for these institutions (i.e., the institutions that are responsible for creating rights in land in the first place). The first objection thus really appears often to rest on the second: that it is not possible to make sense of rights in land outside of a state whose laws establish them; so we naturally can make no sense either

[18] See Stilz's clear characterization of this version of the Lockean view (Stilz [2009b], 190–91). This version of the view is plainly not vulnerable to the "dilemma" that Nine identifies as her reason for rejecting the individualist Lockean view (Nine [2008b], 957–63; [2012], 74–81; Ypi repeats Nine's argument [Ypi {2013}, 244], and Moore accepts it as well [Moore {2015}, 31n14]). The "meta-jurisdictional authority" to secede one's property from one's state's territory is (on this view, as we have seen) one part of that property which is typically given up in the original landowner's consent to be a member of the society. Nine devotes most of her attention to refuting Hillel Steiner's version of the Lockean view (in Steiner [1996]), on which all members instead *retain* the right to unilaterally secede with their land. I agree with some of Nine's complaints about that (in my view, weaker) brand of individualist voluntarism, while acknowledging that members of a society *could* in principle retain such rights for themselves. But her very quick dismissal of the "second horn" of her dilemma—the one actually grasped by Locke (and me)—just seems confused. Those (who desire to own land) who come in the second (or subsequent) generation of members of a legitimate society must typically either acquire (e.g., purchase or inherit) rights to land under the attached ("entailed") requirement that they consent to state jurisdiction over it, or they must find land elsewhere that has not been thus permanently bound to the state's legitimate territories. To this we must add: while, as we have seen, the operation of the Lockean proviso over possessions in land means that such moral "entailments" on particular land do not necessarily result in *permanent* territorial rights for states, they are in no way morally suspicious across generations, *provided* that the proviso's conditions continue to be satisfied transgenerationally.

of grounding a state's territorial rights in the subjection (by willing members) of private rights in land to that state's jurisdiction.[19]

This objection can have a stronger or weaker form, depending on whether it denies all extralegal property rights or only extralegal property in land.[20] Notice, however, that the required skepticism about prelegal rights in land must extend further than mere skepticism about Lockean "natural" property rights. It must extend as well to all conventionalist theories of rights in land (such as Hume's), according to which pre- or extralegal moral rights in land and chattels are possible given the establishment of appropriate interpersonal conventions to define and regulate them.[21] If extralegal property in land is possible—be it naturally or conventionally grounded—then owners' willing subjection of such land to a state can be intelligibly identified as a necessary condition for legitimate state jurisdiction over the land, as the Lockean model requires for justified state territorial rights. Further, the property rights at issue need not be absolutely clear in their precise boundaries, provided that their "cores" are well justified. Even Locke allowed that an important part of each state's job is to "settle" the likely controversial "edges" of natural property claims, just as states collectively settle by treaty the precise boundaries of their territories.[22] So this style of objection to the Lockean position must claim quite a lot about the impossibility of private rights in land outside the state, requiring somewhat more philosophical nerve than at first might seem to be the case.

The third and most fundamental obstacle to the acceptance of Lockean voluntarism, however, is that (as we have seen) the theory offers an account of states' legitimate territorial rights that does not match up very well with the real-world claims made by actual modern states. States are not voluntary associations, nor have the territories states' claim been constructed from the submission of land by willing subjects to state jurisdiction. Lockean theory thus seems to describe

[19] Moore (2015), 16.

[20] On the stronger view, of course, one is committed to affirming that no moral wrong is done to a person (who is outside a state's jurisdiction) even by taking or destroying what that person has crafted or cultivated and harvested.

[21] Moore, oddly, seems to reject this possibility, asserting that "conventions are set by political authorities" (Moore [2015], 19, 153). Such a factual claim seems to ignore the existence of the myriad statutes (both within and without property law) that have been based on preexisting social conventions—useful conventions that were not "set" by any authority, but that simply arose in the ordinary course of social interaction.

[22] "And then, by consent, they came in time to set out the bounds of their distinct territories and agree on limits between them and their neighbors, and by laws within themselves settled the properties of those of the same society" (II, 38). Locke expands on the international version of this "settling" process in II, 45. Moore rejects the Lockean position partly because she (mistakenly) assumes that a defensible natural rights theory of property must have as a direct implication the substance of all familiar aspects of contemporary property law, such as "zoning laws" (Moore [2015], 20, 154).

an extremely demanding ideal that is simply too distant from the hard reality of the world to permit its application to real-world territorial claims and disputes.[23] The plebiscitary voluntarist, functionalist, and nationalist accounts may appear to do better on this score, since they are focused more on states' present characters and capacities and less on the historical processes that produced the present distribution of states' claimed territories. These views thus seem more immediately applicable to real-world territorial claims and disputes, despite their shared theoretical defects (described above), and less likely to require dramatic revisions in our views about the actual territorial rights of real-world states.

To this concern—which is foremost in the minds of many who quickly dismiss any Lockean approach to states' territorial rights—a variety of responses seems appropriate. The first is simply to question such critics' wariness about revisionism. The kind of revisionism being urged here (by Lockean voluntarism) is really no more substantial than would be defending a theory of social or distributive justice that implies that all existing states are unjust, or defending an account of the ideal international order that condemns existing arrangements as unjust or illegitimate. But, at least since Rawls began shaping the political philosophy of his generation, both of these positions have become perfectly familiar. And it is perhaps worth adding that forty years ago philosophers similarly summarily rejected philosophical skepticism concerning states' authority over their claimed subjects. In the intervening years, however, such skepticism about political authority and obligation has acquired a reasonably substantial following.

For those whose concerns about extensive revisionism persist, it should be emphasized again that states can be morally evaluated in many different ways other than by the legitimacy or illegitimacy of their claims to territorial jurisdiction or possession. The possession of the rights in which a state's legitimacy consists is not the only positive moral quality a state can possess. States can be more or less well justified in terms of their justice, their efficiency, the extent to which they help to meet their subjects' needs and those of others in the world, and so on.[24] And even if all actual states fail to live up to Lockean standards of legitimacy, they do not all fail in equal measure. Just as states can more or less closely approximate Locke's ideal of the voluntary political association, so can states more or less closely approximate the Lockean ideal of justified claims to territorial rights. Further, we can surely identify *portions* of existing states' claimed territories that more or less closely satisfy Lockean standards. The failure of some aspects of a state's claim to territorial rights in no way implies the failure of all. The revisionism required by Lockean voluntarism, then, is no more

[23] Miller, for instance, rejects such views as "impossibly demanding . . . putting virtually all borders into question" (Miller [2007], 220). See also Moore (2015), 21.

[24] Again, see my discussion of the relevant distinctions at issue here in Simmons (2001a).

a uniform, condemnatory black brush than is the revisionism required by a reasonable skepticism about the *justice* of modern states, the world economy, or the international order of states.

Finally, we need to keep firmly in mind the theoretical *point* of defending an account of states' territorial rights. Yes, because Lockean voluntarism takes very seriously historical wrongs and the rights of the unwillingly subjected, the theory's practical implications will inevitably be more revisionist than will be those of the alternative theories I've criticized here. But all of the theories we've examined are (or include) *ideal* theories; all describe ideals to which real states' territorial claims will conform only very imperfectly. Many real states' territorial claims will not qualify as legitimate on the terms of plebiscitary voluntarism, functionalism, or nationalism, nor will these theories obviously yield clear solutions to the most pressing of the world's actual territorial disputes. These are, after all, *philosophical* theories.

The job of (ideal) philosophical theories of this sort, in my view, is to identify our moral target, to describe how states' territorial claims could be fully rightful and legitimate. There will then be separate and difficult questions about how, in a distinctly nonideal world, we can approach that moral target in an efficient and fair fashion. That will involve, first, determining to what extent territorial claims made by real-world states count as legitimate according to the ideal theory; and, second, using the ideal to identify the most serious wrongs done by states (and their subjects) in establishing their acknowledged territorial boundaries. Only then can we meaningfully proceed with the business of recommending practical policies that best correct these wrongs, beginning (*ceteris paribus*) with the most serious, and always focused as well on practical and moral limitations on required reforms. (I describe below in part III my view of the actual content of the various aspects of Lockean voluntarism's nonideal theory.)

The true test for an ideal philosophical theory, in my view, is not how closely and comfortably its prescriptions match the ways in which we actually live our political lives, but rather how plausibly it identifies the most grievous kinds of wrongs that we do to each other in the course of those lives. And Lockean voluntarism, I submit, identifies the wrongs that need righting in a clear and compelling way, putting us in position to attempt to redress them and to gradually achieve a more rightful condition. For the Lockean, our political ideal must be a world in which each person is, as fully as possible, treated as a self-governing equal.

The alternative theories I've criticized are theoretically insensitive to too many of the clear wrongs that states do in our names. When states insist on exercising jurisdictional authority over unoccupied land or over land occupied by unwilling subjects, or when they expel or destroy the innocent in their quests for territorial control, they wrong persons in ways that require rectification, either through the adjustment of territorial boundaries or through genuine reparations of some other sort. Indeed (as I suggested above), I think that modern states also frequently do wrong simply in their efforts to control the sites of a wide range of the world's natural resources (through their more property-like territorial claims).

In real-world disputes about territorial boundaries or about rights to natural resources, facts will inevitably be contested, claims will inevitably conflict, and disagreement will inevitably persist. A sound philosophical theory of territorial rights can at best only identify the salient moral vectors in play in such disputes and lay out the general guidelines for pursuing the best resolutions of them. And that, I contend, Lockean voluntarism does admirably. Ease of application and simplicity of resolution are far from the only (or even the chief) virtues a theory of territory (or any theory in moral or political philosophy) should possess. After all, quite silly or clearly defective views can be wonderfully easy to apply to real-world cases and yield stunningly clear conclusions about them. Only some feature that made a theory utterly inapplicable to the real world would appear to constitute a fatal defect, at least in a theory that purports to be action guiding.

And on those grounds, some will no doubt insist that the Lockean voluntarism whose ideal theory I have endorsed must be rejected—precisely because it simply *cannot* be applied in practice and thus cannot hope to yield any even partial or approximate resolutions of territorial disputes (unlike the other theories we've considered). Given the long human history of injustice with respect to land, both by individuals and by states, along with the controversial nature of even many respectable claims to property, we simply cannot expect to be able to untangle the various strands of entitlement to lands in a way that can illuminate any actual territorial controversies. Establishing "innocent possession" of land in the first place, with which the Lockean theory *begins* its explanation of moral right, seems hopeless. This problem appears to be (at least part of) what made Brian Barry call the Lockean account "absurd."[25]

While I do not pretend, of course, that a Lockean account can with no difficulty neatly determine the proper distribution of territorial rights over, say, Palestine, neither, I think, can any of the contending philosophical theories of states' territorial rights. Some of the problems in such real-life cases, of course, are *evidentiary*, which is not a problem with the *theory* at issue. Still, one might reasonably think that these evidentiary problems are far more dire—perhaps

[25] Barry (1999a), 252. Exactly what makes Locke's account "absurd" is unclear from this article. But elsewhere Barry writes that, because of their enormous complexity and controversial nature, adjudicating historical claims to territory is "like asking philosophers and lawyers to rule on the question of whether the number seven is orange" (Barry [1999b], 41). This also, of course, leaves the precise nature of the alleged problem unclear. But it can certainly fairly be said that Barry's language in both articles is far stronger than any arguments he actually advances.

disqualifyingly so—for a theory that relies in its justificatory principles, as Lockean voluntarism does, not only on the routinely obscure actual history of acquisitions and transfers of individuals' property rights and state's territorial rights, but on the shaky counterfactual judgments that seem required in order to determine the proper rectifications of injustices that occurred in that history.

I argue below (in chapter 7) against these charges, in part by showing that in fact many compelling and perfectly valid Lockean claims to land have only vague or "limiting" contents, rather than precisely delineable contents. Even, then, on a perfectly articulated and well-justified Lockean theory, we should *expect* many property claims (hence territorial claims) to be controversial and to require the use of judgment, not merely calculation or principled syllogisms, for their satisfactory resolution. For instance, the compelling historical claims to control over territory made by the descendants of some aboriginal peoples, though perfectly legitimate in Lockean terms, may not be precisely delineable due to the requirement that claims to huge amounts of land (such as those necessary to a large hunter-gatherer economy) may have to be "downsized" in the face of the needs of other potential users (in order to leave "enough and as good for others"). But regardless of how one evaluates those arguments in chapter 7, surely at least this much must still be conceded here: that any theory of territorial rights that *does* purport to offer perfectly simple applications of its ideal principles to—and hence simple resolutions of—the real world's deeply complex and bitter territorial conflicts is for that very reason one about which we should be immediately suspicious.

6

Alternative Approaches

Less Direct Strategies

Do other alternatives remain? Before considering at some length "hybrid" theories of territorial rights, I will just quickly mention (and as quickly dismiss) two possible strategies that might appear to circumvent the problems I've identified (in the "pure" theories), but without yielding to the revisionist Lockean approach. The first employs an approach of "indirection." Instead of trying to directly justify particular distributions of territories to states (by appealing to some nationalist, functionalist, voluntarist, or hybrid theory), we might try to justify these distributions *indirectly*—by justifying the international legal order that has made or confirmed (much of) the extant distribution (through its acceptance and its defense of [many] existing territorial boundaries). The problems with such an approach, however, should be obvious. If the international order is not itself well justified, it cannot convey through its history any legitimacy to its recognition of territorial claims by states. And the international order has been and continues to be indefensibly structured around the interests of powerful states, while its lack of enforcement mechanisms undermines its capacity to uphold any judgments of illegitimacy it makes (judgments that are typically just forgotten, by all but the aggrieved parties, after a suitable passage of time). The international order has permitted states, individually or collectively, to lay claim to all of the usable universe, including that which is unknown and unused (such as outer space and the inner earth). A "legal order" with such a history lacks, in my view, sufficient legitimacy to convey legitimacy to the territorial claims by states that it upholds.

Second (as we saw in chapter 3), it might seem that the problems faced by existing theories of territorial rights could be neutralized if those theories were understood not as *ideal* theories, but as *nonideal* theories of states' territorial rights. A nonideal theory could acknowledge, for instance, that the subjection of trapped minorities or the nonrectification of past wrongs constitutes genuine injustice, while still arguing that accepting (at least much of) the existing distribution of particular territories to particular states is the best course of action under our current morally nonideal conditions. Now, exactly how we should understand the nature of nonideal theory in moral and political philosophy is, of course, far from settled. But my own view (as advanced in greater detail above in chapters 2, 3, and 5) is that we should understand nonideal theory as a transitional theory of justice (or rightness). The rules or principles of nonideal theory, so understood, would be rules designed to direct us on the best (i.e., the most efficient, feasible, but still morally permissible) route to achieving full compliance with the right. And if we understand nonideal theory in that way, I do not think it can be plausibly maintained that simply continuing on our present course is at all likely to bring about full compliance with ideal prescriptions governing states' territorial claims. I have just referred above to my beliefs about the deficiencies of the international legal order in the territorial claims that it upholds. This order has always plainly been, I think, far more clearly oriented toward achieving a stable compromise between the interests of the great powers than it has been toward achieving full compliance with any ideal conception of the right. If so, nonideal theory is unlikely to dictate anything like simple compliance with that order—and with its dictates with respect to states' territorial rights—as the best transitional route to perfect justice.

Hybridizing Kantian Functionalism

As I argued above, the standard reasons for hasty rejection of the Lockean voluntarist position—on both territorial rights and political authority—are less compelling than they might initially seem. Can nationalist, functionalist, or plebiscitary voluntarist theories effectively avoid these perceived "costs" (of embracing Lockean voluntarism) by dealing in other ways with the problems the Lockean view allows us to avoid, such as the problems of trapped minorities and of awkward commitments regarding the supersession of rights? Perhaps those theories could simply be converted into more pluralistic, hybrid accounts by adding a set of new principles designed to correct their core theories' inabilities to effectively address these problems.

I consider in the remainder of this chapter the natures, strengths, and weaknesses of several hybrid theories of states' territorial rights. But I will devote the most attention (and this entire section) to one compelling, sophisticated recent theory: Annie Stilz's Kantian theory of territorial rights. I choose her theory for my focus here partly because its Kantian core offers us the most natural extension (to questions about the territorial dimensions of political authority) of the structuralist, functionalist approach to political philosophy that has dominated the field since the 1970s, as well as the most natural approach to repairing the shortcomings of the Kantian functionalist views that we emphasized in part I. Further, the problems that I believe ultimately undermine Stilz's account are, I think we will eventually see, in many ways representative of those facing hybrid accounts generally.

According to Stilz, a state enjoys "a prima facie claim to territorial jurisdiction" over a particular geographical territory if, first, "the state is in fact legitimate" (i.e., it protects "freedom-as-independence to a sufficient degree") and, second, the state's "legal system defines property rights over [that] particular area of land."[1] The "extent" of states' jurisdictions and the particular "locations" of their territorial rights thus at first appear to be determined simply by the practical "reach" of legitimate states' institutions for administering justice. Legitimate states are morally entitled to govern whatever particular territories they actually effectively govern.

As we saw in part I, it is not particularly uncommon to suppose in this way that part of what we mean when we call a state "legitimate" is just that it rightfully rules where it actually rules. This is precisely the kind of account that we might expect a Kantian theory to offer us (and that we have seen in the other Kantian accounts of states' rights discussed in chapter 3 below). After all, what appears to matter centrally in the Kantian project in political philosophy is that individual freedom be secured by the subjection of all to effective justice-administering institutions, not that individuals be subject to this or that particular political or legal administrative structure. So the problem of identifying the particular territories over which states have de jure territorial rights is again allowed to be settled according to the location of the de facto territorial control exercised by legitimate polities.[2]

Stilz, however, correctly recognizes that "if this were all that mattered . . . there would be no objection to annexation," since the annexing state might be able to administer justice as well as (or better than) the existing domestic institutions of the annexed state.[3] Even structurally legitimate states can wrong persons or groups by "overreaching," by extending their institutional control in wrongful ways (as I argued in chapter 2). Thus, Stilz allows that a legitimate state's prima facie territorial rights can be "defeated" if the particular territory in question (that is, some particular portion of the territory which the state effectively governs) has been acquired by wrongfully displacing other groups from that territory or by wrongfully annexing other groups along with their territories.[4]

[1] Stilz (2011), 587, 590.

[2] In light of its distinguished proponents, this probably qualifies as the "standard" view in contemporary political philosophy: the boundaries of existing states are "accidental" or "arbitrary," but they are not so in any way that obviously challenges their legitimacy. See, e.g., Rawls (1999a), 39; Dworkin (2011), 381–2.

[3] Stilz (2011), 595.

[4] Ibid., 590.

The wrongs involved in the two "defeater" cases are, according to Stilz, different but related sorts of wrongs. The wrongs involved in cases of wrongful displacement are violations of *individuals'* "rights of occupancy." Individuals have not only the right to be *somewhere*, but the right to be in that particular territory in which legal residence "is fundamental to the integrity of [their] structure of personal relationships, goals, and pursuits." Each individual has a right that others respect "the centrality of territorial occupancy for an individual's personal autonomy—his ability to form and pursue a conception of the good."[5] By contrast, the wrongs involved in cases of wrongful annexation are violations of *collective* rights of the *peoples* in the annexed territories—specifically, their rights to an analogous but collective autonomy. Even when peoples' states disappear, the peoples may persist, along with their right to the particular legitimate political institutions "they have created together through their political history." And even when annexation does not involve destroying an existing government, it may still violate a "residual claim" for a people "to reconstitute legitimate political institutions on their territory when their prior state fails, becomes illegitimate, or is usurped."[6]

Both of these accounts (of wrongs that states may do in attempting to establish or extend their territorial jurisdictional) seem to me troubling. We can begin with wrongs of displacement. Because Stilz analyzes the wrong involved here as a violation of individuals' rights of occupancy—and because she defends those rights as based in each individual's "need for a stable legal residence"—Stilz's account requires "a certain balancing" between the competing occupancy rights of displaced persons and those of persons who subsequently (and "without fault") build their lives on the wrongly seized lands.[7] But the actual balancing that Stilz proposes strongly favors the rights of the latter group over those of the former. Indeed, the argument is not so much one in which "balancing" is central, but rather one in which prescription or supersession of the rights of displaced persons takes center stage. "Wrongs of displacement" are superseded where the new residents of seized territories meet Stilz's conditions for having occupancy rights and where the displaced persons are not left stateless (or as second-class

[5] Ibid., 585, 583. It thus remains unclear from Stilz's discussion how, if at all, we are to explain the (apparent) wrong involved in coercively relocating faultless persons or peoples whose goals, projects, and so on are *not* specially connected to the place in which they legally reside. In Stilz's more recent work on occupancy rights, it appears that the only wrong at issue in such cases may be the generic wrong of coercing people without justification (Stilz [2013], 340–41). But if relocation does not involve violating an occupancy right, justifying such coercive relocation may turn out to be quite easy. On the Lockean view, by contrast, persons (and political societies) have rights over all of the land (within their fair share) of which they make productive use.

[6] Stilz (2011), 591, 595.

[7] Ibid., 584.

citizens in some other state). If displaced persons fail to secure equal citizenship elsewhere, they retain a "right of return" to the land from which they were wrongly displaced, but no "right to expel" the current residents.[8]

Stilz defends her position on rights-supersession primarily by citing Jeremy Waldron's account of the matter (which I consider at length in the next chapter). But Waldron's account (like all such accounts) is most forceful with respect to *long-term* supersession, where the issue is one of *ancient* wrongs, where the cast of characters is now completely changed, where facts about the wrongs are obscure, and where judgments about "what would have happened" in the absence of the wrong are very tenuous. In cases of that sort, it is, indeed, very hard to determine the structure of present-day rights by appealing to facts about historical wrongings of the original rightholders. Stilz, however, is offering us instead an account of occupancy rights according to which they can be acquired very rapidly indeed (in "the second or third generation"[9]) by the "innocent" beneficiaries of wrongful territorial seizures.

The *property* principle that would be the analog of Stilz's occupancy principle would work as follows. If you at gunpoint force me and my family from our home and then succeed in raising your children and grandchildren in it (while my displaced family manages acceptably in the new place to which we've fled), your family acquires an uncontested right to my home. Indeed, even if my family *doesn't* manage acceptably in our new location, we retain at most a right to come back and share the house with your family. This to me has less the look of a reasonable "balancing" of competing legitimate claims to the home than it does the look of a disturbingly quick derivation of right from might.[10] Perhaps it might seem that the property case I've imagined must be analyzed very differently from

[8] Ibid., 586.

[9] Ibid., 585. It is not immediately obvious why even the "fault" of the original aggressive displacers should not also be capable of being "superseded" on an account like Stilz's. Her acceptance of the supersession of the victims' rights seems to grow almost entirely out of her concern that once the new occupants are "settled" in the territory, it will be "impossible to move [them] without damage to nearly all [their] life plans" (584); this is "what really counts for supersession" (583). But if wrongful aggressors manage to refocus their life plans quickly enough, shouldn't they also acquire rights of occupancy (that supersede those of displaced parties) in this way? Stilz has more recently added the further requirement that one can acquire an occupancy right only if "his connection to the territory was established without any wrongdoing on his part" (Stilz [2013], 354). But even if historical wrongdoing does, indeed, in this way limit the acquisition of occupancy rights—and it remains unclear why, on the Kantian view, this should be true—it is still unclear why the wrongdoers' second- or third-generation descendants do not also count as complicit in the wrongdoing (like the knowing recipients of stolen goods). They, after all, typically enjoy their ill-gotten territory in full (or at least adequate) knowledge (or at best in deeply negligent and blameworthy ignorance) of the moral impropriety that produced their enjoyment.

[10] Nahshon Perez defends a view that supports Stilz's position here: "by the third generation, I think it is safe to argue that the original property claim has faded" (Perez [2011], 160). I argue against this view in chapter 7.

the territorial cases described by Stilz, possibly because of the great numbers of persons affected in typical wrongful displacement cases. But this would be mistaken. Stilz's right of occupancy is an *individual* right; so greater numbers simply multiply the individual wrongs at issue. In the end, then, while Stilz assures us that her account of territorial rights is not "a mere legitimation of the status quo,"[11] it must be allowed that a very strong conservative bias colors at least her treatment of the "defeater" claims involved in cases of wrongful displacement.

Consider now Stilz's account of wrongs of annexation. Because wrongful annexation is a matter of violating a *people's* right, according to Stilz, it appears to follow that there would be nothing obviously wrong with states annexing as much territory as they please, provided that the territory in question was occupied only by politically unorganized groups or individuals (or by [nonpeople] subjects of some illegitimate state). While Stilz says that annexation must still be "justified" even in such cases,[12] it is very unclear how a legitimate state could *fail* to be justified in such annexations—given the basic Kantian (coercively enforceable) duty on each person to submit herself to legitimate institutions for the administration of justice. But this appears to mean that any legitimate state possesses a more or less permanent right to annex any territory that is occupied only by persons who are not (or who have not recently been) citizens in another legitimate state—even by, say, that land's harmless original occupants—and this despite the fact that such persons may constitute no threat at all to anyone in any legitimate state, at most "threatening" only those who freely choose to share their lifestyle there.

Indeed, given that such persons do not enjoy "legal residence," existing legitimate states would appear to be entitled not merely to annex their land but also to expel the land's inhabitants. Stilz plainly wants to deny this, for she now characterizes individuals' occupancy rights as "preinstitutional" and uses as a central illustration the case of the Navajo tribe, who "were not a politically organized group."[13] But notice how she defines this preinstitutional occupancy right: "the right of individuals to live in a certain area, and, together with others, to authorize a legal institution to enforce rules regarding ownership, or to engage in social practices defining their ownership."[14] Here, first, Stilz at least appears to part company with Kant, for with only "social practices" governing ownership—rather than a definite political or legal institutional structure—the resulting property rights may well lack the clarity, stability, and enforceability required for them to be (for Kant) "conclusive" moral rights. More important,

[11] Stilz (2011), 599–600n42.

[12] Ibid., 598n39.

[13] Stilz (2013), 333, 324n.

[14] Ibid., 333.

though, those individuals who are *not* engaged with others in collectively defining ownership appear on this account to be denied preinstitutional occupancy rights—they are not morally entitled to *be* anywhere, even if they do or threaten no harm to others—making them morally vulnerable, if not to expulsion, then at least to subjection (through annexation of their land) by any legitimate state. But surely it is wrong to take or to subject to outside control land that is being innocently and productively used by individuals, at least so long as there is plenty left for others. The wrong in question here involves neither wrongful displacement of individuals (since such persons may not be displaced but only unwillingly subjected) nor wrongful annexation of a people (since such persons do not qualify as a "people," lacking a "people's" political or legal organization). It is instead a simple case of (what I called in chapter 2) "wrongful subjection."

As examples of such wrongful subjection, consider first an individual, living in isolation from other persons (such as an idealized version of Thoreau), who develops a conception of the good that is both firmly opposed to membership in any political organization and revolves crucially around his relationship to the particular land on which he resides. Consider, next, a loose group of individuals (such as American frontier settlers, living on widely separated bits of land) who mostly just mind their own business, but who also together develop the same kind of ruggedly independent, antipolitical, "geography-specific" conception of the good. Finally, imagine a socially well-integrated group—but one that lacks the formal, rule-centered structure necessary for legitimate government and law (being, e.g., both antidemocratic and "impressionistic" with respect to property and basic rights)—that also has an antipolitical and geography-specific conception of the good (such as the Seminole "nation," prior to its expulsion from Florida). Now suppose that these individuals and groups are forcibly subjected from outside to (structurally just) institutions of government and law, making a good life for them impossible.

Stilz appears to be committed to denying that these acts of forcible subjection are wrongs (except, perhaps, in the case of the Seminole, depending on how we understand their social practices regarding property). Her reason, I suppose, must be that where people live outside of legitimate states (or legitimating "social practices"), they live in a condition of injustice with respect to those around them. If legitimate states subject (or expel?) such persons, their doing so is defensible as an act required by justice. But if that is indeed her answer, surely it is an answer that misses at least one very important part of what makes the wrongful subjection or displacement of innocents wrong. While sometimes doing so robs the expelled of a "stable legal residence" that is central to their lives, the deeper wrong is surely that it simply wrecks their lives by robbing them of a firmly (and apparently innocently) entrenched way of life. Geographically grounded conceptions of the good typically structure and help to give meaning to the lives they guide, and they do this regardless of whether those lives involve acting with others to "authorize legal institutions" or to engage in "social practices" that define ownership. Peoples are not all that matters. People matter too. Individuals' interests in the land on which they live and work can be of the same kind and urgency whether or not they are socially engaged with others in "defining ownership"; in either case, "occupancy of a particular place is of central importance for an individual's life-plans and projects."[15] *Where* they live can matter deeply even to solitary individuals.

In Stilz's treatment of annexation, then, just as in her treatment of displacement, she seems to take only a half-step toward acknowledging the moral relevance of the history of states' acquisitions of territory. In both cases, individuals and groups with strong and innocent-looking connections to particular portions of the earth are denied (by Stilz's account) rights to control or (when wrongfully displaced) to regain that land. But even such half measures appear to sit very uncomfortably with the Kantian foundations of Stilz's position. As we have seen, the core of her position is a Kantian functionalism: states' legitimate authority over us and our duties to uphold our states derive from the state's performing its mandatory function of making justice possible. How we happen to find ourselves subject to some legitimate state's justice-administering institutions seems simply beside the point. "If a state exists and enforces a legitimate system of property law, it necessarily represents me," Stilz says; "we have a duty to support and comply with legitimate institutions where they exist" (and, we might add [to complete the Rawlsian thought] where "they apply to us").[16]

Nowhere in this basic line of argument is there any obvious motivation for concern about *how* we came to be subject to a just state (or for the "fault" that might be ascribed to those who do the subjecting), and Stilz dismisses as "misguided" voluntarist worries that we (typically) have no choice in our inclusions in our various political collectives.[17] Yet in her treatment of the two defeater claims, she attempts to take seriously some of the nonfunctionalist, historical considerations that are crucial to any adequate understanding of states' claims to legitimate authority. And there, perhaps surprisingly, it turns out that even "an absolutely perfect state," one that performs its mandatory justice-related functions as well as a state could, nonetheless lacks territorial rights if it has acquired its control over territory in the wrong way.[18] History does matter—but apparently only sometimes and only for some people.

[15] Ibid., 334.
[16] Stilz (2011), 581, 582.
[17] Ibid., 597.
[18] Ibid., 583.

My deeper worry about Stilz's position, then, is that its historical side cannot be adequately motivated by its core functionalism, but operates simply as an ad hoc addendum to it (designed to try to avoid the counterintuitive implications of that position). If I am right in this, then Stilz's own theory is an "unstable hybrid," like the plebiscitary voluntarism she rejects for this reason.[19] My suspicion—which we will test in the following section of this chapter—is that the same will prove true of all other efforts to avoid the counterintuitive implications (outlined above) of the other, nonfunctionalist alternatives to Lockean voluntarism.

Pluralist theories are not, of course, indefensible simply in virtue of their pluralism. But defensible pluralism requires a unifying overall motivation, not simply a convenient conjunction of elements deriving from views that are essentially in tension with one another. The Lockean theory I favor is itself pluralistic, since it limits individuals' historical claims to land and resources (and thus also limits legitimate states' claims to territory) with the nonhistorical requirement that each person (and, so, each person's state) take no more than a fair share of the earth (to which no person naturally has better claim than any other). But this pluralism is taken seriously from the start in the style of Lockean theory that I support: our most fundamental moral duty is not to harm (innocent) others; and, in keeping with this duty, we may not acquire parts of the earth in ways that do harm (by leaving others a less-than-fair share). Other hybrid views, like Stilz's, appear to define a "default" position on state territorial rights first, appealing only to the core orientation of the theory (e.g., pure functionalism). Only later, in the face of concerns about the pure theory's disturbing implications are other considerations (e.g., about historical wrongs) allowed to have "defeating" moral weight within the theory, thus creating the impression of merely convenient conjunction. A defensible hybrid theory must be pluralistic from the start, driven by a compelling unifying motivation and defending an ideal of rightful territorial claims that takes seriously throughout all of the factors that help to define that ideal. Lockean voluntarism, I believe, unlike the rival theories of state territorial rights I've considered here, satisfies that most central theoretical requirement.

Hybrids of Other Kinds

Can other kinds of hybrid theories do better? I very briefly consider here the theories of territorial rights defended in two recent books that are devoted entirely to the territorial dimensions of political authority: the broadly nationalist hybrid theory supported by Tamar Meisels[20] and the broadly Lockean hybrid at work in

[19] Ibid., 600.

[20] Meisels (2009).

Cara Nine's writings.[21] It may seem inaccurate to describe Meisels's theory as a "hybrid," I suppose, since it appears to appeal only to nationalist considerations throughout: each of the arguments she considers is characterized by her simply as one type of nationalist argument for territorial rights (from a "liberal nationalist" perspective).[22] I treat her theory as a hybrid—though what we choose to call it, of course, matters not at all to its merits—largely because of its inclusion of, in addition to "pure" nationalist arguments for states' territorial rights, Lockean (or "quasi-Lockean") bases for acquisition of territory, as well as acknowledgment of persisting historical claims to rectification for past wrongs. Admittedly, Meisels never comes close to endorsing any individualist or voluntarist claims about territory;[23] the Lockean acquisitions she takes seriously are only preexisting *nations'* collective acquisitions of territory, and the claims to rectification she discusses are only preexisting *nations'* possible claims to (some of) the territory of which they were unjustly deprived.

But if Lockean grounds for *national* territorial acquisition are in fact defensible, as Meisels insists—that is, if adding value and creating new things are ways in which nations can acquire moral claims over land and resources[24]—then it would surely be perverse to deny that adding value and creating new things may be defensible bases for the acquisition of *individuals'* moral rights over unowned land or objects; it is, after all, the analogy with *individual* acquisitions that gives the *nationalist* argument whatever plausibility it has in the first place. And if moral claims to the rectification of distant past wrongs to *nations* can persist, unsuperseded through generations—as Meisels insists[25]—it would again seem perverse (for the same reason) to deny that the moral claims of individuals to rectification of past wrongs may likewise persist. If this is so, though, then a theory like Meisels's will have great difficulty denying that not only past wrongs to nations, but also past wrongs to individuals (including the wrongful subjection of their property to state authority) can bear directly on the legitimacy of states' current

[21] I will focus primarily on Nine (2012).

[22] Meisels (2009), 12.

[23] Indeed, as a nationalist, Meisels presumably takes herself to be committed to denying both. A nation, of course, could, at least in principle, arise through universal consent and could, at least in principle, come to regard as its homeland only what was formerly the privately owned land of its willing members. But nationalists typically regard such (possible) facts about nations as uninteresting—that is, as completely irrelevant to what actually grounds nations' moral (including territorial) rights.

[24] Meisels (2009), esp. 120–24. Meisels takes settlements to be "brought into being" by settlers, who in the process improve their land over its natural condition and form the land "into something new" (124). This is part of her case for the moral priority of the territorial claims of present possessors of the land.

[25] Ibid., esp. 62–9, 87–8. Historical injustice, she insists, can create a "prima facie case for partial restitution" of long-lost lands (68–9), grounding "historical claims [that] can endure with great force over time" (88).

claims to territorial rights. So despite Meisels's having no apparent interest in such individual cases (or in possible voluntarist views of the legitimacy conditions for political societies)—being distracted from such possibilities, I think, by her insistence that territorial rights must be viewed as *collective* rights (which, of course, they are even on the Lockean individualist voluntarist theory)—her theory in fact appears to be *committed* to accepting the forcefulness of individualist challenges (or challenges by nonnational groups) to states' territorial claims.

Meisels's failure to see (or, at least, to take seriously) this fact is, in my view—as was true in the case of Stilz's hybrid Kantian theory—an important part of what makes her theory untenable in the end. The deep problem (for nationalist and other theories) of trapped minorities is nowhere discussed or even acknowledged as a problem by Meisels. From the start, no agents other than nations are taken at all seriously as having morally considerable connections to land and resources. But if (as I have argued) individuals and nonnation groups, along with the land on which they innocently live and work, can be wrongly subjected to the territorial control and jurisdiction of states, then surely such wrongs must be in some ways relevant to an understanding of the proper extent of states' legitimate territorial claims. Meisels's unremitting focus on nations thus plays much the same role in her theory as does Stilz's unremitting focus on states and peoples. The "primacy of individuals and their well-being" that Meisels avows and rightly locates at the heart of liberalism[26] is thus actually cast in a distinctly secondary role in the theory of territorial rights that she ultimately defends, a role that appears almost exclusively in the standard nationalist observations about the value of national cultural in individuals' lives (and to individuals' identities).

Even were Meisels to more centrally acknowledge the relevance of individual and (nonnational) group claims within a satisfactory theory of territorial rights, however, her overall strategy in her book would undoubtedly force her to relegate such claims to the status of prima facie claims only. Meisels's strategy, recall, is to enumerate (in her individual chapters) the variety of possible nationalist arguments for territorial rights—including historical arguments from "formative territories" and rectification of injustice, arguments from efficient use, from improvement and creation, and from the roles of land in cultural expression and cultural identity. Each line of argument purports to ground an interest that a nation can have in a particular territory (and thus, according to the Razian interest theory of rights Meisels embraces, to possibly ground a right to that territory). But, in the end, the balance of interests turns out, unsurprisingly, to favor (necessarily?) the interests of the present possessors of the land. The interests

[26] Ibid., e.g., 4.

"of current and actual settlers take priority over the potential interests of another national group" in determining territories.[27]

It is not entirely clear how Meisels thinks such conclusions can be established across the board, especially in light of her earlier insistence that her "pluralistic" approach to the topic offers no "neatly formulated recipe" for the right answers in balancing competing interests in land, that her approach doesn't just "endorse the status quo" (by regarding existing boundaries as "sacred").[28] Perhaps Meisels's apparent "blanket" conclusions are not really intended to describe the proper balancing in all cases. Nonetheless, despite her conviction that supersession arguments are insufficient to eliminate from serious consideration historical claims to rectification (or to formative territories),[29] such historical claims appear in her discussion to virtually evaporate in the face of current settlers' interests in their value-adding creations and their geographically located cultural identities.[30] There appear to be no "defeating" conditions (to nullify such claims) involved in even the most egregious wrongs that might be involved in nations' or states' acquisitions of their claimed territories.[31] As in so many of the other views we've examined, then—and despite her denials—the same strong theoretical bias in favor of the status quo ultimately seems to determine her conclusions throughout. As Meisels puts it, "the forward-looking considerations . . . ultimately prevail."[32]

In the end, then, there may not be much to distinguish Meisels's approach from the "pure" theories we examined above (or, at least, from their most problematic aspects). Her "heavy reliance" on "the work of John Locke"[33] turns out not to produce much theoretical movement toward a genuinely Lockean view, and her modest resistance to Waldron's supersession thesis seems in the end to give way to a position that in fact closely approximates Waldron's own. There is, of course (and as we will see in the next chapter), a significant difference between claims being genuinely superseded and claims simply being outweighed or overridden by competing moral considerations. Meisels appears to appreciate this difference,[34] and her conclusions seem to be based only on the

[27] Ibid., 161. See also 130–31.

[28] Ibid., 3, 10–11.

[29] Ibid., 160.

[30] Meisels does say: "some claims to territorial restitution based on historical events are well-founded, even if, when all is said and done, justice often requires them to be put aside in favour of the weightier claims of settlers" (ibid., 87). The use here of "often," of course, suggests the possibility of nonconservative conclusions in some cases. But her other claims in the book make it quite clear that she thinks such conclusions at least *extremely* unlikely.

[31] Ibid., 132.

[32] Ibid., 161.

[33] Ibid., 6.

[34] Ibid., 62.

idea that historical claims will be (routinely? always?) outweighed by the interests of present possessors, not on the idea that these historical claims have been superseded. She also, on the other hand, finds Waldron's supersession arguments "undeniable" and "irresistibly convincing."[35] So it remains a bit unclear exactly why the claims of the national present possessors of territory are really thought by Meisels always to prevail.

This much seems clear, however. Meisels cannot plausibly maintain that the interests of "current and actual settlers" always, or even routinely, "take priority" over those of competing claimants until those settlers have been in possession for quite a long time. For neither of her two principal arguments for the priority of current settlers' interests works as a "short term" argument for grounding entitlements—and one of them doesn't appear to work at all, even over the long term, at least in the absence of genuine *supersession* of rival claims. Meisels's identity argument—roughly, that territory is significant to national culture, which is in turn central to the identity and welfare of members of the national group[36]—surely has force, if at all,[37] only over the long term. The claims of decimated and expelled former residents are, on this score, likely to look *stronger* than those of present possessors for a considerable period of time, since their (disrupted) attachments to the land will likely persist even through decimation or expulsion, while the new attachments of settlers will likely develop only gradually. Only after a considerable period of time will the settlers' cultures and identities be likely to be more firmly tied to the land than the cultures and identities of those they subject or displace. And no such superior tie seems at all *necessary*, no matter how much time passes.

And Meisels's "Lockean" argument—that current settlers have changed and improved the land, creating new things—might well serve to bolster in certain ways her identity argument (since we often grow attached to and identify with things we've created), but appears to lack any independent force of its own. Making new things or adding value to existing things is simply not a way of acquiring rights over them, at least unless there are no prior claims to

[35] Ibid., 74, 77.

[36] Ibid., 129.

[37] Frankly, I'm not sure I understand the force of "identity arguments" for rights even in the cases most favorable to their proponents. The mere fact that my identity is tightly bound to some place or thing—so that I would suffer great loss and disorientation were I deprived of it—does not obviously give me any special rights over that place or thing. This seems especially true of places and things that *belonged* to others and were unjustly acquired by people (like many settlers) who deliberately chose to tie their identities to their unjust gains. You cannot acquire rights over the Maserati you stole from me, no matter how central "Maserati owner" becomes to your identity (or to the identities of your heirs).

those things (and unless appropriation does not treat others unfairly).[38] I cannot acquire rights over the new and valuable sculpture that I create if I create it out of the stone that I illicitly pried out of the foundation of your house. And settlers, for all the value they add and the new things they make, also regularly make their creations on land to which others had prior claims.[39] Perhaps (as we will see in the next chapter) those prior claims might have had to yield in part or diminish in certain ways in response to the needs of the settlers. But the claims of prior rightholders surely do not simply dissolve for the benefit of settlers in response to settlers' injustices, giving those settlers superior rights to all the value they add to and all the new things they create on their ill-gotten lands.

Things might seem different, of course, if the prior rightholders' claims were said to in fact be genuinely superseded by—as opposed to being said to be merely outweighed by—the claims of settlers. Then there would be no (continuing) prior claim, no ongoing injustice to nullify or undermine the settlers' claims, nor would there be any negative moral weight of wrongs from the past to be overridden by the settlers' positive moral claims in the present. But Meisels declines to take the strict supersessionist line. Or does she? The arguments she offers for settlers' superior rights, like the arguments for genuine supersession, plainly have more force as the relevant injustices become older and the cast members change (as we've just seen). And while historical claims are said by Meisels to persist into the present, those claims seem to have virtually no bearing on any of her conclusions about territorial rights. As we've seen, she finds arguments in favor of rights supersession to be "undeniable" and "irresistible." So perhaps it is most reasonable to read Meisels as really favoring something very close indeed to simple supersessionist reasoning. However we read her arguments, though, she appears to be locked into the very same kinds of implausible, counterintuitive commitments regarding the force of historical claims as were the other theories of territorial rights that I discussed and rejected above.[40]

[38] Despite the popularity of reading Locke's theory of property as appealing to such claims (and despite Meisels's taking herself to be following [part of] Locke's reasoning in these arguments), Locke is in fact not best interpreted as appealing to either value-adding or creation as the ground of property (as I argue at length in Simmons [1992], esp. 256–64, and Simmons [2001c]). And (as I also argue there) we do Locke no favors by mistakenly ascribing to him arguments appealing to features of actions that are only irregularly conjoined with the feature (namely, simple labor-mixing) that genuinely grounds property rights for Locke.

[39] Meisels admits that settlement often involves the destruction of previous "arrangements" that were valuable for others (Meisels [2009], 126), but she treats such cases as simply involving the creation of "competing claims" to the land.

[40] It is also unclear whether we should read Meisels's conclusions as conclusions in ideal theory or in nonideal theory. Much of the argument seems to be premised on her belief that we all agree that there should not be "massive reversion" of land to (e.g.) the aboriginal owners from whom it was

Cara Nine has also defended an approach to states' territorial rights that she takes to be heavily influenced by Lockean considerations—indeed, she calls her view "a Lockean theory of territory"; and, like Meisels, Nine uses an analogy with Locke's theory of property to explain (aspects of) territorial rights.[41] But the theory she defends, again like Meisels's, in fact rejects both the kind of individualism and the kind of voluntarism that motivate the position I defended in chapter 5 as the (best) Lockean view.

Nine disparages (for reasons discussed and rejected in chapter 5) Locke's derivation of territory from property (through Locke's mechanism of political consent and incorporation of land), the centerpiece of his theory of legitimate territorial rights for states. And the Lockean (individualistic) voluntarism I endorse, of course, is expressed most directly in the Lockean commitment to the consent theory of political obligation and authority. Nine, of course, also objects to Lockean consent theory, apparently because she believes it cannot explain the legitimate rule of a government that is guided by the will of the majority of citizens.[42] As we saw above, though, part of the implicit content of consent to membership in a political community, on the Lockean model, is consent to majority rule going forward (unless some other nonunanimity decision rule is explicitly adopted instead). So legitimate government by majority rule is perfectly consistent with—indeed, it is the default requirement of—Lockean consent theory. Perhaps Nine's more substantial objections really lie elsewhere, less prominently stated (e.g., in the apparent potential, on the Lockean consent view, for geographically discontinuous territories; or simply in the basic Lockean refusal to accept Nine's functionalist criteria for legitimate political authority over nonconsenters; or in Locke's false factual claims about the contemporary applications of his ideal principles).

In any event, the "Lockean theory of territory" actually advanced by Nine is "Lockean" only in a fairly thin sense. Indeed, the core of her theory is a quite straightforwardly *functionalist* account of political legitimacy (and thus of the

stolen by settlers (e.g., Meisels [2009], 161). This makes more sense as a premise in a nonideal argument about feasible and fair paths to a perfectly rightful condition than it does as an ideal principle of some (odd) sort. And Meisels does in fact claim that her "level of inquiry . . . is non-ideal." But that appears to be because she (confusedly) associates ideal theory just with "utopian" challenges to the international order of multiple sovereign states (10–11), rather than understanding ideal theory as setting the requirements for perfect political justice or rightfulness. If Meisels's work is, indeed, to be taken as nonideal theory, however, it is nonideal theory that proceeds (unfortunately) without any clear statement of the ideal principles that should be structuring the discussion and providing her nonideal theory with its target ideal.

[41] Her original statement of this analogy (revised somewhat in her book) was this: "the state acquires territorial rights in much the same way that individuals acquire property rights . . . States change the land . . . via labour . . . by creating, adjudicating, and enforcing laws" (Nine [2008], 155).

[42] Nine (2012), 56.

most basic qualification for a people's possession of territorial rights). According to Nine, a "collective" or "people" qualifies for territorial rights—and so may be justified in exercising rights of jurisdictional authority over persons and resources (that is, justified in being "self-determining")—if it demonstrates the capacity to meet "minimal standards of justice" and if its members share a conception of justice.[43] "Legitimate" political societies, as in Altman and Wellman, protect and respect human rights (or are "capable" of doing so),[44] thus discharging their "morally mandated" functions. As we saw, however, functionalist accounts of this sort face immediate particularity problems, since such successful functioning does not appear to tie the polity to any particular geographical area. Nine, accordingly, tries to particularize territorial rights by adding that collectives that qualify (functionally) as rightholders can actually *claim* territorial rights only if they have an appropriate historical connection to a particular region—if they are capable of changing the land in morally valuable ways. This "Lockean" connection to a particular region is accomplished by "using" (or being "capable" of using?) the land—that is, by providing "rule of law," by "establishing justice in a region."[45]

But this, of course, is just the same "particularizing" move that we saw at work in Stilz's account (and those of other Kantian functionalists). The de facto reach of a polity in administering justice—in "using" the land, to employ Nine's language—is allowed to determine its particular de jure territorial rights. So the "quasi-Lockean," particularizing part of Nine's theory seems to quickly transform itself into something more closely resembling the Kantian view explored in chapter 3. But that, of course, would seem to leave Nine facing the same "boundary problem" that confronts Kantian functionalists (along with Kantian hybrid views like Stilz's). Seemingly legitimate states (or "collectives"), we might again

[43] Ibid., 3, 45–7. The "common conception of justice" requirement is Nine's (broadly Rawlsian) way of understanding the unique identity of a particular unified people with "common sympathies," but doing so without any appeal to national or cultural qualities.

[44] Ibid., 49.

[45] Ibid., 3–4, 41, 71, 83–5. I confess to not understanding how a people could *fail* to be historically tied to a region, given Nine's characterization of a people as a "geographically defined" cross-generational group (66). And the use in these claims of "capacity" and "capable" seems to me to introduce the same kinds of problems that we saw facing Altman and Wellman's account. A group's mere capacity to establish a property regime and administer justice accomplishes no morally valuable function. And groups can plainly be *kept from* "demonstrating"—or even developing—the capacity (which they would otherwise possess) to administer justice and secure human rights simply by the coercive interference of other states or groups. So it would appear that powerful existing states can (legitimately?) at will short-circuit the process by which a group might qualify for territorial rights. Similarly, merely being "capable" of changing the land in some valuable way—rather than *actually* changing it—neither grounds Lockean property rights in it (or even "desert" claims to property in it) nor "establishes" any morally valuable "relationship" with the land.

conclude, are empowered by such a view to simply *make* themselves the providers of just institutions to a region, acquiring by force legitimate jurisdictional authority over unwilling subjects and other groups' lands. This (deeply counterintuitive) commitment seems to be supported by Nine's acceptance of the same, coercively enforceable duty that is at the heart of the Kantian theories—namely, the moral duty of all to leave the state of nature and submit to collective justice-administering institutions.[46]

How could such conclusions be avoided? Nine might (but, so far as I can see, does not) adopt "defeating" principles like Stilz's, denying new territorial rights (albeit temporarily) to those states that achieve territorial control unjustly. Or she could (as we saw in chapter 3) argue that historical injustice in its acquisition of territory in fact makes a contemporary state *unjust* in its institutional administration of the rule of law (no matter how perfect its institutions might appear). In either case, though, it would then be necessary to somehow render the move consistent with the embraced functionalist criteria for legitimacy (and with the generally desired conservative conclusions about the legitimate authority of existing decent states), a step that (I've argued) is distinctly unpromising.

Or perhaps Nine would choose this strategy: given that peoples, on her view, are both "geographically defined" and must have a single, shared conception of the good in order to be morally qualified to hold territorial rights, any people that coercively extends its administration of justice beyond its current region must lose its status as qualified to hold territorial rights (having undermined its own "identity definition"). Perhaps peoples would still be entitled to "redefine" themselves by expanding to take new, vacant territory; and perhaps peoples could without consequence subject to their jurisdiction individuals who happen to share their defining common conception of justice. But without a very robust account of rights supersession at work in her theory, such a line of argument would have deeply anarchistic implications, of a sort to which Nine seems strongly opposed throughout (as indicated, among many other things, by her frequently expressed concern that a valid theory of territorial rights must have adequate "coverage"). Given her acknowledgment "that most territorial borders have been formed unjustly,"[47] it seems likely that many, many peoples will have "undone" themselves along the way to their current claimed territorial boundaries, unless there has been regular and widespread supersession of this injustice. It would be necessary to see the details of such a theory of supersession before we could evaluate her theory's ability to support even broadly nonrevisionist results.

[46] Ibid., 35–6.

[47] Ibid., 96.

Unfortunately, Nine's book does not centrally develop any of these themes. The "problem of trapped minorities" (and that of "wrongful subjection" more generally) goes almost undiscussed in her work—perhaps because she is so closely focused on the idea of peoples who share a unifying conception of justice. My own view is that few if any real states, even among the most admirable ones in the world, are entirely populated by subjects who adhere so uniformly to one conception of justice—even to one Rawlsian "political" conception of justice—as to really eliminate the problem of trapped, unwilling individuals and groups.[48] And the problem of rights supersession is dealt with by Nine in a couple of pages, without any obvious position being taken (other than a remark that Waldron-style supersession is "mysterious").[49] In the end, we are simply left unclear about Nine's overall view of the relevance of historical and enduring wrongs (done in the acquisition of unwilling subjects, land, and resources) to the legitimacy of current polities' claims to territorial rights.

It must be said that the overall tone and orientation of Nine's book do not look especially sympathetic to the claims of trapped minorities or wrongly subjected groups. Nine does mention in passing the importance of redressing harms done in unjustly establishing boundaries in the past, seems peripherally interested in arguments for mandatory downsizing of holdings (that I develop and explore in the next chapter), and very quickly notes the possibility that rectification of wrongs might require adjustments of territorial rights.[50] But surely the main line of argument in the book is the familiar functionalist one: that existing political societies that have successfully administered justice on a particular territory have, as a result, jurisdictional authority over that territory. In exercising such territorial jurisdiction, decent states interact with their territories in morally valuable ways, allowing group self-determination and promoting the satisfaction of basic individual needs.

History matters to territorial rights. But the history that matters centrally for Nine's account seems to be (once again) only a group's history of institutionally administering justice—its "using" and "improving" its territory (through

[48] "Given that territorial groups are necessarily culturally diverse," Nine observes, we need to find their unique unifying conceptions of justice in their "overlapping consensus" on a "common good idea of justice" (ibid., 64). But as was true of the same kind of appeal to "shared political identity" in nationalist theory, even "fair" political institutions that avoid dependence on national or cultural values cannot avoid the problems of relatively permanent (and systematically outvoted) minorities and powerless individuals.

[49] Ibid., 168–70, 176.

[50] Ibid., 98, 176–7, 180. The mention (on 180, in the book's concluding substantive paragraph) of territorial rights as required compensation for past wrongs, however, may be intended to apply only to the "ecological refugee" case, in which another territorial group is responsible for completely eliminating the territory of the wronged group.

this administration) in ways that deserve recognition (in the form of territorial rights). This, in my view, is yet another example of a theoretical focus on only the most comfortable and tidy part of our political histories. Our political philosophy needs to take seriously the full moral import of how we have arrived where we find ourselves. The wrongful subjection of subjects and lands, the trapping of unwilling groups and individuals in the process of territorial acquisition and concentration—these are also parts of our political histories, parts that have enduring consequences in the present. We feel shame when we witness these consequences and read about the histories, even when we were not ourselves involved in them. And we may suspect that somehow rectification is required for these wrongs, even if that suspicion derives only from reasoning by analogy with our everyday lives of wrongs and repairs. That nagging suspicion will be explored in the next chapter.

Our past, current, and ongoing institutional administration of justice is undoubtedly of enormous moral importance, and it should certainly not be jeopardized. But it is in most societies an important structure that is built upon morally unsound foundations. And the enterprise of administering justice need not be jeopardized, rather than merely inconvenienced, by recognizing this fact. It seems clear, though, that none of the theories of territorial rights we've examined other than Lockean individualist voluntarism—not plebiscitary voluntarism, nationalism, functionalism, or the attempts to hybridize those pure strategies—has the resources to adequately recognize the moral importance of these unsound foundations. Perhaps, though, those foundations have, as it were, repaired themselves through the passage of time and the changed circumstances that time has brought about. It is to that possibility that I turn next.

PART III

PROPERTY AND TERRITORY

7

Rights Supersession

Supersession and Its Relatives

I have suggested throughout part II that non-Lockean theories of territorial rights are seriously weakened by their untenable commitments concerning the supersession of historical rights (and wrongs). I've suggested as well that one of the great virtues of the type of Lockean voluntarism I favor lies in its ability to successfully and plausibly avoid such commitments. But to this point, I have not provided much in the way of argument for those suggestions. I've merely pointed to the absence of any real theory of supersession at work in the writings of those who centrally rely on the idea of rights supersession; and I've trusted the reader to share my reactions to what I've called the counterintuitive implications of the kinds of claims about supersession that are made by theorists of territorial rights. But I plainly need to do better than that. So I offer here a more detailed account of the problem of rights supersession, hoping that it will make plainer and more convincing my criticisms of the ways in which the idea of supersession is employed in non-Lockean theories of territorial rights.

It was Jeremy Waldron who, extending more technical ideas of supersession in law,[1] introduced into the literature on historic rights and reparations the idea of *moral* rights supersession (in his 1992 paper "Superseding Historic Injustice"). It is nearly always to Waldron's account of supersession, as developed in that 1992 essay and in a series of closely related subsequent pieces, that those who utilize the idea of supersession in their theories point in explaining themselves. So I will here pay central attention to Waldron's arguments concerning supersession. Before doing so, though, we would do well to be clear about where the idea of supersession will fit in a theory of rights (and wrongs) and about ideas with which we should be very careful not to confuse the idea of supersession.

[1] When an older law is repealed by a more recently enacted statute, the latter is said to supersede the former. Similarly, third-party actions or intervening events that prevent my being held liable for what would otherwise have been tortious are sometimes referred to as superseding causes. Waldron's use of the idea of supersession, however, relates more closely to *prescriptive* doctrines in property law.

If, as I believe, there are three general ways in which rights can be lost,[2] supersession would fall under the broad heading of *prescription*.[3] *Alienation* of right is loss of right through voluntary transfer or renunciation (as in contract or abandonment). *Forfeiture* of right is loss of right through wrongdoing or negligence (as when criminal conduct makes punishment permissible). *Prescription* of right (in this broad sense) is loss of right that is both nonvoluntary (unlike alienation) and not based in some wrong by the rightholder (unlike forfeiture). Standard instances of prescription of institutional (including legal) rights involve governmental withdrawal or suspension of rights (in times of social emergency, say) or loss of property right (or of certain of the "incidents" of fee simple ownership) through long passages of time without legal claims or enforcement—as in cases of adverse possession (involving, e.g., "squatters rights" or rights of way established by long and unchallenged trespass).[4] It is less easy to list the standard instances of prescriptible *moral* rights, many (or all) of those rights having been regarded as "imprescriptible" in the great early modern tracts and manifestos on rights.

There are, of course, familiar philosophical puzzles about promising (and other activities involving the deliberate alienation of rights), however unquestioningly we accept these practices in our daily lives. And philosophers and legal theorists have, of course, had deep worries about the alleged phenomenon of rights forfeiture.[5] But surely prescription of rights is the most puzzling (or, at least, the most troubling) of the three categories of rights loss. How, one might reasonably ask, can I really count as having a *right* to something—a weighty, enduring claim to it—if my right can not only dissolve in the face of wrongdoing by others (that is, in the face of others' persistent ignoring or violating of that very right), but actually pass to the wrongdoers (the "disseisors," in legal jargon) as *their* right? This, initially at least, has the look of a malicious forced taking,

[2] I discuss this view more fully in Simmons (1983). The view can be found in Locke; but Joel Feinberg was, I believe, the first contemporary philosopher to clearly state it (in Feinberg [1978], 110–14).

[3] This, I should emphasize, is a general and nontechnical use of the idea of "prescription." In contemporary law, "acquisitive prescription" is usually distinguished from "adverse possession"; but both count as "prescription" in the sense used here. The former legal notion is based on the Roman law doctrine of "usucaption" (or "usucapion"), though Roman law also distinguished this from a form of prescription that primarily gave the present possessor of a thing the right just to resist the claims to recovery of it by the former owner.

[4] The desired analogy with these particular prescriptive doctrines in property law is, of course, a happy one for those who employ a thesis of supersession in discussing *territorial* rights. For the law is much more generous with those who unjustly occupy *real* property (in land) than it is with those who seize (and thereby hope to effect a supersession of) existing property rights in *chattels*.

[5] I have tried to address many of these worries about rights forfeiture in Simmons (1991).

the kind of act for which the wrongdoer seems to merit punishment more than reward.

We can, perhaps, understand the point of this phenomenon when we are dealing with the loss of *institutional* rights after lengthy periods of unchallenged violation. In the case of "prescriptible" *legal* rights, we may take prescription to be justified by "procedural difficulties about evidence and memory" and by the new "structures of expectation" that arise around originally wrongful arrangements.[6] But the appeals to rights supersession in Waldron (and in the work of the other theorists we've examined here) are appeals to the supersession of *moral* rights, where justifications in terms of administrative convenience (or "institutional pragmatism") seem completely beside the point.[7] We must in the moral case understand how there can be moral justification for depriving an unwilling, innocent rightholder (or his heirs) of rights whose possession by that very person we take to have been fully morally justified in the first place—then handing those rights to the wrongdoer who violated them (or to his heirs). What could such a justification look like? I will consider momentarily a set of possible answers to that question.

First, however, we should be certain that the arguments we employ are in fact arguments for rights *supersession*, rather than arguments for the existence of related and far less controversial moral phenomena. For a right to be superseded—in the literal sense—is for that right to not only be nullified or set aside, but for it to be "forced out" over time as inferior to (and for it to be replaced by) another's claim of right. Importantly, a genuinely superseded right is one that is lost *nonvoluntarily* by the original rightholder. Consider a few related ideas with which that idea of supersession might easily be confused—always remembering the kinds of real-world, territorial rights cases in which the phenomenon of rights supersession is said to be operative.

One is the idea of "tacit dereliction" or implicit abandonment. When a thing has for a long time been possessed by one who is not the original rightholder, it might be thought that the original owner of the thing can be assumed to have abandoned or "quitted" the thing. It is hard, of course, not to suspect that most actual cases will simply involve unjustified and self-serving assumptions made by the present possessors. But even where this is not the case, it is important to

[6] Waldron (1992), 15. Pufendorf famously "excused" prescription in terms of its utility: "some feel that this custom is opposed to equity, since it is absurd to build upon continued license and injury as upon right and justice, yet it can be excused by reason of the general advantage which follows from it to the public" (Pufendorf [1934], 647 [4, 12, 2]). To the utilitarian advantages mentioned by Waldron we can add finality of litigation and productive use of unused resources.

[7] As Grotius put it: "the right of prescription . . . receives its being from the *civil* law [as opposed to the *natural* law] (time, as such, having no power to produce any thing . . .)" (Grotius [2005], 483 [2, 4, 1], my emphasis).

see that abandonment or dereliction of right is conceptually quite different from supersession of right.[8] Abandonment of right is a voluntary act that requires for its accomplishment clear signs of rightholder intent (such as leaving unwanted property curbside). Supersession involves a nonvoluntary loss of right, typically just through passage of time (without possession of the thing) and the associated changed circumstances.

Another idea related to—but not identical to—rights supersession is that of forfeiture of right through negligence. Just as a criminal might be thought to forfeit (parts of) his moral right to liberty in virtue of his wrongdoing, a property owner who neglects to look after or safeguard his property might be thought to forfeit his claim to that property. A central part of Pufendorf's defense of prescription, for instance, combined an argument from the original rightholder's negligence—he "having for so long time neglected claiming what was his"—with one from the new rightholder's innocence—"he who by honest means and a just title hath gotten possession of what was really another's."[9] There is little doubt that such arguments from rightholder negligence (like those from tacit dereliction) have motivated aspects of prescriptive doctrines in the law. But they have little relevance to the kinds of cases of purported moral rights supersession that have produced contemporary interest in Waldron's supersession thesis.[10] Familiar instances of lands taken by aggressive military conquest or wrongs done to native peoples in colonial settlement typically have had little to do with negligence or dereliction on the part of the original rightholders (nor have they involved innocent acquisition[11]). The rights supersession alleged to have occurred in such cases of historical wrongs is not a well-deserved penalty for negligence, but a simple fading of rights and wrongs through passage of time and changed circumstances.

[8] In one of the earliest defenses of the prescription of rights, for instance, Pufendorf mistakenly appeals to tacit dereliction as a basis for prescription. But he acknowledges that it is "certain that prolonged silence does not always avail for a presumption of tacit dereliction . . . Therefore, this basis for prescription will not hold good in all cases" (Pufendorf [1934], 654 [4, 12, 8]). His chapter "On Usucapion" gives Pufendorf's full views on prescription (646–60).

[9] Pufendorf (2003), 135 ([bk.] 1, [chap.] 12, [sec.] 12).

[10] Pufendorf, in fact, allowed that such a combination of justifications does not apply in many familiar cases of alleged prescription of rights.

[11] As we have seen (in discussing Stilz's view), one standard argument by "supersessionists" identifies as the "innocent acquirers" the second- or third-generation descendants of those who have wrongfully seized others' lands. But the wrongdoers' second- or third-generation descendants in such cases will, in my view, typically count as complicit in the wrongdoing, as the knowing (or negligently ignorant) recipients of stolen land. While they are not "personally to blame" for the original injustice—as Margalit and Raz insist in supporting prescription (Margalit and Raz [1990], 143)—they are not thereby rendered perfectly "innocent" or "blameless."

A third idea with which supersession might be confused we can call *presumptive justification*. One might reasonably suppose that certain kinds of epistemic limitations (such as theoretical or empirical ignorance) argue for simply following institutional practice or for upholding present possession. If, for instance, we lack an adequate philosophical theory of the possession and loss of right, this might seem to dictate that we take a conservative stance on acknowledging and upholding moral rights in practice (if only because of the transaction costs and frustrated expectations involved in upsetting existing arrangements). More commonly, we might think that certain kinds of *factual* ignorance—such as ignorance or reasonable disagreement regarding the factual history of acquisitions and transfers of land, of the sort often at issue in actual territorial disputes—argue for upholding those rights of present possessors in cases where the relevant property cannot be *shown* to have been unjustly acquired. While I believe that appeals to presumptive justification do, indeed, have a role to play in a defensible theory of property (and, by extension, in a defensible theory of states' territorial) rights,[12] the only point that needs to be emphasized here is that presumptive justification of present possession is a quite different idea than that of the actual supersession of historical rights by contemporary ones. Supersession, properly understood, involves the replacement of one rightholder's older claim by another's newer claim. Presumptive justifications, by contrast, may turn out not to be defensible after all in the end—presumptions are, by definition, defeasible—and so they in no way presuppose that older rights have in fact been extinguished.

Related arguments supporting rights of present possession can be understood in a variety of ways. It is not uncommon, for instance, to find arguments to the effect that the values of social peace or stability or the promotion of general social utility favor the claims of present possessors. Such arguments might, of course, be understood just to point to implications of a direct consequentialist theory of rights—though the well-known difficulties involved in defending such a theory of rights (or the prospect such a theory seems to promise of rapid supersession of all kinds of rights) will be sufficient to deter most theorists from that path. Or such arguments might be intended simply to establish a presumptive justification, suggesting that present possession should win the day absent compelling countervailing considerations. Or, last, such appeals to stability or utility might actually be intended only as claims that these considerations (in favor of yielding to present possession) will reliably *outweigh* or *override* claims of past or historical right (as we saw in chapter 6, this is the kind of argument made by Meisels).

[12] See my discussion in Simmons (1994), 76–8.

It is a relatively simple business to fall into confusing genuine supersession of moral right with the idea of moral rights merely being defeasible or overridable. But no plausible theories of rights—including the kind of Lockean theory I have defended here—deny that genuine moral rights can sometimes be overridden by competing moral considerations (such as those of social stability or large-scale utility). Moral rights, while they have great moral weight, do not have absolute or "trumping" weight with respect to other things of moral importance.[13] Sometimes we ought, all things considered, to do what secures social stability or what produces important utility gains, even at the cost of violating (or infringing) someone's moral right. It is important to see, however, that when a right is merely overridden—rather than genuinely superseded—first, that right persists through the overriding and has its full weight afterwards, and, second, the violation of that right calls for further action to in some way mitigate the impact of that morally unfortunate (but morally necessary) violation and to make clear its temporary and regrettable nature. The overriding leaves, in the language of ethicists, a "moral residue." Rights that are genuinely *superseded* neither persist through the supersession—they are simply replaced by newer rights—nor leave afterwards a residue that calls for mitigation or apology: if there is no right remaining, we no more owe mitigation in such a case than we would owe it to someone who was never an interested rightholder in the first place or who had freely alienated the relevant right to us.

We should not, then, confuse our eminently plausible conviction that moral rights may be overridden with a commitment to some more controversial doctrine of the supersession over time of moral rights (of the sort embraced in non-Lockean theories of territorial rights). But even in Waldron's very influential work on supersession, these two ideas—of rights being overridable and rights being supersedable—seem sometimes to be run together, permitting the plausibility of our shared commitment to the former notion to appear to provide support for the latter. Notice that Waldron not only uses the languages of "trumping," "overwhelming," and "having priority over" in discussing the grounds of supersession, but he also writes as if, after supersession, there is a significant moral residue that demands mitigating action—both of these being appropriate to a discussion not of genuine rights supersession, but only of the defeasibility of rights.

In the absence of "an honest attempt . . . to arrange things justly for the future," Waldron says, "there is nothing to overwhelm or supersede the enterprise of

[13] As we saw earlier, Locke accepts the defeasibility of moral rights. And the contemporary rights theorist most often accused of treating rights as absolute—namely, Robert Nozick—does not in fact hold that view, nor does the rights theorist who is generally credited with inventing the idea of rights as normative "trumps" (namely, Ronald Dworkin). See Nozick (1974), 30n, 41; and Dworkin (1977), 191–6.

reparation" (for past violations of rights). Only such a "committed resolve" can "trump that enterprise," giving it "priority over [some] rectificatory actions."[14] Similar things are said by Waldron about nations' or peoples' violated rights to sovereignty or self-determination: "Responsiveness to present circumstances may trump or supersede any claim for reversion to an earlier form or heritage of governance."[15] And there could hardly be a clearer affirmation of the presence of post-"supersession" moral residue than this: "I do not mean to say that we should forget about historic injustice. Apologies and acknowledgments are properly demanded, and at least symbolic compensation may be due to descendants of those who were originally treated unjustly."[16] The claim here does not appear to be that mitigating actions would be a "nice" thing to do, just to make the former holders of superseded rights feel better—as might be appropriate in a case of genuine supersession. Rather, the claim is that such mitigation is "due" those (former?) rightholders and may be "properly demanded" by them. So if we agree with Waldron's claims here, we are not really agreeing, I think, with any claims he is trying to make about genuine supersession of violated moral rights. We are really only agreeing, instead, with the far more plausible claim that we may sometimes have to violate moral rights in the interest of pursuing a more pressing, competing moral goal.

Arguments for Supersession

None of that, however, shows that there *are* no compelling arguments for the claim that some (or all) moral rights are in principle supersedable. It shows only that we should be careful to distinguish claims or arguments that actually bear on a thesis of moral supersession from those that bear only on related theses (such as the defeasibility of some [or all] moral rights). In this section, I try to summarize and assess various lines of argument that have been adduced to support rights supersession, though these lines of argument are not always clearly distinguished from one another by their "supersessionist" supporters.

One familiar argument that rights are supersedable, of course, just rests on the observation that "it is widely believed that some rights are capable of 'fading' in their moral importance by virtue of the passage of time and by the sheer persistence of what was originally a wrongful infringement."[17] Even if we accept the idea

[14] Waldron (1992), 27.

[15] Waldron (2015), 13.

[16] Waldron (2004), 237–68, 244. Similarly: "Like the gift I buy for someone I have stood up, the payment is a method of putting oneself out, or going out of one's way, to apologize" (Waldron [1992], 7). See also Margaret Moore's similar claims (Moore [2015], 148–9).

[17] Waldron (1992), 15.

that a proposition's being "widely believed" provides real support for its truth (at least in moral matters), it is not obvious to me that the relevant proposition is in fact widely believed. We do, of course, "widely believe" that some *legal* rights are prescriptible or supersedable—for the excellent reason that this is plainly true in the law, where some rights have simply been *made* prescriptible by legislative or interpretive legal acts—but it is far less obvious (to me, at least) that we "widely believe" any such thing about our *moral* rights. Most (of my) students, when introduced to the fact that I can acquire legal rights in your land or your building by unlawfully and openly trespassing for long enough, find the idea morally outrageous, even though they understand the "administrative" reasons for such legal policies. Indeed, their objection is typically precisely the objection that Waldron guesses people will raise to his claims about rights supersession—what he calls the "moral hazard objection": that supersession seems to offer a reward, and so a persistent and perverse incentive, for injustice, including a reward for sustaining (rather than rectifying) the injustice long enough that the superseded rights can be reaped by the wrongdoer (or his heirs).[18]

This objection aside, I suspect that most nonphilosophers will simply give a different answer than Waldron's to his question about one of his central examples of rights supersession: that of a stolen car, kept by the thief for years and finally handed down to the thief's descendants.[19] Who has the moral right to the car? Waldron is not "so sure" what the answer is; but most of us will be surer, I think. The original owner has the right, just as that owner would if the thief had sold the car to an unwitting third party the day after the theft. That the third party (or the thief's heir) has perfectly innocent expectations of legitimate ownership, that she has quickly built her life around her new car, will all be regrettable and will give the third party solid claims to reparation *from the thief*. But that is neither here nor there in determining where the true right to the car lies. Passage of time or multiplicity of unlawful transactions will not affect this judgment, even if they may make it difficult in practice to determine the facts or to produce legally respectable evidence of them. But perhaps those, like Waldron, who disagree with me on this can agree at least on something more modest: belief that *moral* rights are supersedable is at least not so "wide" as to constitute a "provisional fixed point" in our views about justice or right, a point with which a valid theory of rights must strive to remain consistent.

[18] Waldron's repeated response to the "moral hazard objection" is to say: "But I do not see how this difficulty can be avoided" (Waldron [1992], 19; [2002], 158). The best way to avoid the difficulty, as I hope my arguments here will show, is simply to avoid Waldron's commitments regarding moral rights supersession.

[19] Waldron (1992), 14–15.

One might, I suppose, believe (relatedly) that some moral rights *should* come with time limits or expiration dates, like statutes of limitations or the time limits on copyright in the law.[20] We would presumably not want to apply such a rationale for supersession to basic *human* rights; but we might well think that in cases of property (or territory) such limits on rights would serve an admirable end in offering a fair deal to new generations of persons (or peoples), who mostly come into the world with many things (or everything) already owned and unavailable for use—just as copyright limits open up opportunities for subsequent generations. To this line of argument, at least two responses seem apt. First, even if we think that moral rights should have—and, so, *do* have—expiration dates, this would not be an argument for the *supersession* of moral rights, but only for their periodic *dissolution*. The argument provides no justification at all for allowing the particular claims of the *present possessor* (to property that was, at some point, unjustly acquired) to supersede those of the original (unjustly deprived) owner, nor does it justify preserving intact the specific content or extent of the original right. Second, Waldron repeatedly emphasizes that supersession is not (on his view of the matter) about *mere* passage of time.[21] What matters to rights supersession is instead the changing, morally relevant circumstances that passage of time routinely (but not necessarily) produces—changes that also change what justice requires, that change the distribution of rights that is morally required. So I will focus here not on mere passage of time, but on trying to understand exactly how we should take rights to be sensitive to such changes.

Waldron in fact mentions two different kinds of morally relevant changes of this sort, two "principled" (i.e., non-"pragmatic") reasons why we should accept that moral rights are supersedable: (a) rights must be sensitive to "changes in background social and economic circumstances" (what I'll call the "changing circumstances" claim), and (b) any plausible "basis of the rights themselves" will inevitably be "weakened by the historic persistence of dispossession" (what we can call the "fading basis" claim).[22] I will focus briefly initially on the second of these claims, before discussing the first at much greater length.

[20] Buchanan (1991), 88.

[21] And legal doctrines of prescription, after all, are primarily based on concerns about evidentiary difficulties and on the plights of innocent third parties or nonculpably ignorant wrongdoers, whose lives have been built up around legally indefensible expectations. The doctrines are not motivated by any concern for time limits on rights: they were never intended, for instance, to benefit those who maliciously seize another's property and just cleverly manage to hold it long enough for the prescriptive legal rules to apply. George Sher argues that there are "necessary conditions for desert of compensation which become progressively harder to satisfy over time." But his arguments lead only to the conclusion that entitlements are very *likely* to diminish over time; and this diminution has nothing to do with the *mere* passage of time (*simpliciter*). See Sher (1981), 6, 13.

[22] Waldron (1992), 16, 18.

The second ("fading basis") claim about "change" appears to amount to this: any (plausible) ground for the possession of (property) rights that might be specified by an historical theory of rights—that is, any relationship between person and object that the theory might identify as giving rise to the person's rights over the object—will very likely (or inevitably?) be undermined by long periods of time without possession of the owned object. Consequently, the right itself must "fade," replaced (perhaps?) by rights for those who in fact later come to stand in that relationship to the object. So if my right over something (or over some parcel of land) is based, say, in that thing's centrality to my ongoing plans or projects—or if it is based in its importance to my personal autonomy—this relation to the thing is bound to change if the thing is unjustly taken from me and kept from me for a long period of time. My plans and projects will inevitably change, being deprived of one of their central components, while the thing may instead come to play a central role in the plans of those who have actual access to the thing. The same will be true if the original right is based on my important expectations, on my central interests, on my sentimental attachment to the thing, and so on.[23]

This "fading basis" style of argument for supersession is a very popular one, and we have seen uses of it before (e.g., in chapter 6[24]). The argument's intended (or, at least, its most plausible) conclusion, I take it, is that while rights to unjustly taken things will not *necessarily* be superseded over time, in favor of those with present possession—the original owner could, after all, continue to have plans in which the stolen object (e.g., the tribe's stolen lands) plays a central role, while the present possessor might develop no plans at all for its use—there are no moral rights to things that are *in principle* immune to supersession.[25] For whatever the relationship between person and thing that our theory alleges grounds rights over things, that relationship at least *could* fade with respect to the original (just) owner and *could* arise with respect to a later (unjust) possessor.

But "fading basis" arguments for moral rights supersession seem to me to rest on a very peculiar—or a very partisan—picture of how the bases for rights-claims relate to the retention of rights. Fading (or faded) bases for rights seem pretty clearly to be neither necessary nor sufficient for loss of rights, at least on any even remotely generous understanding of how those bases are intended to function in a theory of rights. That fading bases are not necessary for rights-loss is obvious (in light of the possibilities of alienation or forfeiture of rights).

[23] Ibid., 18–19.

[24] Stilz employs a similar argument involving autonomy (Stilz [2011], esp. 583–4). Meisels ([2009], esp. 66–7) and Moore ([2015], 143–4) also use this style of argument.

[25] "The normal line of argument for property entitlements is simply insufficient to establish imprescriptible rights" (Waldron [2002], 158).

Far more important for present purposes, it seems clear that they cannot be sufficient either (on any plausible theory). For most of the relevant bases for rights can surely fade regardless of whether or not we retain possession of the thing over which we have rights; and in cases involving continued possession and use (of legitimately acquired things) virtually nobody believes that rights over those things are all superseded if and because the bases for the rights have faded. Suppose that I have a right over something—say, over the table I built—in virtue of its centrality to my plans or my sentimental attachment to it. And suppose that, while I continue to possess and use the table, it gradually loses the centrality and sentimental value it used to have for me. Surely only a bizarre theory would commit itself to the conclusion that, simply on the strength of these "faded bases," I automatically lose all of my rights over the table, despite my continued possession of it. Even more bizarre would be the suggestion that the true owner is now some (any?) person (or persons?) whose interests in the table are now keener than my own, despite her (their) lack of possession (say, a would-be table thief who became fixated on the table while peeking through my window). If *that* is how the fading-basis argument must imagine that bases or grounds for rights function in a theory of rights, then the argument is plainly attacking a straw man (or attacking only exceptionally strange theories of property rights).

Waldron, of course, excludes from the start the Lockean ground or basis for property rights that I favor. He has been for many years a well-known critic of Locke's (and Lockean) "labor mixing" arguments for property rights. I have argued elsewhere that Waldron's criticisms of the Lockean approach are unsound and that a Lockean labor-mixing argument for property rights can in fact be convincingly stated, motivated, and defended from the standard objections.[26] I will not repeat those arguments here, but will instead try to briefly illustrate the approach—and the response to this kind of fading basis argument for supersession—that I have in mind. Suppose with me, then, that our "principle of acquisition" maintains that rights over previously unowned land or natural resources can be acquired by usefully employing these things in our projects and purposive activities—by "mixing our labor" with those things, in the sense of bringing them within the scope of our purposive, productive activity (i.e., our labor)—at least provided that a strong Lockean proviso is satisfied, so that others will have similar opportunities to acquire such goods by their own labors. This mixing, as Locke suggests, "marks" the thing as belonging to the laborer—marks it for exclusive use in that specific person's projects—thus distinguishing it from those things that remain in common for the use or appropriation of others.

[26] See Simmons (1992), chap. 5.

Importantly, this "mark" on the thing can remain through any number of unjust transfers of the thing over any period of time, provided that the original owner does not at some point indicate that he no longer wants the thing (for any potential use).[27] To deny this is to simply deny the moral distinction, crucial to Lockean (and all other plausible) theories of property, between abandonment and theft. Both involve loss of possession of a thing. But my abandonment of property is accomplished by clear signs of my intention no longer to try to use it in my plans or projects. Theft of property, by contrast, may make it impossible for me to immediately use that property in my projects; but it will still leave that property as a potential part of my ongoing or long-term plans, provided only that I would be happy to get back and use that property (perhaps only because I could advance my ends by *selling* the property or by charitably *giving* it away). When my wife tries to collect for Goodwill my seldom-used things, my reply is sometimes that I still *want* these things (I may want to use them some day). They have not been abandoned, nor would they count as abandoned by me if they were gathering dust instead in some *thief's* basement. But even if they *did* count as abandoned by me, my rights over them would not have been *superseded* (and replaced by the claims of the thief, as the present possessor). My rights over those things would instead simply have been deliberately *alienated* (in this case, "renounced") by me, with any subsequent *innocent* claimant (who could *not* therefore be the thief) counting *not* as a beneficiary of rights supersession, but only as a new appropriator of unowned (because abandoned) things.

Further, of course, while theft normally eliminates one's ability to immediately *use* the stolen item—and so to employ it in projects in the standard ways—depriving a rightholder of the ability to use property, even for an extended time, is plainly not sufficient to deprive her of rights over that property. Imagine, for instance, that you attempt to extinguish a property right of mine—by eliminating my capacity to use the property—through some means other than theft. If I have negotiated an unlimited *contractual* right to, say, enter your studio to view your art collection whenever I please, this right cannot then be extinguished by your subsequently crippling and blinding me. The right remains a moral asset of mine, even if I cannot presently exercise it. (The contract might, for instance, permit me to sell the right to some third party who *could* exercise it.) It would be most odd, then, if *theft* of property, *merely* by preventing the property from being immediately used or controlled by its owner, affected the owner's rights over the property.

[27] Pufendorf put the point thus: "no man ever loses against his will dominion over a thing, even though its actual possession is lost . . . but he keeps the right to recover it so long as he has not actually given up the intention of recovering it" (Pufendorf [1934], 580 [4, 6, 12]).

The more general worry about "fading basis" arguments for rights supersession at work in the background here is that such arguments uniformly involve assuming without warrant—and typically without argument—that the conditions for continued possession of a right must (in historical or in all rights theories) mirror those for the initial acquisition of a right, so that when the "acquisition relationship" is altered or diminished, so must be the rights implied by the "continued ownership" relationship. But no plausible rights theory will hold a view like this, since doing so would incapacitate it even in relatively simple cases of rights retention—such as the retention of promissory rights.[28] *Acquiring* a promissory right from another requires the other's intention to convey the right to you (or at least the other's intention to use signs that he knows will lead you to believe he intends to convey it). *Continued possession* of a promissory right, however, clearly does *not* depend on the promiser's continued intention that you should enjoy the right. The promiser's further intentions, after the binding promise is made, are irrelevant to your continuing to have a right that he perform as promised. Further, promissory rights, *acquired* by another's alienation and one's own acceptance, can be *lost* (forfeited) by one's own wrongdoing (which involves neither alienation nor acceptance). The supposition of a required symmetry in such matters is plainly misguided.[29]

Must it be otherwise, as "fading basis" arguments suppose, where it is specifically *property* rights that are concerned? I do not see why we should believe this. Why, after all, should we think that the grounds for morally separating something from what was available for common use should be identical to the grounds for continued exclusive possession of it? But even if we *do* believe that property rights are special in this way, the Lockean labor-mixing basis for the acquisition of property rights is one basis that *still* defeats the "fading basis" argument for supersession, since things not only can, but often do, continue to be "mixed" with my labor—by still being in some way incorporated into my long-term projects (the "mark" that stays with our property)—long after they have been stolen or possessed by others.

Before proceeding to my extended discussion of Waldron's (and others') "changing circumstances" arguments for supersession, I want to mention just

[28] See my discussion of this issue in Simmons (1993), 111–12. Meisels also comments on a case in which the "triggering" conditions for the acquisition of right are quite different than the conditions for continued possession of the right—namely, the "consummation" requirement for the acquisition of marital rights (Meisels [2009], 103).

[29] Moore criticizes autonomy based accounts of rights of residency and return (such as the ones in Lefkowitz [2014] and in Stilz) specifically because on such accounts the conditions for acquiring and for losing the rights are not "symmetrical" (Moore [2015], 143–4). The considerations adduced here show that, on the contrary, it would be only a very odd theory of rights that satisfied such a symmetry requirement.

one other point in favor of rights supersession that comes up both in Waldron's and in others' discussions of the problem. Waldron puts the point perfectly clearly:

> I should add that the Supersession Thesis is not just a technical theorem in political philosophy. It expresses a certain attitude towards justice. The spirit of the Supersession Thesis is that people who are thrown, in Kant's phrase, unavoidably side-by-side, have no choice but to share the resources that surround them justly among themselves as though they were a new community, even if the presence of some of them in that situation is a result of injustice. Justice may make reference to the past, through principles of desert and Lockean entitlement; but its primary focus is on the present—present-day people, present-day resources—and on the circumstances of the present inasmuch as they affect who should get what.[30]

Waldron is undeniably correct that his (and, e.g., Stilz's) stance on rights supersession is one more expression of this Kantian functionalist approach to questions about right or justice. The body of the present work, of course, has been intended to show that this association should not be counted as a point in favor of "the Supersession Thesis."[31] But it is worth noting as well that, just as Stilz seeks in the end to make room for concerns about historical wrongs in her theory of territorial rights (as we saw in chapter 6), Waldron also here indicates more pluralistic inclinations in his concession that, even though we should *primarily* "focus upon present and prospective costs," our theory of justice "may" also "make reference to the past. The brand of Kantian functionalism to which Waldron intends to subscribe thus may in fact be more pluralistic (involving some sort of balancing between structural and historical principles of justice) than many of his remarks on supersession suggest—thus, perhaps, narrowing in that way at least the distance between my own Lockean views and Waldron's.

[30] Waldron (2004), 245–6. Similar observations by Waldron: "Claims about historic injustice predicated on the status quo ante may be superseded by our determination to distribute the resources of the world in a way that is fair to all of its existing inhabitants" (Waldron [1992], 26; [2002], 157); and "Behind the thesis of supersession lies a determination to focus upon present and prospective costs" (otherwise, Waldron suggests, the conception of justice at work in one's theory isn't "practically relevant" [Waldron {2002}, 159]).

[31] Waldron states this specific "thesis" as follows: "In some recent writings, I have explored the proposition that certain things which were unjust when they occurred may be overtaken by events in a way that means their injustice has been superseded. I call this the Supersession Thesis" (Waldron [2004], 240).

Changing Circumstances: Shaky Counterfactuals

There appear to be three "themes" that are joined in (what I've called) Waldron's (and others') "changing circumstances" arguments for moral rights supersession. One is a general skepticism, due to the unpredictability of change, about the kinds of counterfactual judgments that are required to make sense of persistent rights to the reparation of past injustices. The second concerns the ways in which, over time, the changing cast of characters and the alteration or destruction of the relevant property affect the persistence of rights to those things. The third focuses on the ways in which changes in the overall availability of resources and the numbers of those needing access to resources will change what justice demands in the distribution of property rights (and, by extension, territorial rights). I will try to address these themes in turn.

We can begin with the worries about the counterfactuals involved in specifying the substance of historical rights to reparation.[32] While Waldron (with other Kantians) rejects both the ideal and the nonideal principles of historical entitlement theories,[33] the most obvious difficulties appear to most theorists to lie in historical theories' nonideal accounts of reparation or rectification.[34] Historical principles of rectification, for situations of partial compliance, are designed to specify the enduring rights of persons who have suffered *violations* of their rights, as defined by the ideal principles of acquisition and transfer.[35] If you steal my bicycle, say, I have a right to the rectification of this wrong—usually assumed to be a return of the bicycle, along with compensation for any loss I suffered as a result of being temporarily deprived of its use. The standard idea, familiar to us from the civil law, is that in order to rectify a past rights violation, we must, as far as it is within our power, "make it now as though the injustice had not

[32] While many theorists have strong opinions about the required language in such cases, I will not try to legislate here any particular uses for terms like "reparation," "rectification," "restoration," "restitution," "compensation," and the like. Since different theorists insist on using such terms in many different ways, there seems little point in aiming at anything more precise than the understanding that context will provide here.

[33] My guess is that Waldron might concede that the intuitions underlying Lockean ideal theory make it harder to resist than Lockean nonideal theory. If I am the first settler of a vast, uninhabited territory (in another solar system, say), and I build a home and cultivate the land needed to comfortably support me, surely the settlers coming after would wrong me (violate my property rights) if they simply seized my land and home, with ample and equally attractive land and resources available to them.

[34] "The rectification principle . . . seems to be the most problematic part of the entitlement theory. It is certainly an essential part; for, without it, . . . if there has been a single injustice in the history of a state, no matter how far back, the state will not be able to achieve a just distribution of goods in the present" (Davis [1976], 839).

[35] Nozick (1974), 152.

happened."[36] We cannot undo a past wrong, but we can try to "make up for it," perhaps by minimizing the effects of the wrong.[37]

It was noticed long ago (by Lawrence Davis) that where stolen goods were destroyed, no rectification seemed possible on an historical entitlement theory (like Nozick's). It was noticed as well that the most obvious addition to make to his theory to handle such cases would be some sort of indifference principle:[38] where the stolen good is destroyed (or irreversibly altered), the victim's right is to some share of the wrongdoer's goods that raises the victim to at least as high an indifference curve as had the theft not taken place. The obvious worries about introducing an indifference principle are that (a) it leaves many possible just rectifications between which we must somehow choose, and (b) it ceases to preserve entitlements to particular objects.[39] Indeed, we might suppose that endorsing such a principle within an historical entitlement theory would mark a shift from a "deontic" to a consequentialist or "outcome-oriented" conception of rights. And then all historical entitlements to particular things would be threatened, since no rights would ever count as violated if the victim's well-being were simply appropriately enhanced during the course of the apparent right-violation.[40]

These worries will be lessened, I think, by noting that rights of rectification in such cases may be more specific than the discussion has thus far indicated. In particular, if the motivation in rectifying wrongs is to as nearly as possible nullify the effects of the wrongdoing (i.e., to make it as if the wrong had not occurred), the best rectification in cases of theft will be that which returns the victim to the closest possible approximation of the condition that would have obtained in the absence of the theft. If you steal my bicycle and *don't* destroy it, I am entitled to the return of my bicycle (plus additional compensation for loss). I am *not* entitled to demand instead the cash amount that raises my indifference curve to an appropriate level. Nor are you entitled to decide to keep the bicycle and instead pay me that cash amount. This suggests that if you steal my bicycle and

[36] Waldron (1992), 8.

[37] We are speaking here, of course, only about questions of *reparation*, which are *independent* of further questions about whether or what *punishment* is appropriate for the wrong. It is possible, of course, that reparation or compensation may be due the victim of a wrong simply for the breach of his rights, even when this breach is accompanied by no loss of wellbeing (or by a *gain* in wellbeing). I do not consider such cases here. For discussion, see Lomasky (1991), 28, 33 and Gaus (1991), 67, 69–72.

[38] Davis (1976), 840–41. As Davis notes, Nozick seems content to employ an indifference standard (earlier in his book) in formulating his Principle of Compensation.

[39] Ibid., 842, 844.

[40] Mack (1981), 186–7. See also Wolff (1981), 86; Paul (1990), 569–71; O'Neill (1987), 78–80; Lomasky (1987), 143.

do destroy it, a genuinely historical theory must say that appropriate rectification is not just the return of *any* share of your goods that meets an indifference standard, but rather the return of a share which effectively facilitates my transition to the state I would have been in but for the theft. If you have another bicycle of comparable quality, or you have the cash to allow me to replace my stolen bicycle with a similar one, giving me these would be better rectifications of the wrong than would giving me a pile of books that I would value as highly as my bicycle. I am not entitled to demand the books *instead* of an identical bicycle, nor are you entitled to insist on providing the books as compensation instead of exercising one of the other options. I conclude from this that (a) historical rights theories need not embrace a *pure* indifference principle (with all of its attendant difficulties) in cases of destroyed property, and (b) claims to (what I will call) *particularized* shares in such cases, while not always claims to *particular* shares, will normally be claims to something in a relatively narrow range of options.

This idea seems quite appealing in relatively simple cases of short-term rectification. But any of a wide variety of complications can quickly diminish its appeal. What if, instead of just stealing my bicycle, you then melt it down and turn it into cufflinks, various pairs of which are bought by innocent third parties and later left to their grandchildren as family heirlooms? What if I die or you die before rectification occurs? What if the injustice remains unrectified for several centuries? And how confidently, in any event, can we make the relevant counterfactual judgments even in relatively simple cases? For to make it as if the wrong had not occurred, we must judge what would have taken place in the absence of the wrong. But what would have taken place may depend on what choices people would have made and on other changes in context and circumstances that seem quite unpredictable.[41] Would I have met the perfect mate or found the perfect job had my mobility not been impaired by the theft of my bicycle? Or did the theft save me from being crushed by a delivery van while out riding?

Destruction of stolen property, changes in the cast of affected parties, innocent third parties, and the simple passage of time complicate the already complicated counterfactual judgments until we seem to have passed the breaking point. It is popular, for instance, in criticisms of historical theories of property rights, to cite instances of massive historical injustices—such as the theft of tribal lands and resources from aboriginal peoples—and then to note that all of these complications are present. It seems impossible to say with any confidence just what kinds of property transfers would satisfy a plausible historical principle of rectification in such cases. Must the struggling Asian immigrant return her hard-earned holding in commercial land, land which is now

[41] Waldron (1992), 8–13.

deforested and developed, to the distant descendants of the hunter-gatherers from whom the land was once stolen? The problems here are not just epistemological or *evidentiary*. It is not just that we lack all of the relevant historical data to unravel the chains of historical entitlements (though, of course, we do).[42] The problems are also substantive difficulties of *principle*. It is very hard in such cases to see how we could find any satisfactory basis for specifying the exact *content* of historical rights to rectification. Someone was clearly wronged by someone somewhere in the murky past. But who has rights to what now? The players are now very different, the land is irreparably altered, and legitimate expectations of myriad sorts surround the present set of holdings. If just rectification is in many cases impossible in principle, because of the indeterminacy of the principles defining historical rights, such rights begin to look like only wishful shadows of real rights.[43]

A variety of responses to these difficulties seems possible. Defenders of historical rights might reply that *any* moral theory will face these kinds of problems in moving from ideal to nonideal theory. Any theory, historical or not, will have a hard time determining how to remedy injustice when faced with widespread, innocent expectations founded on the anticipated continuation of unjust arrangements. But this response is too feeble. The problem for historical theories seems not to be just that situations of partial compliance require inevitably very complicated principles of rectification. The problem seems to be instead that historical theories cannot even state the desired principles of rectification in any plausible way. There is, for instance, no clear *end* toward which these principles *aim* us, as there is a clear end toward which end-state nonideal principles aim (namely, the achievement of a just structure of holdings in society). The nonideal theory of an historical account cannot be (as in an end-state account) a complicated set of practical rules for minimizing harm in the transition to a more perfectly just arrangement. Historical accounts, having no ideal just structure of holdings to aim us at—having only, instead, principles for identifying rightful acquisitions and transactions—must defend the content of their principles of rectification in a way which is compelling *independent* of structural goals. And the complications we have been discussing seem to stand in the way of such a defense.

As a result, of course, a very common response to historical theories is simply to reject altogether the idea of historical entitlements, as Waldron does (or, at

[42] Despite Nozick's apparent belief that this is the only real problem. Nozick suggests using nonhistorical patterned principles of distributive justice as "rough rules of thumb" for approximating *historical* rectification in real-world cases where information about the past is incomplete (Nozick [1974], 230–31).

[43] Davis (1976), 844.

least, comes close to doing). In anything but a world very close to moral perfection (in which the principles of ideal theory are fully satisfied), historical rights will have no determinate content and hence will not be real rights at all. But this simple rejection of historical rights *also* seems feeble. For in our anything-but-ideal actual world, in both law and morals, we still take historical rights to rectification very seriously. Given the many reasons we have for taking practice to be relevant to theory, the best response to the problems of historical theories would seem to be neither to rationalize away the problems nor to dismiss the theories, but to see whether further clarifying our conception of historical rights can make the problems more manageable.

I will respond to such worries in the next two sections not by arguing that historical theories can specify precise contents for these rights, but rather by arguing that their inability to do so constitutes no defect in the theories. Historical theories can be coherent and plausible, I will suggest, and can thus define real rights, even when those rights do not have a perfectly determinate content. The best historical theory will entail that persons can sometimes have rights that give us only imprecise, but nonetheless principled, guidelines for rectification, rather than giving us determinate entitlements to particular things or performances. Before proceeding to defend that view, though, I think it important to observe that many who write about historical theories of rights seem to me to be a bit *too* eager to give in to skeptical doubt, both about the possibility of making reliable contrary-to-fact judgments of the kind required by historical theories and about the moral importance of such judgments.

While the truth conditions (or assertability conditions) for various kinds of counterfactuals is obviously a controversial issue, it is clear that we do regularly make counterfactual judgments with a high degree of confidence and take them to be centrally relevant to determinations of praise and blame and moral or legal liability. "If he hadn't stolen my bicycle, I would have been better off (by so much and in these ways)." (Or: "If my father hadn't argued against it so passionately, I would have married that good-for-nothing bum.") We are not bothered by the fact that, during my bicycle's absence, I *might* otherwise have been shot by a deranged hater of bicyclists or *might* have been discovered by a talent scout for the Olympic cycling team. We do not hold the thief liable for dashing my Olympic hopes or reward him for saving my life. For purposes of assigning blame and liability we *assume* a normal, unsurprising course of background events, roughly like the one that actually occurred. And we *assume* that our and others' choices would have likewise been more or less the same.

In saying "If he hadn't stolen my bicycle, I would have been better off," I am saying that those of my possible histories that most resemble my actual history (as closely as their including the nontheft of my bicycle allows them to resemble it) involve my being better off.[44] Possible worlds with Olympic talent scouts noticing my bicycling do not sufficiently resemble the actual world in which my bicycle is stolen to belong to the relevantly similar class of histories. Often, of course, our judgments concern not what would certainly have happened in any relevantly similar history, but rather what would have been most likely to have happened. The vagaries of individual choice and the complexity of background conditions often make stronger claims indefensible. They also force the moral (and legal) uses of counterfactual claims to be essentially conservative in nature. In ascribing blame or liability for losses, we take ourselves to be bound both to show a high probability that the losses would not otherwise have been suffered and to make only conservative assumptions about choices and background conditions.

In the absence of full knowledge of what would have occurred had a wrong not been committed, blaming a wrongdoer conservatively constitutes a fair compromise between assuming that his wrong would have had horrible consequences for the wronged party and assuming that his wrong would have had wonderful consequences. We instead conservatively assign him liability only for those losses that we can confidently attribute to his wrong, against background assumptions that things not directly affected by the wrong would in its absence have gone on more or less as they in fact did. We know that in the absence of the wrong, the wronged person (or some other) might have made wild or unpredictable choices, and that others might have been influenced to act differently because of this. But since we cannot know the likelihood or the consequences of such choices, we assume that rash choices would not have been made, trying to be fair in our determination of the extent of reparation required. If you hadn't stolen my money, I might have used it to rashly buy a stack of lottery tickets that included the winner, or I might have rashly invested it in penny stocks and lost everything. Even if I am a rash person, then, we assume an absence of rashness in our counterfactual judgments.[45]

None of this seems to me arbitrary or ad hoc. The difficulties of assessing counterfactual judgments are very real and substantial. But they are not theoretically insuperable; nor, I think, do they cast a pall over the whole project of explaining historical rights to rectification. People do make choices, and choices

[44] This is, very roughly, the analysis of counterfactuals suggested in Lewis (1973).

[45] Obviously, our assumptions will be different if rash choices were made in the *actual* history, at least if these rash choices were not a direct consequence of the wrong. More generally, we assign moral liability to the wrongdoer only for those of the victim's subsequent losses which we take to be direct causal consequences of the wrong itself. To the extent that these losses are taken to follow from the victim's own free choices and actions, we compare the actual history that includes those choices and actions to the closest possible histories that also include them, in order to determine the truth of counterfactual judgments about the consequences of wrongdoing.

are sometimes unpredictable. Sometimes we will simply be unable to say what conditions would most likely have obtained in the absence of a wrong (perhaps because there simply is no fact of the matter). But nothing in that admission (or in the nature of human freedom) justifies any stronger skepticism about counterfactuals involving persons or about their employment in moral judgment. Persons often have a (legal and/or moral) right to what they would have enjoyed in the absence of a prior wrong, according to our best conservative estimate of what that would have been. Nothing here involves assuming without warrant that "rational choice predictions" are "normatively conclusive," nor should such worries motivate a retreat from our efforts to understand historical rights counterfactually.[46] Indeed, even within nonhistorical, end-state conceptions of rights and justice, these same kinds of counterfactual judgments will very likely have to be relied upon to determine entitlements, even if these determinations are taken to have force only in the context of a just basic social structure.

Changing Circumstances: New People, Different Stuff

We have already seen some ways in which the alteration or destruction of property or the death of victims and/or wrongdoers can complicate the counterfactual judgments required to understand the content of rights to the reparation of past wrongs. In some such cases, it seems undeniable that rights to reparation can simply dissolve. If you steal my banana, eat it, and die immediately (from an allergy to bananas, say), leaving no property behind with which to compensate me, my right to reparation seems to simply disappear. This is not exactly a case of supersession, of course—since nobody else's right to the banana supersedes my own—nor does my right to reparation for the theft exactly "fade" (unless you take a very long time to die). But perhaps this counts as a related moral phenomenon. Similarly, some cases involving property wrongs conjoined with (or followed by) the death of the victim may involve rights to repair that dissolve with the victim's demise. Again, however, the right in question would not be

[46] Waldron (1992), 13–15. We can, for instance, confidently claim about Native American tribes that, in the absence of the deception and violence that in fact typically caused their loss of territories, they would not have given away or sold the land or resources necessary to the survival of their tribe or culture. This judgment is based not on some simple assumption about the authority of (hypothetical) rational choice, but rather on our knowledge of the actual prior histories of tribal choices and the vitality of their cultures, and on conservative assumptions about background conditions (and thus about the consequences of choice).

superseded (in any literal sense), and it would certainly not be superseded by (or in favor of) any new right for the present possessor. Rather, in such cases the stolen things are best understood as simply "reverting to common" and becoming available for morally permissible acts of appropriation by others.

Changes of cast through death are obviously complicated cases for historical theories of rectification (as they are as well, I think, for nonhistorical theories). And many of the cases that historical theories most hope to illuminate typically involve serious past injustices that either involved or were followed by the death of victims and/or wrongdoers. When the wrongdoer dies, he may leave behind nothing that could adequately compensate his victim for the wrong, in which case rectification will simply be impossible. Where land is at issue, of course, this will generally not be the case (though we will still need to deal with the conflicting claims on the land of the children or dependents of the wrongdoer or of innocent third-party holders of stolen land). But set all of this aside for now; the impossibility of full rectification in certain kinds of cases is not, I think, any more of a problem here than is the impossibility of *retributive* justice in cases where offenders die before they can be punished. The more troubling questions, I believe, clearly concern those cases in which the *victim* of wrongdoing dies. If the victim's rights die with him, of course, then historical rights to reparation cannot possibly persist through the years in the ways my arguments here have suggested.

Like most Lockeans, I believe that rights in things—importantly including rights in land—are heritable and do not simply disappear as the specific rightholders and wrongdoers die off. But why should we suppose this, suppose that rights of rectification descend down family lines, from the original victims of injustice to their current descendants? After all, those original victims might, in the absence of the injustice, have later sold their holdings or lost them in a poker game or given them to a needy friend, so that the relevant rights never would have passed to their children anyway. Why should *inheritance* of rights to rectification simply be *assumed* in this way,[47] particularly when we know that inherited property is the source of many apparent social injustices?[48] To this I think there are two appropriate responses. First, our counterfactual judgments about how things would have gone on in the absence of the wrong should be conservative, as I argued earlier.[49] Second, I think children have *rights* against their parents to

[47] Waldron (1992), 15.

[48] Lyons (1977), 258.

[49] A special problem with such judgments arises where the children (who are alleged to inherit rights to reparation) are conceived after the relevant injustices. For in those cases, it has been argued, some of the counterfactual judgments necessary to the case for historical reparations are simply (necessarily?) *false*. Following the lead of Parfit, a number of philosophers have pointed to a set of "existential" difficulties allegedly involved in attempts to apply the historical theory of rectification to such cases. The central objection is put most clearly by Chris Morris. If the idea of rectification is to

the receipt of property (including in this "property" parental rights to the return of stolen property) that is needed by those children for a decent life, and this will often include rights to stolen land, stolen resources, or stolen wealth. Indeed, even if the parents *did* (before their deaths) freely give away or sell the land their children needed for a decent life, the children would *still* have claims against the recipients of that land to the portions they needed.[50] Their parents were not *entitled* to dispose of the land without regard for the needs of their offspring.

Some of the changes relevant to reparation, though, are not changes to the cast of characters, but instead involve changes to the things unjustly appropriated. Stolen things can be destroyed or altered. Stolen land can be stripped or irreversibly changed (e.g., by farming, or commercial or residential development). Such land cannot subsequently be returned to the rightful owner in any way that will make it as if the wrong had not occurred. How can an historical theory of reparation deal with such changes? We have already seen (in the previous section) a start to the answer. But a further important point relevant to the problem here is this: I believe that the most prominent contemporary *defenders* of historical rights have importantly misdescribed such rights. Nozick, for instance,

restore victims to the conditions they would have enjoyed in the absence of the injustice (or to the closest approximation thereof), the historical theory cannot, Morris claims, sanction rights to rectification for persons conceived after the injustice occurs (e.g., the descendants of decimated aboriginal peoples). For insofar as the injustice certainly changed the conditions under which the children of victims were later conceived, those children are different persons than the ones who would have been born in the absence of the wrong done to their parents. There is, then, *no* condition that actual children would have been in had injustices prior to their conceptions not occurred; nor is there any sense in which they can claim that *they* would have been better off in the possible world without the injustices (Morris [1984], 176–7). I can only quickly sketch here what I take to be the correct response to Morris (et al.). There can be no denying (and Morris does not try to deny) that Morris's conclusion is counterintuitive. Common sense has no trouble with the claim: "If my parents had not had all of their property stolen (before my conception), I would have had an easier life as a child." Yet on Morris's analysis, this claim is straightforwardly false. His analysis fails, I think, because it involves one or more of the following: (a) a tacit assumption that a significant injustice *necessarily* alters subsequent conditions for the conception of offspring; (b) an assumption that the relevant claims always concern identity across possible worlds, rather than some version of the "counterpart" relation across worlds (see Lewis [1973], 39–43, 67); (c) an assumption that perfect identity of genetic makeup is the single privileged criterion of personal identity; or (d) some combination of these three assumptions. I reject all three of the assumptions. The best analysis of the counterfactual above, I think, sees it as equivalent to: "In those possible worlds in which I (or my counterpart) exist and my parents do not have all of their property stolen (before my conception), I have an easier life as a child (than that which I had in the actual world)." Since there certainly *are* such possible worlds (i.e., since, contrary to assumption (a) above, the absence of the theft could not be claimed to *necessarily* exclude my existence [or the existence of my counterpart]), the counterfactual at issue will be perfectly capable of being true. For a more skeptical examination of and conclusion concerning these questions—but one that is too quick with the idea of a "counterpart—see Sher (1979), 381–83.

[50] I discuss this view in Simmons (1992), 204–12.

suggests that what is distinctive about the historical conception of rights is that thus conceived rights are to *particular things*; whereas on end-state conceptions of rights, rights are to *shares* of the total social product.[51]

On Lockean historical accounts, the labor that grounded a property right in the first place is invested in some specific object, establishing a connection between the person and the object that persists even if the object is well traveled afterwards. Rights depend on the actual history of acquisitions and transfers of particular things. When you steal my bicycle, my right to that particular bicycle persists not only through wrongful expropriations, but also through acquisitions by innocent third parties. Injustice permanently taints goods, because those particular goods are (as we've seen) morally *marked* by the labor of their original legitimate owners.[52] Rectification calls for a return of unjustly appropriated objects to their rightful owners. By contrast, on end-state conceptions of rights, since rights are to shares of goods (i.e., to shares that satisfy the structural distributional requirements of the end-state theory in question), rectifying injustice is a simpler matter of adjusting the relative sizes of shares of goods. To rectify the theft of my bicycle, we need not return to me that particular bicycle, or *any* bicycle at all, provided that my overall share of goods is readjusted to its appropriate size and shape, the one specified by the favored pattern.

Nozick attempts, of course, to make the end-state view seem ill motivated and oppressive, since it gives people claims on a share of the goods produced through the honest labors of other individuals. It pries apart production and distribution, treating created goods as if they were manna from heaven. But many of his readers respond instead by noticing that the end-state view makes the project of rectifying a long history of social injustice seem possible and attractive. We "simply" bring the shares of oppressed people into the range of those acceptable under the relevant end-state principle. On the historical view, on the other hand, this rectificatory project seems impossible, both for evidentiary reasons—we have no clear records of the complicated strands of entitlements to particular things—and for reasons of principle—the change of cast, the irreversible alteration or destruction of the things people were once entitled to, the passage of time, and so on, make it impossible even in principle to specify the holders or the contents of historical rights. If historical rights simply "dissolve" in these ways, why should we take them seriously as real rights at all?

An important part of the problem here for historical theories of rights is that the contrast with end-state theories has been badly drawn. Most obviously, of

[51] Nozick (1974), 238, 171–2. See also Lomasky (1987), 142: "Persons' rights are rights to particular performances and are rights over particular items of property."

[52] As Locke puts it, "this labor being the unquestionable property of the labourer, no man but he can have a right to what that is once joined to" (II, 27).

course, end-state theories will often *also* advocate the use of historical criteria for rights. If the end-state principles are taken as guides only for the basic structure of society (as on Rawls's view, for example), entitlements *within* a just structure of basic institutions will be historical claims on particular objects, *not* rights to *shares* of the total social product.[53]

Less obvious, perhaps, is the fact that no adequate historical theory can do without the idea of *historical* rights to *shares* of goods. This is most evident in two kinds of cases, the first of which I deal with here (while the second, which involves what I'll call mandatory "downsizing" of legitimate holdings, I discuss in the next section). In the first kind of case, the object to which I have a right is destroyed or irreversibly altered by some wrongdoer. You steal my bicycle and run it through a compacter or melt it down. What becomes of my right? How is the theft to be rectified, on an historical theory of rights? Surely my right in such a case is not any longer a right to a particular object, nor is it a right to a certain share of the total social product. It is rather a right to a certain-sized share of a particular set of holdings—namely, to a share of the holdings of the wrongdoer. This is what I earlier called an historical right to a *particularized share*. Now it may seem that such a right could not *be* an historical right at all, since I have no historical connection (say, through my labor) with the object on which I have a claim in this case. But this appearance is mistaken. One needn't oneself have any deep historical connection with an object, beyond a *transactional* connection, in order to have an historical right to the object. If you give me an object you own (or sell it to me), my right to it is perfectly historical, despite my having no prior connection to it.[54] Similarly, in the present case of theft and destruction, you forfeit to me rights over a certain share of your legitimate holdings, by virtue of your illegitimate theft and destruction of my property. But the right to this share is still perfectly historical. The claim in question depends on the past

[53] Nozick, of course, treats patterned theories as if their favored principles were intended to govern *all* distributions of goods within societies. Thus, in a perfectly just society, if you give me a more expensive gift than I give you, or if a judge awards compensation for an unintentional wrong, a patterned theory would require redistribution to restore the initially just pattern (since shares have now changed size). This understanding of patterned theories reduces them to a rather silly straw man. No real defender of a patterned theory believes that Christmas is a time for the redistribution police to be especially wary. As the discussion below indicates, I believe that Nozick's characterization of historical and end-state theories in fact badly distorts *both* approaches.

[54] Historical theories are also sometimes criticized, of course, for their apparent inability to explain how even *alienation* (transfer) of property is possible. If my labor is mixed with an object, thus preventing any legitimate nonconsensual appropriation (i.e., theft) of the object by another (since taking the object would involve taking my labor as well), why doesn't my labor continue to inhere in the object even when I try to alienate my rights to the object, rendering *consensual* transfer impossible? (e.g., Waldron [1988], 259–62; [1992], 17). The answer, I think (and as we saw above), involves reinterpreting the Lockean idea of mixing one's labor with a thing in (slightly less literal) terms of

history of holdings and is justified by the importance of free acquisition and transfer. The claim is *not* based on any patterned or end-state insistence that the resulting shares meet a favored structural requirement—that they end up being equal, say, or that they be proportionate to the overall moral desert or virtue of the parties.

Changing Circumstances: Justice for All

I turn now (finally) to what I take to be the central theme of "changing circumstances" arguments: that who is entitled to what—and, by extension, which group or state is entitled to what territory or resources—is (at least primarily) a function of how many people are around now, what they're up to, and how much (and what kind of) stuff is around now for them to use. Since all of these things will change with the passage of time, so must our conclusions about who is entitled to what. Entitlements based on legitimate claims from the past—and entitlements to reparation based on past wrongs—will often be superseded by the present demands of justice. Waldron (repeatedly) puts the point as follows (indeed, he appears to want to *define* supersession in these terms, despite his occasional use of other examples of supersession that do not precisely fit this model):

> I do not think this possibility—of the supersession of past injustice—can be denied, except at the cost of making one's theory of historical entitlement utterly impervious to variations in the circumstance in which holdings are acquired and withheld from others. If circumstances make a difference to what counts as a just acquisition, then they must make a difference also to what counts as an unjust incursion. And if they make a difference to that, then in principle we must concede that a change in circumstances can affect whether a particular continuation of adverse possession remains an injustice or not.[55]

incorporating that thing into legitimate purposive activities. The nature and extent of the rights one acquires over a thing is (in part) determined by the *role* it is intended to play in the specific pursuits or projects (as we will see below). Since one purpose we may have for a thing is that it be available for transfer to another person as a legitimate holding, as a thing over which that other has undiminished rights, our purposive incorporation of the thing (our "labor" in it) can end with such a transfer. No "residue" of our "labor" then persists in the thing, any more than it does when we *abandon* property and thereby allow it to "revert to common." Cases of deliberate transfer of a thing—where the thing is not abandoned and hence does not revert to common—involve intentionally "directing" the thing to its incorporation into the new owner's plans or projects.

[55] Waldron (1992), 25; virtually identical passages are in Waldron (2002), 152 (and, oddly, again on 156), and Waldron (2004), 241–2.

And Waldron's further elaboration:

> I inferred that an initially legitimate acquisition may become illegitimate or have its legitimacy restricted (as the basis of an ongoing entitlement) at a later time on account of a change in circumstances. By exactly similar reasoning, it seems possible that an act that counted as an injustice when it was committed in circumstances C_1 may be transformed, so far as its ongoing effect is concerned, into a just situation if circumstances change in the meantime from C_1 to C_2. When this happens, I shall say that the injustice has been *superseded*.[56]

Now any Lockean (like myself) who believes in a proviso that governs both acquisitions and holdings is committed to accepting claims very similar to those made by Waldron in the passages above. Moral entitlements are, indeed, sensitive to changing circumstances; changing circumstances do, indeed, change the contents of our rights, making new distributions of things just. The question for the Lockean is whether accepting such claims really does commit one to the kind of supersession thesis Waldron defends—as Waldron plainly thinks it does. My own view is that the fact that "changing circumstances" may change the specific contents of our property rights in no way entails that moral rights are supersedable, at least given Waldron's (or a proper) understanding of supersession. Changing circumstances entail *none* of the following: that rights over stolen things are lost by the original rightholders, that rights to reparation for past wrongs "fade" over time, or that the present possessors of things enjoy any privileged position with respect to rights over those things.

To see this, consider two points. (The first, largely ad hominem, point I will make quickly; the second, more general, point I will discuss in more detail.) The first point is just this: it is important to notice the very significant extent to which Waldron's argument here constitutes a kind of preaching to a very particular choir—namely, to those (like his fellow Kantian functionalists) who are committed to a purely *structuralist* account of justice. An injustice in "circumstances C_1," Waldron says, "may be transformed, *so far as its ongoing effect is concerned*" into "a just situation" at a later time (my emphasis). What can this possibly mean, other than the following: that the overall distribution of holdings at that later time has come to count as just (because of changed circumstances), according to some structural principle of justice—that is, according to a principle of justice that purports to assess distributions *independent of* the histories that produced them? The new situation cannot have "become just" in any other sense. The original

[56] Waldron (1992), 24; (2002), 155.

injustice has never been remedied or "made up for" by anyone. No deliberate rectification has been attempted or accomplished. Surely Waldron must mean here just that the "ongoing effects" of that injustice—that is, the holdings that the victims (or their descendants), the wrongdoers (or their descendants), and others end up having in its aftermath—may come to count as structurally just shares of societal land and resources.

But if we think that the history of a distribution can matter to its justice—and if we think (as I do) that a wrong amounts to more than just its costs and its ongoing effects[57]—then Waldron's points look like a non sequitur, at least as support for the idea of genuine moral rights supersession. It is certainly true that the specific shares to which one may be entitled—as a matter of *structural* justice—can be affected by changing circumstances. If I am entitled to an equal share of my society's distributable goods, say, what counts as an equal share will obviously change in size or shape depending on the changing numbers of persons in my society and the changing amount and kinds of stuff to be divided between them. But this should in no way affect our position on questions about the persistence of claims based on historical wrongs, unless we have already begged the main question by just assuming the *irrelevance* of historical wrongs to contemporary justice.

Nor does insisting that history *does* matter to the legitimacy of contemporary holdings mean that *structural* justice is not *also* important. My arguments have throughout favored a pluralistic approach to such questions.[58] If one prefers to reserve the adjective "just" for possible application only to the structural or institutional dimensions of states, then we should simply refer to the morally relevant historical facts about states using some other suitable moral language. Interestingly (and as we have already seen), Waldron does not seem *himself* to be committed to pure structuralism in his account of justice, since the kinds of historical "*injustices*" that he believes can be superseded by changed circumstances

[57] According to the Lockean view I have defended here, rectification of past wrongs may be required even where victims are *not* currently suffering as a result of those wrongs. The well-off, for instance, may be owed restitution for wrongs against them even if those wrongs have no persisting negative effects on them. This fact is important in considering the claims of groups of people against whom historical wrongs were committed but who are not today worse off because of them. Native Americans would still have been entitled to rectification, in my view, even had they prospered on the reservations to which they were forcibly removed.

[58] "Robin Hood principles," of course, always tempt us here. It is hard not to be sympathetic to the simple reduction of inequality, say, even if it involves stealing (from the rich). But the appeal of such principles in no way affects my case here. Simple structural justice *does* matter morally. And theft is plainly *less* of an historical wrong—if, indeed, it is wrong at all—in social circumstances (like those in the story of Robin Hood's England) that include huge, brutally imposed, and intransigent inequalities.

are primarily wrongs of a *nonstructural* sort—such as theft of land, which is wrong for reasons quite different than that it might upset a favored, just distributive structure. But whatever *language* one chooses to employ to discuss historical and structural wrongs, the persistence of rights based on the former can surely not be denied simply by observing that later sets of holdings may eventually come (without attempts at rectification) not any more to constitute the latter.

The second, much more general, point that undercuts Waldron's attempts to motivate the supersession thesis (by appealing to "changed circumstances") is this. Theories of persisting historical rights—like my Lockean theory—can appeal, in resisting supersession claims, to a second kind of case of rights to "particularized shares" of goods: namely, the rights at issue in cases of mandatory "downsizing" of legitimate holdings. Even many of the most thoroughly libertarian historical rights theorists acknowledge that historical rights must be sensitive in certain ways to changes in circumstances. Property claims that were once perfectly legitimate may cease to be so with decreases in the pool of resources or increases in the number of persons needing to draw on those resources. Thus, even Nozick allows that his Lockean proviso applies to holding as well as to taking goods. If I legitimately appropriate a desert waterhole, and all the other water holes subsequently dry up, the *content* of my rights over the water hole changes with the changed circumstances. I can no longer charge whatever I wish for the water. Nor does my legitimate appropriation of a desert island permit me to later deny a new castaway access to the island's meager resources.[59] Even Nozick, then, concedes that no historical rights theory is defensible unless it incorporates some version of a Lockean proviso for takings and holdings—that is, unless it limits historical rights by some reasonable requirement that we leave "enough and as good" in common for others.

I take the best Lockean position on this issue to be something like the following. Persons have rights of fair access to available land and natural resources. These rights are *opportunity* rights to, not rights of *property* in, a fair share of the earth. Property rights in the earth and its resources are acquired by the incorporation of things (that fall within our fair shares) into our legitimate purposive activities. But changes in circumstances may change what constitutes a fair share. Thus, both access (opportunity) rights and property rights may change in their extent or content as circumstances change.

In the Nozickean example, simply imagine eight castaways, each of whom has an access right to one-eighth of the island's land and resources. Each of the eight labors on and takes property in his or her full fair share. But children, grandchildren, and additional castaways increase the population without

[59] Nozick (1974), 180.

any corresponding increase in land or resources. The original eight must then "downsize" their previously legitimate holdings, giving the new population fair access to their shares of the island. If the original owners refuse to yield, those of their holdings that exceed their fair shares may be justifiably seized by those who have rights of access (that is, seized through incorporating that surplus into their legitimate projects).[60]

As in the kind of case analyzed in the last section (involving altered or destroyed stolen property), the point to notice here is that the mandatory downsizing both creates for the newcomers access rights to a share of the island and sustains for the original castaways historical rights to a portion of their original just holdings. But in both cases, the rights are to what I called a "*particularized* share." The newcomers, for instance, have neither a right to just any fair share of the whole island nor a right to a particular piece of land or property. Their rights are rather rights to some appropriate share of the specific original just holdings of the original castaways.[61] Once again, as in our first kind of case

[60] Lyons suggests that in such a situation it may be legitimate to require the original castaways to give up their *private* property altogether. If all the islanders are *better* served by a system of collective ownership, all may be obliged to pool their resources (Lyons [1977], 263). My own view is that mandatory downsizing is the *typical* requirement in such circumstances; a collective property regime may be *required* only in certain very specific kinds of cases (including, of course, those in which there is voluntary joining of individual holdings or in which the relevant purposive activities are all themselves collective). To suppose otherwise is, I think, to suppose—mistakenly in my view—that justifications of property must always be *optimality* justifications (which mandate the *best* property regime) rather than *permissibility* justifications (see Simmons [1994], section II). There may, of course, be some things that are not privately appropriable in the first place (because they are indivisible or because fair shares are unusably small, say). Locke, for instance, discusses the English commons partly in these terms (II, 35). And downsizing may in certain cases result in individual rights in *undivided* shares. Finally, considerations of *charity* may in some cases require that private property be surrendered. But while these kinds of possibilities may *motivate* a voluntary move to collective ownership, I take only the creation (through mandatory downsizing) of unusably small fair shares to actually *require* the nonvoluntary conversion of private to collective property.

[61] This, I think, is how we ought to assess many of the historical claims to land and resources made by decimated, expelled aboriginal peoples: they are required to share with the many who came later, but not required to surrender their claims to everything of which they were unjustly deprived. Treating their claims in this way preserves the *particularity* of those claims without allowing that their claims are still claims to all the land of which they were unjustly deprived (on which so many others now live and work). Their rights are not, I think, just rights to *some* fair share (*any* old fair share) of their countries' land and resources; they are rather rights to a *particular* (or a *particularized*) fair share. For example, treating Native American rights as exclusively end-state rights would mean denying that the actual arguments made by Native American tribes for historical rights to *particular* lands and resources have any moral force at all or any appeal beyond ungrounded emotionalism. I do not think most of us regard Native American demands for control over portions of their historical homelands as just unmotivated, sentimental nonsense. One great virtue of the historical approach, then, is its ability in this way to make good moral sense of the particularity of Native American claims, without accepting what seem to be ridiculous demands. For an extended defense of this approach to Native

(involving destroyed or altered property), it may be thought that the rights in question could not count as genuinely *historical,* since they must rest on some apparently end-state idea of a fair division. Some of Nozick's critics, for instance, suggested that his use of the Lockean proviso undermined his theory, incorporating end-state considerations into what is supposed to be a purely historical theory.[62] Nozick explicitly *denied* that this was the case,[63] but the disagreement here may be largely verbal. The idea of a fair division used in Nozick's (and in my own, Lockean) account is motivated *not* by the need to insure some pattern of holdings (as Nozick rightly maintained), but by the requirement that our appropriations and holdings not *harm* or unfairly disadvantage others. Further, the idea of a fair division, on this model, is used only in determining rights of *access* to land or resources. Actual *property* rights continue on this account to be based in the actual *history* of acquisitions and transfers, *not* in the desirability of achieving any favored pattern of distribution of property rights. While rights of fair access *limit* the possible scope of property rights, they do not *determine* the content of those rights or the relative sizes of individuals' rightful shares of property. Who owns what (if anything) *within* their fair shares is still determined by what has actually taken place, by the specific history of actions and transactions.

Whether or not such a position is counted as "purely historical" seems far less interesting (to me, at least) than does the fact that the position treats historical rights and wrongs as the principal determinants of the legitimacy of contemporary claims over things. Such historically based (even if not, perhaps, "purely historical") claims still sharply *contrast* with moral demands based in structural theories about who should have what, theories oriented by (what we saw Waldron call) a "primary focus" on current or forward-looking considerations. Perhaps (as I suggested above) historical claims of legitimacy and structural claims of justice can both have their places in a pluralistic theory of rightness. But the Nozickean (or Lockean) employment of a limiting proviso does not simply turn the former kind of claim into a species of the latter.

If I am right about this, then a properly developed historical theory of rights will accept the idea of property rights in *shares* of goods. But the historical rights in question will be to *particularized* shares—not rights either to particular objects or to general shares of the whole of the divisible resources. Such an historical theory will thus still motivate some of the essential particularity

American claims to reparation, see Simmons (1995)—an article from which some of the other arguments in this chapter have been drawn.

[62] See, for one among many such arguments, Sarkar (1982).

[63] Nozick (1974), 181.

of historical claims.[64] But by acknowledging that some historical rights are not rights to particular things, the theory also gives us some reason to believe that the problem of rectifying complicated injustices may not be insoluble in *principle*. For even if we cannot say precisely to what particular thing some individual or group is entitled, we can now see that just rectification may be achieved in such a case by redistribution within a *range* of appropriate outcomes. And the theory now has something intelligent to say about *why* the content of historical rights is not always determinate—something to say, that is, that should not just lead us to conclude that the historical rights in question are not real rights at all (or that if real, they are only real because *reducible* to *end-state* rights). But it will undoubtedly seem that I have still left the content of historical rights to particularized shares too vague to do any real work in explaining the requirements of historical rectification of injustice. So let me add a few very brief remarks on how I think the idea of rights to particularized shares can be more fully specified.

Return with me to our example of the desert island castaways. When the island's population increases, just what may the needy newcomers lay claim to and what must the original islanders surrender? My view is this: the original islanders must make available to the newcomers some portion of their holdings that will allow the newcomers access to a fair share of the island's land and natural resources. But the original islanders have the right to choose *which* portions of their holdings to relinquish, and they retain their rights over even the relinquished portions so long as the newcomers opt not to make property in them. The original islanders may choose to keep the fair share of their original holdings to which they feel most attached, for instance, or in which they have invested the most labor. And they are entitled to compensation from the newcomers for improvements they have made in the portions of their holdings they are obliged to surrender.

The newcomers, on the other hand, are entitled to take in their purposive activities their fair shares of the original islanders' previously legitimate holdings. But they may take only from the relinquished portions. If the original islanders resist downsizing their holdings and refuse to choose which portions to surrender, the newcomers may seize their shares without the original owners' consents. But they may not seize just whatever portions they choose. They must take those portions that are *least* central to the original owners' pursuits and that carry the least investment of labor by the original owners. The newcomers may not seize their shares without indicating to the original islanders their intention

[64] Some resources, of course, are not divisible into shares. And where (if ever) the downsizing of *artifacts* is at issue, division will routinely be pointless. In such cases the relevant rights to shares will still be particularized in the right sense, even if they are rights only to undivided shares.

to do so and their need for fair access. And they must compensate the islanders for any improvements previously made to the portions seized.

Finally, both parties must compensate the other for any losses caused by holding or seizing property in a fashion that is illegitimate at the time, but that later *becomes* legitimate through changes circumstances. For instance, an original islander might retain control over more than his fair share, denying the newcomers full access; but later developments might increase the available land (a drought dries out swampland, say) or decrease the demand (some of the islanders die), rendering the retained share *fair* at this later time. In that case, compensation is owed the newcomers for losses suffered by not having had access to their fair shares during the intervening years. Or the newcomers could seize more than their fair shares, gradually distributing portions of these illegitimate holdings to their children or to other newcomers, until the shares they all hold *are* of an appropriate size. In that case, compensation is owed to the original islanders for the losses they suffered from having, for a time, less of their original property than that share to which they were entitled. In neither case has the historic injustice simply been "superseded," as Waldron suggests is true of such cases,[65] for compensation is still due for unjust losses suffered during the time before which circumstances (and fair shares) changed.

If I am right about this, then we should once again conclude that rights to particularized shares can in fact be given some reasonably specific content. The original islander's claim to a share of her initial holdings (in cases of mandatory downsizing) is not necessarily a claim to an antecedently specifiable holding, but it is a claim that is far more specific than simply a claim to any appropriately sized share of the island. Further, if my remarks here are plausible, we can see at least part of what an historical rights theorist should say about the effects on our rights of passing time and changed circumstances. This has always been a sore subject for historical rights theorists, for it has seemed to many ad hoc to claim that rights simply expire or fade away if we ignore or complicate injustices for long enough. In the face of an entire society historically descended from unjust land acquisitions, say, Nozick can hardly say, "We will take historical entitlements very, very seriously starting *now*; those old historical entitlements don't count any more. But these *current* entitlements, grounded in precisely the same way as the old ones that we'll ignore, are supremely important morally."

We can now see some ways in which historical rights can change, shrink, or expand, and so be sensitive to passing time and changing circumstances, without their simply "fading" away. My own view, like Waldron's, is that *mere* passage of time, considered strictly by itself, can have *no* effects on the substance of our

[65] Waldron (1992), 24–5.

moral rights, including our rights to rectification of past injustices. But against Waldron (and many other functionalist and nationalist theorists), I've argued here that acknowledging the sensitivity of justice to changing circumstances in no way requires our committing ourselves to the view that moral rights are supersedable (at least, in the literal sense outlined above).

One could, I suppose, just choose to call all required changes in the content of moral rights instances of "rights supersession," though the cases of required change described above appear to have very little in common with the "fading" (prescription) of *legal* rights over time (that originally motivated Waldron's discussion of moral rights supersession). The "trimming" of the full extent of our (originally legitimate) moral rights has nothing to do with either "procedural difficulties about evidence and memory" or the new "structures of expectation" that arise around originally wrongful arrangements. It has to do only with guaranteeing that all are treated fairly (both in compensation for destroyed goods and in access to the earth and its resources). If there is some sense other than this in which moral rights "fade" with passing time, this sense has not yet been clearly defined or plausibly justified by the proponents of rights supersession.

True, where changing circumstances entail that some portions of historical entitlements are lost, portions of rights to reparation (for violations of those entitlements) will be lost as well. And new people will then be able to acquire property rights in (through mixing their labor with) things that were originally legitimately owned by others. But if these phenomena resemble anything, it is surely not the prescription of legal rights. Rather, they resemble the simple outweighing of our property rights by a more imperative moral requirement—as when some new humanitarian disaster requires of us all that we surrender some of our property to assist those in dire need.[66] In any event, even should we decide to just *call* "supersession" this sensitivity of the content of rights to changing circumstances, supersession of this feeble sort will not suffice to support the theories of territorial rights that centrally rely on some thesis of moral rights supersession. Functionalist, plebiscitary voluntarist, and nationalist "supersessionists," as we've seen, support not just *revisions* in historical holdings based on changed circumstances. They support, in effect, a new start: a comprehensive redistribution of claims to land or territory—typically beginning (in legitimate polities) with present possession—in those ways that best satisfy their favored moral imperatives. And we have seen no reason in this chapter to suppose that such a systematic supersession of historical moral rights can be morally justified.

[66] This is, I take it, consistent with the spirit of Meisels's claim: "some claims to territorial restitution based on historical events are well-founded, even if, when all is said and done, justice often requires them to be put aside in favour of the weightier claims of settlers" (Meisels [2009], 87).

8

Resource Rights

Jurisdiction and Exclusion

Modern states, as we have seen, claim legal jurisdiction over particular geographical areas of the earth's surface, claiming in the process political authority over persons located within those areas. Most of this book has been thus far devoted to evaluating these claims by states. But in addition to such jurisdictional rights ("of control"), states also claim rights that more closely resemble the kinds of claims to landownership made by individuals (which we discussed at some length in chapter 7). These property-like ("exclusionary") rights include, first, the right to control the borders of the territory, as a landowner has the right to fence or otherwise exclude others from entering or using his or her land. And relative to those borders, second, states also make (and international covenants confirm[1]) property-like claims over the nonhuman, physical stuff in, around, and comprising their areas—the things often referred to as "natural resources."[2] States typically claim rights of control over resources (if any) that are not privately owned and rights to tax and regulate the uses of resources (if any) in private hands. In the final two chapters of this book, I will explore and assess (in reverse order) these two kinds of property-like claims made by modern states.[3]

[1] The United Nations' *International Covenant on Civil and Political Rights* (1966), for instance, states that "all peoples may, for their own ends, freely dispose of their natural wealth and resources" (Article 1).

[2] Cara Nine defines natural resources as naturally occurring nonhuman things that are or may be of use or value to persons (Nine [2012], 117). Chris Armstrong defines them as "any raw materials (matter or energy) which are not created by humans but are available to sustain human activities" (Armstrong [2014], 3). Either of these definitions will suffice for my purposes here.

[3] Nine rightly notes that groups' claimed rights over natural resources include *both* jurisdictional rights—such as rights to regulate, determine a property regime for, and tax resources—*and* exclusionary "ownership" rights (Nine [2012], 117–120). The same is plainly true of claimed rights to control their borders. I focus here (and in chapter 9) just on the property-like aspects of states' claimed rights over resources.

The claimed rights over resources at issue here emanate from, but are not confined to, the surface shapes of states that we draw on maps and globes. In the same way that states claim rights to a bounded surface and to the things on it—the land and surface water themselves, the timber, plants, and animals found there—they also claim rights over what lies beneath that surface—the rocks and dirt, the metals and minerals, the oil, gas, and water. And, of course, states claim rights over more than just this, including much of what is located above and around their surface shapes.

National airspace is generally recognized as part of the sovereign territory of each state. But "remarkably, there is no agreement as to the location of the boundary between airspace and outer space" (the latter being part of the "global commons").[4] Existing states make claims to airspaces ranging from 30 to 160 kilometers above the state's surface claims (including the space above its claimed territorial waters). Since it makes little sense to claim as property the fluid and fast-flowing air itself, states' claims in this area are normally understood simply as rights of exclusion and control (with respect to particular air-filled spaces) and are usually limited to prohibiting activities that compromise either national defense or domestic "traffic coordination" within the airspace. So, for instance, flyovers by military or spy planes are generally prohibited, while innocent flyovers (under domestic supervision) are normally permitted[5] (as are the activities of spy satellites that merely view surface spaces *through* that controlled airspace).

Claims over moving water made by contemporary states include, for similar reasons (of defense and coordination) and with similar restrictions, both the state's interior waters (i.e., water that is landward of the low-water seaside baseline for the state) and its exterior territorial waters (if any). Most states currently claim twelve nautical miles beyond the low-water baseline as territorial waters over which they have sovereign rights.[6] A tiny handful of states still adhere to the old (and much more obviously defensively motivated) three-mile "cannon shot" rule, designed initially to permit states to exclude warships from those surrounding waters within cannon range of their coastlines. International accords now, however, recognize as well states' claims to large "exclusive economic zones" (EEZ) ranging out to 200 nautical miles from the state's sea baseline, as well as continental shelves beyond the EEZ.[7] Such EEZs give states control over seabed resources and marine economic activities.

[4] Sprankling (2014), 171.

[5] Under Article 1 of the *International Air Services Transit Agreement*, each signatory state guarantees the others "the privilege to fly across its territory without landing."

[6] In accordance with the 1982 *United Nations Convention on the Law of the Sea*, Article 3.

[7] Sprankling (2014), 154. See the *United Nations Convention on the Law of the Sea*, Part V and Articles 76–7.

In these kinds of cases, of course, states' territorial claims appear to be driven not by any special concerns about national defense or traffic control (as might be true of more tightly defined territorial waters), but simply by concerns to maximize national control of possible sources of wealth. But that is hardly true only of states' claimed rights to the seabeds. It is plainly true as well of at least the more extended claims states make to land and air as well. By way of illustration, let us focus for a moment on just one of those extended claims.

To the Center of the Earth?

Sometimes the implications of a principle are best explored through a story. In 1864, Jules Verne, the father of science fiction, published his novel *Voyage au centre de la Terre*, the first of a remarkable series of books that he called *Voyages Extraordinaires* (a series which included other journeys around the world, to the moon, and to the bottom of the sea). In Verne's "center of the earth" story, a German professor, his nephew, and their guide descend to the earth's center through the crater of a volcano in Iceland—encountering along their way various marvels, including prehistoric plants and animals—before eventually being safely delivered back to the earth's surface courtesy of the eruption of a different volcano, this one in southern Italy. *Voyage*, for all its entertainment value, has, alas, aged poorly in its science by comparison with Verne's other novels.

To be fair to Verne, though, until early in the twentieth century, we knew almost nothing about the interior of the earth. Before then, most (including Verne) assumed that the earth was mostly composed of earth and rock throughout, a composition which could in principle permit humans to reach its center. While we still know surprisingly little about the interior of the planet on which we reside, we do at least have reliable evidence that the earth's solid crust is a relatively thin shell—twenty to thirty miles in depth at its thickest—and that the interior 95 percent of the earth is of a very different and far less hospitable character. The earth's large mantle layer is (depending on the science to which one subscribes) fluffy, gooey, or molten, very hot and in motion around the core,[8] while the inner and outer cores are a moving layer of molten metal surrounding a (possibly) solid metal sphere[9]—with temperatures approximating those on

[8] Recent discoveries (announced in March 2014 and March 2015) strongly suggest the existence of a large layer of moving water (a "wet zone") located between 250 and 410 miles underground and a "stiff" layer somewhere near the middle of the mantle.

[9] Also in March 2015, a team of scientists at the University of Illinois announced their finding that the inner core in fact has an "inner inner" core, whose iron crystals are oriented differently than those of the "outer inner" core.

the surface of the sun and pressures approaching fifty million pounds per square inch. Needless to say, humans cannot now, and probably will not ever be able to, visit the earth's center.

Indeed, despite all our contemporary technologies, to this date, no hole made (or explored) by humans has penetrated through even one-third of the earth's crust. The deepest mining operations in the world's history (in one of today's South African gold mines) take place less than two and a half miles beneath the surface, while the depth record for drilling sits at less than eight miles. These are hardly more than scratches in the earth's crust. A much-publicized project is, of course, underway, in which scientists hope to drill through the earth's crust to the mantle sometime during the next decade or so, by doing their drilling on the ocean floor where the crust is much thinner—though they appear to have a disturbingly modest understanding of this experiment's potential for unpleasant side-effects (which have been loudly predicted and graphically described by other scientists).

Jules Verne's characters encountered many problems in their explorations of the earth's interior; but one problem they decidedly did *not* encounter was any suggestion, during or after their journey, that in the process they had violated any individuals' property rights or any state's territorial sovereignty. The characters did, after all, travel through parts of the earth, gather samples from the earth, eat and drink from it, and eventually blow up and reconfigure a goodly chunk of it. That it never crosses our minds (or the characters' minds) that any of these activities are wrongful or illegal suggests that we think, while reading, what the characters think: namely, that no one else has a prior claim of right over what Professor Lindenbrock and his companions are using.

It is, however, a commonplace of Anglo-American property law that an owner of land has rights over all that lies beneath that land (*ad inferos*), descending in a rough cone with its point at the center of the earth. Similarly, international law operates on the presumption that individual nation-states have *territorial* rights over all that lies in the (very) rough cone that extends from the boundaries of their surface territories to the center of the earth.[10] By these principles, of course, Jules Verne's characters were violating rights left and center. And at the conclusion of their descent, nearly 4,000 miles beneath the earth's surface, they were trespassing on the property of every landowner in the world and had unlawfully crossed the borders of every one of the earth's sovereign states.

Of course, the legal principles that have these implications seem preposterous, perhaps even more preposterous than Verne's story. Contemporary

[10] Landowners have also, of course, in the past been supposed to own all that lies *above* their land, extending to the heavens (*ad coelum*). Neither property law (for individual landowners) nor international law (for state territories) any longer adhere to that principle (and have not done so at least since the advent of manned flight).

landowners and nation-states cannot now reach and—barring the development of truly surprising technologies—will probably never be able to reach, let alone use, the central portions of the earth, for the same reasons that Verne's adventurers could not have explored there. Worse, however, the legal center-of-the earth principles run squarely into the facts that much of the earth's interior is fluid and in motion, so that different materials compose each rough cone at different times—despite those cones supposedly belonging to the same landowners and states at all times. Claims to property or territory deep beneath the earth's surface thus more closely resemble claims to ownership or jurisdiction over the skies or the seas than they do claims to surface land. Of course, as we've seen, states make certain kinds of claims over the skies and the seas as well (a point to which I'll return momentarily).

Though often assumed to be quite ancient, the center-of-the-earth *property* principle actually appears to be of relatively modern origin. While there were some suggestions of the principle as early as the mid-thirteenth century (in Accursius and in English common law), it did not begin to be widely accepted until the seventeensth century. Samuel Pufendorf wrote in 1660 that the "proper space" associated with land ownership is a four-sided pyramid, extending from its point at the center of the earth through the four corners of the surface property, with its base indeterminate in the heavens.[11] The most influential formulation of that idea, though, and one probably borrowed from Pufendorf, was William Blackstone's in his 1766 *Commentaries on the Laws of England*.[12] Before Blackstone, references to subsurface property rights in English law were almost always very restricted, focused only on the rights at issue in controversies over near-surface areas of economic activity, such as wells, pipes, or mines, or over mere extensions of surface objects, such as tree roots or buildings' foundations. After Blackstone, however, lawyers and judges began to cite the center-of-the-earth principle as though it were a revered principle of ancient Roman law.[13] And it was through colonial America's reverence for Blackstone's *Commentaries* that the center-of-the-earth principle made its way into early American law, remaining firmly ensconced ever since in American legal reasoning about property.[14]

[11] "I might lawfully build a structure above my ground, even beyond the lunar heaven, if that were possible . . . ; so, likewise, I might lawfully dig down until I reached only as far as the centre of the earth" (Pufendorf [2009], 83–4 [1, 5, 29]).

[12] Blackstone (1765–9), 18 (2, 2): "Land hath also, in its legal signification, an indefinite extent, upwards as well as downwards . . . ; downwards, whatever is in a direct line between the surface of any land and the center of the earth belongs to the owner of the surface."

[13] See the discussion of the principle's history in Sprankling (2008), esp. part I.

[14] On Blackstone's profound influence on early American law, see Glendon (1991), esp. 22–5. Many agree with Glendon that the *Commentaries* was, after the Bible, the most important book to the American colonists.

Later international law concerning state territory, of course, was more or less obliged to follow property law in this matter, also using the center-of-the-earth principle to locate the territorial rights of the modern state. For a state can hardly allow that its citizens possess domestic property over which that state has no jurisdiction, over which it has no rights to enforce its laws, over which it has no rights of taxation or of regulation of use. So the preposterous "center of the earth" principle became as well a common feature of discussions of state territory in the international sphere.

Justifying States' "Extended" Claims

We now have before us a reasonably complete picture of the range of property-like territorial rights that modern states claim and that international law confirms.[15] Should we regard these claims of right as well-grounded or justified? In a world of rapidly increasing population and gradually decreasing areas of dry land, states' claims to exclusive control over potential living space on the earth's surface may look increasingly self-serving and ill justified. And this model of states' rights—that is, of states having exclusive rights over the natural resources on, under, or around their lands—is one that is implicated in some of today's worst human tragedies. In the grips of this model, local political factions in poorer nations, competing to fully exploit (what they take to be) their own territories' resource rights, have produced extensive oppression, disorder, and bloodshed. Meanwhile, wealthy nations, vying to secure reliable access to valued resources in poor countries, have created or propped up willing and often quite brutal regimes—largely because doing so was necessary to create the appearance of dealing for resources with the representatives of a sovereign territorial state, a state that had exclusive rights over those resources.[16] Most developed countries (along with their corporate citizens) have participated in these practices.

How shall we approach the issue of trying to justify states' property-like territorial claims to nonhuman stuff in the world (as opposed to their more jurisdictional territorial claims)? I want to start by distinguishing what I'll call the "extended" territorial claims that states make to the air above, subsurface below, and sea around their land from what we can call their "core" territorial claims to their bounded portion of surface land. And I'll consider these claims in that order, since it seems clear that the most plausible of the claims to extended

[15] As we've seen, of course, some of these claims by states are diminished or shared in cases where states have entered into unions or confederations with other states. We should think of these claimed rights just as the "starting point" in states' territorial claims.

[16] See Wenar (2008).

territorial rights are precisely that—that is, only a kind of extension of the more basic, core territorial claims by states that we mostly take for granted. If we think of these extended claims as property-like claims in their own rights, they will inevitably appear confused or ill-motivated. That is partly because property claims over things like air, water, or much of the earth's interior immediately raise the question: how can a person—or a nation—*own* a spatially fixed cone- or pyramid-shaped piece of something when that something is a fluid in constant circulation, so that the composition of one's cone or pyramid changes from moment to moment?

Historical debates about such questions were confined almost entirely to debates about the sea. When theorists first began to think about the territorial rights of the modern state (and the property rights of the modern citizen), the "center-of-the-earth" and "up to the heavens" principles of property law still were in their infancy. And, in any event, nobody was going to worry very much about the fluidity of the heavens above or the subterranean world below, so long as these domains remained so inaccessible to us (and so long as the earth was assumed to be mostly solid throughout). Indeed, it was not really until the twentieth century—when manned flight became a serious social issue and we learned a bit about the earth's interior—that claims over such unbounded fluid domains began to seem troubling.

But there were in fact, from the very start of our thinking about the territorial rights of modern states, politically charged and quite bitter theoretical debates about the possible ownership of the sea. The first and most famous of these again involved Samuel Pufendorf. Pufendorf's famous natural-law predecessor Hugo Grotius had argued in 1609 that the sea, having no fixed portions or natural limits, is incapable of appropriation and must remain in common for all to use freely. More precisely, the sea (in Grotius's view) can neither be properly occupied or possessed (being fluid and constantly changing, like the air) nor properly used (being "infinite").[17] Since possession and use are the principal requirements for transforming what is held in common into what is "proper" (i.e., subject to the exclusive control of some particular party), any nation that claims dominion over any part of the seas should be accounted "an ambitious seeker of excessive dominion."[18] The English jurist and philosopher John Selden (known today mostly for his influence on Hobbes) argued in reply (in 1635) that the sea is as "capable of private dominion or propriety as well as the land," that the sea can be owned by persons or states (and he invented the term *mare clausum* to oppose Grotius's *mare liberum*).[19] The sea, Selden maintained, though fluid and

[17] Grotius (2004), 25–7.

[18] Ibid., 33.

[19] Selden (2004), e3. On this one occasion at least, Selden agreed with his king, Charles I, who had loudly condemned the activities of Dutch fisherman poaching in English coastal waters.

continually reconstituted, remains the same thing through its changes (like "the ship of Theseus"); and portions of that thing, like other fluid and changing things—such as rivers (which are only "lesser seas") and fountains, or the air above a house, which the house's owner has the right to control—can still be the property or territory of a person or a people.[20]

Pufendorf, sensible as always, on this occasion largely agreed with Selden against Grotius, but suspected that each "had rather the advantage of his own state before his eyes, than the zeal for truth."[21] Portions of the sea (in particular, the coastal waters of states) can be possessed[22] in the relevant sense, if they can be rightfully used and if others can be rightfully excluded from them. And the sea plainly not only can be used but was intended by God to be used by us, since God filled it with tasty fish over which he explicitly gave Man dominion—just as God gave man dominion over the land, which we can carve up into private shares. One may claim ownership of or dominion over a thing where "he has the right of so completely appropriating to himself the uses of it that . . . he may be able with justice to keep [others] out."[23] In short, the rights to use and exclude, if systematic and legitimate, simply add up to rights of ownership or dominion for Pufendorf. And one can legitimately use the sea (for fishing) and exclude others from the sea (for defense), just as one can with the land.

There is, I think, something correct about both positions here. There would be something deeply odd (as Grotius thinks) about claiming a property right—or a property-like territorial right—over a particular, geographically located set of water molecules (or over a particular, geographically located school of fish), if these things remained very likely to—and perfectly free to—immediately migrate to other locations, intermingling with others of their kind that were unowned or owned by other persons or states.[24] The absence in such cases of anything like a real period of stable *possession* of a specific thing (when that thing keeps changing its composition)—a standard requirement for establishing first-acquisition ownership of a thing—is what makes this idea odd. And it is that, I think, that also explains the initial oddity of states, claimed territorial rights to the air above, sea around, and earth beneath their lands. But there is nothing at all odd about claiming the right to use spaces, or to exclude persons from or prohibit certain kinds of activities within a geographically fixed portion of a

[20] Ibid., 127–34.

[21] Pufendorf (2009), 50 (1, 5, 7).

[22] Possession being the element through which "proprietorship begins fully to exert its effects" (ibid., 55 [1, 5, 11]).

[23] Ibid., 52 (1, 5, 7). See also Pufendorf (1934), 558–68 (4, 5).

[24] As Blackstone observed (following Grotius), "water is a moveable, wandering thing and must of necessity continue common by the law of nature" (Blackstone [1765], 18 [2, 2]).

fluid domain, particularly where the activities bear on important human interests. And such claims to exclude will look legitimate precisely to the extent that they are required for the success of activities that are themselves legitimate.[25]

In this way, then, we can try to think of at least some of states' claims to control airspaces and territorial waters as simple extensions of states' presumably legitimate tasks, such as traffic control, border control, and territorial defense with respect to their primary surface territories. These tasks, notice, are primarily jurisdictional in nature—or involve just the defense of jurisdictional claims—making the extended territorial claims at issue also look more jurisdictional than property-like. If states are entitled to control and coordinate domestic movement by those over whom they have jurisdiction—by imposing traffic schemes, enforcing safety provisions, restricting vehicle types, and so on—and if some of this movement by their subjects (or others) takes place in the air above and sea around their core land territories, then states look entitled as well to control airspaces and coastal waters for these purposes. Similarly, if states are entitled to defend their core territories and their jurisdictional authority over them—and if attacks on these things can come from air or sea—then states look entitled to take reasonable means to prevent the air above and the sea around their lands from being used for such attacks. But it is the right to govern the surface land that gives these extended rights over air and sea. Merely having the right to extend jurisdictional claims over the land to areas beyond the land still appears to fall far short of anything resembling real ownership of the air above and sea around one's territory.

The legitimacy of *fencing* is often a good test for the presence of property-like rights over an area.[26] Private landowners, for instance, are normally entitled to fence their just holdings, in order, say, to keep in pets or livestock or children or to keep out thieves or trespassers. You may not, to be sure, build your fence in a way that ruins your neighbor's permissible activities (by blotting out his sunlight or entangling his livestock, say), or top your fence with poisonous vipers. But provided only that in fencing your land you do not unduly endanger others or the environment, or diminish the value of others' holdings, fencing of privately owned land usually seems unobjectionable.

[25] While I do not discuss here the more complex cases of rivers that cross national boundaries, some of the reasoning defended in this section plainly also applies in those cases. The central concerns for a Lockean in such cases will be with guaranteeing fair access to all and with prohibitions on uses that harm or unfairly disadvantage others.

[26] Blackstone, in fact, defines landownership in terms of fencing: "every man's land is in the eye of the law enclosed and set apart from his neighbor's; and that either by a visible material fence, as one field is divided from another by a hedge; or, by an ideal invisible boundary, existing only in the contemplation of law, as when one man's land adjoins to another's in the same field." (Blackstone [1765], 209–10 [3, 12]).

And we seem prepared, as well, to treat states' core territorial claims to surface land and interior water in this property-like way, assuming that border fencing is at least not inherently illegitimate. The Great Wall of China is the most impressive historical example of such territorial border fences, but many contemporary states have similar, though far less cool, barriers. The United States has a largely ineffective fence along some of its southern border with Mexico and is constantly considering proposals to build more. Israel has somewhat more effective barriers along its borders with the West Bank and Gaza, as well as slowly disintegrating barriers at its borders with Egypt. India has fences between its territory and those of Pakistan and Bangladesh, Iran has one along its border with Pakistan, Saudi Arabia has fortified its border with Yemen, Turkey has built and maintained a barrier that divides Cyprus, and the two Koreas have long been separated by a very strong and tightly guarded set of border defenses. And so on around the world.

There are, of course, many objections to border barriers. But the standard objections seem to be of two sorts: either the complaint is that the barriers are bad items of their kind or the complaint is that the very task of border control that these barriers assist is itself an illegitimate task. As an example of the first kind of complaint: in the United States, among the standard worries about the barriers at the Mexican border are (a) that they are ineffective; (b) that they unnecessarily endanger those attempting illegal entry, by channeling illegals into dangerous routes (as we might object to your viper-topped fence); or (c) that they destroy animal habitats and landscapes. And complaints of the second kind tend to rest either on the general (e.g., cosmopolitan) position that all national borders ought to be open (or "softer") or on charges that the particular barriers in question defend unjustly established borders (as in the familiar objections to the barriers in Israel,[27] Saudi Arabia, and India). But complaints about border fences almost never take the following form: the control of those very borders is a legitimate task, but fencing the borders as a way of securing them would be illegitimate. That such complaints are so uncommon again suggests to me that we are mostly comfortable with the idea that otherwise-legitimate states have property-like claims to their core surface land territories.

What, though, would we say of treating the air above and sea around as "owned" by states in this way? Enclosure is surely the most natural answer to the problem of marking off for ownership portions of a fluid domain. So suppose a state could build a massive fence or wall from the ocean floor to well above the sea's surface, enclosing all of its coastal waters and its claimed EEZs. Or suppose that it could build a massive dome that entirely enclosed its claimed airspace,

[27] For instance, in 2004 the International Court of Justice ruled that Israel's West Bank barrier was in violation of international law.

reaching many miles above the earth's surface (to the border of "outer space," wherever that might be plausibly located). If intuition can manage to reach past the science-fiction character of these suppositions, my suspicion is that most will find such imagined enclosures by states morally dubious, at least largely because of the ways in which they would exclude innocent, nonthreatening activities in the relevant spaces. Denying a passenger plane an innocent flyover or a yacht an innocent sail-through[28] has more the look of greedy grasping for control of the world than it does the look of legitimate pursuit of morally unblemished state goals.[29] It would, of course, be unacceptable for Mexico and Canada to build a very long suspension bridge over the United States, linking Mexico City to Montreal—for the same reasons that it would be unacceptable for your two neighbors to build a large bridge between their houses that goes directly over your yard. Still, though, forcing innocent flights from Mexico City to Montreal to fly around or to fly high enough to get above all areas of air and sea over which the United States claims control looks at least equally unacceptable.

And *without* massive walls enclosing portions of the ocean or domes enclosing a states' airspace—which is, of course, our condition for the foreseeable future—there is a further obvious concern about states claiming ownership of sea or air, a concern that returns us to the issue of their fluid characters. Sometimes individual owners claim the right to damage or pollute what they own, if doing so somehow advances their ends. They are, however, typically forbidden to do so or are required to pay damages if their pollutants are allowed to escape and to adversely affect the property of others. States often display a disturbing tendency to treat local pollution as a merely local problem—just as a landowner might say "I can do with my land what I please." But because of their patterns of movement, the air and sea surrounding one state can only very rarely be polluted without eventually causing problems for other states. The same is true of pollutants that can migrate underground (or in water that flows) across national borders. Encouraging states to think of their claims over air and sea as less property-like—and more as mere extensions of core jurisdictional claims—might conceivably encourage in them as well a greater sensitivity to the ways in which local polluting is often not a local problem.

If all that is true, of course, it suggests that because states' extended territorial claims—its claims over what lies around its core surface spaces—fail the "fencing test," they probably cannot be defended if they are characterized as

[28] This is part of the "right of innocent passage" guaranteed in Article 17 of the *United Nations Convention on the Law of the Sea*.

[29] Sidgwick says this of territorial waters: "the marine dominion of States is restricted . . . to a narrow belt of water along the coast of a State's territory; and this is only allowed to be appropriated subject to a general right of peaceful navigation" (Sidgwick [1897], 253 [15, 4]).

anything like claims of ownership or property.[30] And that fact casts into serious doubt many specific aspects of the rights that states claim over sea, air, and subsurface—in particular, those aspects of those claims that cannot be justified as extensions of states' jurisdictional and defensive tasks. State claims over everything on and beneath the ocean floor, for instance, extending hundreds of miles from the state's coastline, plainly cannot be justified as simple extensions of jurisdictional requirements. Further—and here we return to the theme with which I began—there is plainly no need for states to coordinate traffic, to monitor border crossings, or to establish territorial defenses in the deep interior of the earth beneath their territories. Even at the US-Mexico border, where drug traffickers' tunnels seem to virtually exhaust the available subsurface spaces—or at the border between Egypt and Gaza, where new smuggling tunnels are dug faster than the Egyptians can flood the old ones—only the very near subsurface of the territory needs to be monitored and controlled for jurisdictional and defensive reasons. And it is thus only in the very top layers of the earth's crust that states' property-like claims look even potentially defensible, at least using this rationale for them. States' claims over the vast majority of those rough cones or pyramids, extending to the center of the earth, again (at least so far) have the look of mere greedy grasping.

In order to justify states' claims over the deep earth beneath or the ocean floor surrounding their core territories, it would appear that we are obliged to argue that each state is somehow entitled to reserve for itself all of the known and unknown natural resources that merely happen to lie closer to their surface land than to the surface land of any other state. But it is very hard to see how we could go about arguing for such an entitlement, especially in light of our extraordinarily unequal and historically stained distribution of state territories. It might initially seem, I suppose, that states' claims over their subsurface cones (and over all the resources located therein) might be legitimated by the fact that outsiders cannot gain access to these areas without disrupting surface activities above them, thus interfering with the lives of the citizens who live on the surface or with the jurisdictional tasks that states perform on their surface territories. But this would be a mistake. Nonvertical wells and mines—which are now perfectly familiar—can enter subsurface areas and harvest resources without disturbing the surface areas directly above those resources. Similarly, activities on or beneath the claimed surrounding seabed need not disrupt the activities of a

[30] This appears to be consistent with Mathias Risse's conclusion about "airspace control" (which is drawn from quite different premises): "Although the skies *as such* should neither be legitimately appropriated to the exclusion of some nor be left in common ownership, this convention [that "control of airspace above a country belongs to it"] . . . is . . . a demand of reasonable conduct" (Risse [2012], 194).

state's citizens in objectionable ways. And, in any event, many of the resources deep beneath their territories in which states are most interested—such as groundwater, natural gas, and oil—often exist in reservoirs that extend across subterranean national borders and can be harvested from multiple surface territories (and thus are referred to as "common pool" resources).[31]

Justifying States' "Core" Claims

Given the doubts I've raised about treating states' extended territorial rights as property-like rights—doubts which I find it very difficult to resist with plausible argument—I want to turn now to the far less obviously contestable cases of the property-like claims that states make, namely, states' core claims to the resources located on or near the surface of their claimed land (which seem, initially at least, to *pass* the "fencing test"). We tend, of course, to think of natural resources as comprising such things as metals, oil, water, arable land, or timber. But equally important as territorial resources are things like coastlines, navigable interior waterways, defensible boundaries, interior terrain suitable for domestic infrastructure, and so on. All of these, of course, are distributed in dramatically unequal fashion between the various states in the world.

Even were states' unequal allotments of such natural resources simply a matter of good or bad fortune in a morally impeccable history of the world, there is a well-known argument against allowing this distribution of resources to simply stand as is. This argument attempts to extend, in a cosmopolitan direction, Rawls's famous claims about the moral arbitrariness of the distribution of personal assets in (what he called) "the natural lottery."[32] When we drop into the world at birth, complete with our inherited genetic make-ups and social positions, these initial endowments are plainly just a matter of good or bad luck. The distinctions between us in these matters are arbitrary from a moral point of view, in the sense that they are not to the credit or discredit of those who inherit them.

[31] Finally, while states' resource-control rights may now be conceived of territorially, it is important to remember from the start that this connection between territorial rights and rights over all resources around the relevant territory is not obviously (morally, physically, conceptually) necessary. For example, we often recognize (special or exclusive) rights for those who simply discover new things, regardless of *where* (within limits at least) they happen to have done this. So it would not be morally odd if we recognized my (or my group's) right to resources that I or we discovered first—or even just harvested first—even were those resources discovered beneath (say, through data collected by satellite) or harvested from beneath or around some alien state's claimed territories. While the current legal distribution of state resource rights might be convenient in many ways—especially for some states—it is not the only possible distribution that could look morally respectable.

[32] Rawls (1971), 74.

Social institutions that treat any of these differences between persons as if they *do* reflect the merits and demerits of persons—by including rules that permit people's life prospects to be importantly determined by these differences (as is the case, for instance, in free-market economies)—are unjust in the same way that institutions that discriminate on the basis of differences in skin color or gender are unjust. Persons deserve to neither profit nor suffer from such arbitrary differences between them, and societies should not institutionally reinforce these unearned differences.[33] The result of societies' accepting this constraint, we can assume, would be a far more equitable distribution of basic social goods than we see at present.

But we can, in this same way, treat nation-states' ample or scanty resource endowments as important, but morally arbitrary and undeserved, influences on their residents' life prospects. From such a theoretical starting point, it is natural to suppose that nations, not deserving their particular (good or bad) resource endowments, have no special claims over them (as they might if an *international* free market were just) and are morally required to treat all persons in the world as equally entitled to access to all of the world's natural resources (or to the value of these resources). Rather than exclusive control by sovereign states over territorial resources, such arguments suggest a duty on states or peoples of global sharing of resources, through redistributive taxation or other effective means. Cosmopolitan political philosophers (most prominently Thomas Pogge) have argued in roughly this fashion for a "global resources dividend," a tax to be paid by nations on the natural resources that they use or sell, with the resulting funds to be redistributed in the interest of securing basic rights in developing countries.

Similarly, left-libertarians (most prominently Hillel Steiner) have argued for related conclusions—that is, that those using more than a fair share of the earth's land or resources must pay for this use to those who get less—but they've argued from different premises. Left-libertarians typically begin by affirming natural rights of *self*-ownership, while denying any private rights to *the earth and its resources*. The earth is viewed as either naturally unowned or naturally owned in common, with no individual entitled to appropriate more of it than any other.[34] Individuals may legitimately use or control no more than an equal share (at least absent compensation to all others for taking more than that); and collections of individuals (such as political societies) can legitimately establish exclusive control over no more than the sums of the legitimate shares of their

[33] Societies that ignore this fact permit "distributive shares to be improperly influenced by these factors so arbitrary from a moral point of view" (ibid., 72).

[34] Nine rejects "common ownership" starting points for arguments to cosmopolitan-style conclusions about territorial rights (Nine [2012], 160–61). She appears to believe (mistakenly, I think) that cosmopolitan conclusions cannot be reached from "negative community" premises; and she

members. It follows, of course, that the extent of states' justified resource rights cannot be any simple function of the resources that happen to lie on, under, or around their claimed territories.

And that, of course, is only the start of the problems we confront in trying to justify the core resource rights that states claim. The unequal distribution of resources between states is hardly just a function of good or bad luck, of the various nations having simply been plunked down where they currently are (in the way that individual persons are plunked down into their bodies and their social circumstances). Much of the world's impressively bloody history has been a deliberate product of nations seeking to acquire and control such resources by force of arms, so arbitrariness has been compounded by injustice. The colonial histories of the great European powers were regularly driven by the desire to control and exploit the natural resources that were arbitrarily placed far away from their core territorial claims, often with quite grim consequences for the native inhabitants. Similarly, most of the worst episodes in the United States' expansionist period were motivated by the ambition to control North American resources, including not just gold and silver, but fur-bearing animals, timber, arable land, navigable waterways, and finally Pacific harbors. And it continues to be routine in the contemporary world for the great powers to exploit the resources of poor nations through the monopoly that wealthy nations possess over the expertise and technology necessary to harvest those resources. Already-affluent nations then reap unconscionably large shares of the profits from such joint enterprises, often sharing those profits with corrupt and autocratic regimes.

Problems with the Standard Approaches to Resource Rights

In the face of such concerns, how can even states' core claims to resources be defended as morally justified? The natural place to turn for counterarguments, of course, is the standard philosophical approaches to justifying states' territorial

regards "positive community" starting premises as resulting in "incoherence" (for what she takes to be Lockean reasons). But Locke himself was quite clearly arguing *from* an assumption of a special kind of original positive community: a kind of "joint property" that is unilaterally divisible into private shares under certain conditions (including the satisfaction of the proviso)—joint property, that is, that is legitimately divisible into private shares *without* any need for consent from the other commoners. That is the whole point of the "meat-cutting" passage (II, 29), oddly cited by Nine in support of her opposed reading. The "father" or "master" (read "God") has provided meat (read "the earth") for the children or servants "in common"; yet they may each, in Locke's view, still plainly cut the meat and appropriate a part, without the consent of the other "commoners." See my discussion of this problem—and the implications of these arguments—in Simmons (1992), 236–41, 279–81. On the kinds and logic(s) of common ownership arguments generally, see Risse (2012), esp. part II.

rights. We explored in part II the defenses of states' *jurisdictional* claims that are offered by voluntarist, functionalist, nationalist, and hybrid theories of states' territorial rights. But those kinds of theories are, of course, designed to justify as well the more property-like, exclusionary territorial claims that states make. Can they do so successfully? In the defenses of these theories in the existing literature on territorial rights, there is a surprising paucity of discussion of resource rights. The silence, indeed, at times looks almost embarrassed; and it seems to me clear why this should be the case.

For it is very hard, indeed, to see how *any* of these philosophical approaches to justifying states' territorial rights could be thought sufficiently powerful to defend *resource* rights for states that even approximate those that states actually claim (and that are actually granted by international law). Plebiscitary voluntarist theories, for example, must be guided in their reasoning about states' territorial rights by what is required for respecting the free political choices of groups and by what is necessary for allowing them to function as self-determining polities. But while groups may need *some* resource rights in order to maintain a level of societal wealth sufficient to remain self-determining—and while they may need to *control* access to resources in various ways in order to be acceptably self-determining—it is extremely difficult to see how respecting groups' political choices and rights of self-determination could justify anything like group ownership of all natural resources on or around the particular territory the group occupies. Having the right to be a legitimate self-determining polity entails neither that control over any *particular* set of resources is essential to self-determination nor that there are no other-regarding restrictions on how that polity may act with respect to resources.[35]

What about the nationalist approach to states' territorial rights? One basic aspect of many nationalist accounts appears initially to be promising with regard to justifying states' particular and more extensive claims to resource rights. Nations very often engage in harvesting, developing, protecting, or actively stewarding natural resources in their homelands, and such activities not only add value to their territories, but may be important to both a nation's ability to be self-determining and to its national history or identity[36]—these being, remember, what nationalists say ground rights of territorial control. Similarly, nationalists argue that nations have rights to those features of their home territories that are in other ways—for instance, in religious or symbolic ways—significant to their national identities.

[35] Which perhaps explains why Altman and Wellman simply assert legitimate states' claims to rights over all resources in their regions in a single, short footnote (Altman and Wellman [2009], 200n14).

[36] Miller (2012).

But while such arguments might appear to point in a promising direction, surely they cannot do all of the justificatory work required here. The vast majority of natural resources in the world do not appear to have religious, historical, or symbolic value for the nations within whose territories they happen to be located, or to have played a central role in the formation of national identities. And even if, say, an OPEC nation's identity were tied tightly to its control over and harvesting of large local oil reserves, it seems unlikely that this identity would be greatly threatened if it were required to share with other nations some of (or some of the proceeds from) its happy resource endowment. Further, while nations may often identify with or endow with cultural or religious significance certain resource-rich geographical features of their "home" territories, they are far less likely to have done this with those parts of their states' claimed territories on which few of their people reside or which they seldom visit—nor are they likely to have added value to such regions in any interesting way. And resources beneath the state's surface territory or that are as yet undiscovered seem almost never to be claimable by appeal to these kinds of nationalist justifications. Similarly, while nationalist appeals to self-determination in support of resource rights look more plausible than those of the plebiscitary voluntarist—since the nationalist can at least say something about which particular resources should belong to the group—such an appeal must still fall far short of doing the required work. For a nation can plainly be self-determining in quite a robust sense even if it lacks property-like rights over all (including undiscovered) resources in its vicinity or lacks rights to the full profits yielded by their harvested resources.

Perhaps another nationalist approach to resource rights might work better.[37] Even if nations don't have special attachments to the natural resources themselves, they may well have attachments to things or to ways of life that would be damaged or disrupted in harvesting, using, or selling these resources. If some particular part of the national homeland (or all of that homeland, for that matter) is taken to be sacred in some way, harvesting resources from that land might well be regarded as defiling what is sacred. Or if the national lifestyle would be forced to change were available resources harvested, used, or sold, there might appear to be quite reasonable nationalist objections to such resource-related activities. But the conclusion we should reach from taking seriously such considerations would surely be not so much a national property-like right over the relevant resources, but rather a national right to reasonable control over how

[37] See the papers by Avery Kolers and Margaret Moore, along with my reply ("States' Resource Rights: Locating the Limits"), in "The Symposium on Resource Rights," *Territory and Justice: A Research Network* (January 2012). The print versions of Kolers's and Moore's papers are Kolers (2012) and Moore (2012). My paper is available at http://eis.bris.ac.uk/~plcdib/territory/papers/SimmonsMooreReply.pdf.

(or if) the resources are harvested. And that, again, falls far short of the kinds of property-like rights over local natural resources on which contemporary states insist.[38]

This brings us to functionalist approaches to resource rights. But, like plebiscitary voluntarism, functionalism appears to be severely limited from the start in justifying states' claims to resources. Functionalist theories seem able to defend states' legitimate claims over natural resources only to the extent that they are necessary to the state's performance of its morally mandated functions. While this, again, may yield *some* claims to some resources—such as claims to what is necessary to produce sufficient societal wealth for political viability, and claims against others' uses of local resources that disrupt local life or that threaten societal defense—these rationales seem very unlikely to justify states' claims to either *all* resources within or around their claimed territories or to any *particular* (i.e., local) resources, unless these are relatively central to the lives of the states' members or the security of their states.[39] Doing justice does not, on any plausible rendering of that idea, require the right to maximize societal wealth or to control any particular set of resources. Even a consequentialist version of the functionalist argument would not appear to legitimate anything like the very extensive resource rights to which actual states lay claim.[40] The simple fact of massive and dire need in the world appears to dictate that the best outcome will almost always require considerable redistribution of the wealth derivable from natural resources. While some efficiencies (derived from transaction costs and possible disruption of local economies) will, of course, favor local control over local resources, these considerations seem plainly insufficient to very regularly

[38] Margaret Moore, who at first appears to be arguing for robust states' (or peoples') rights over natural resources (in roughly "nationalist" terms), in fact seems to accept most of the skeptical arguments that I've raised in this chapter. She concedes that her arguments from collective self-determination establish "at best" only a "presumption in favour of control over resources" and denies that peoples have rights to the "full stream of benefit from the exploitation of resources." And she allows that the deep earth, seabeds, polar regions (and other uninhabited regions), airspaces, and coastal waters ought not to be automatically under the control of the states closest to them (Moore [2015], 184–5). She seems principally to want to insist that peoples must have the (presumption of a?) right to make the rules governing the extraction and use of resources in their domains, because which rules are chosen will affect the collective life of the community (there being a "cultural dimension of different rules regarding land") (166, 175). While I would insist that a state's moral right to self-determination, properly understood (see chapter 9 below), typically implies only very limited property-like territorial rights for states, Moore's actual conclusions about resource rights seem at least broadly consistent with those that I accept here.

[39] See the similar arguments against functionalist theories in Armstrong (2014).

[40] Sidgwick, on utilitarian grounds, defends the view that landowners do not have a "right to extract the minerals which lie below the surface" (Sidgwick [1897], 75–7 [5, 4]). The logic of his arguments commits him to saying the same of states' rights to what lies below the surface of their territories.

outweigh the desperate need for much broader allocation of the value of natural resources. So strong, exclusive rights for states to all of their local resources seem very unlikely to fall out of functionalist theories of states' legitimate rights.

Cara Nine, as we've seen, adds some Lockean twists to a functionalist account of political legitimacy, and one of these twists is at the center of the discussion of states' claimed resource rights in her book. So perhaps her hybrid arguments will take us further than pure functionalism. Nine's account is "based loosely on the Lockean theory that agents acquire exclusive rights over goods if they interact with the good in a way that is value-generating"—which they do by "deserving" such rights for their "efficient" establishment of "legitimate rule of law over resources within the region."[41] Collectives that administer "justice for geographically situated groups" have jurisdictional rights over all natural resources in that geographical area if those "resources are used to generate justice in the best possible way" and because "jurisdictional rights over resources are necessary for collectives to secure the objects of individual basic needs for their members."[42] And collective *ownership* of the resources is justified where "ownership rights over resources are necessary for or directly derived from jurisdictional authority"—as when groups need to use or extract resources for ordinary economic activities or to fund the provision of essential public goods, or when groups change or improve the resources in their areas.[43]

Nine's arguments here might seem to help explain why polities have claims on *particular* sets of resources, rather than just claims on whatever resources would be sufficient to discharge their responsibility to administer justice. But the "quasi-Lockean" appeals to societal use and improvements that are meant to accomplish this particularizing again look disturbingly in tension with the functionalist spirit of Nine's overall project. If use and improvement are what particularize resource claims for functional collectives, why didn't *historical* use and improvement—by conquered peoples and unjustly subjected persons—also establish rights for them over resources, rights that stand in the way of contemporary, functionally based territorial claims over resources made by collectives? To employ the analogy with Lockean property-acquisition arguments in the contemporary collective case, but to at the same time largely ignore the Lockean

[41] Nine (2012), 139–40. Nine again, curiously, insists on equating such efficiency with "demonstrating the capacity" to establish just institutions (4, 140). But merely having a "capacity" to accomplish something, as we saw in chapters 4 and 6, does not ground any *actual* Lockean claims, create any value, or make a group morally "functional." Further, the best understanding of Lockean arguments for property rights does not in this way centrally refer to any notion of *desert* (see Simmons [1992], 245–7).

[42] Nine (2012), 138, 139, 142.

[43] Ibid., 142.

arguments' relevance to individual or historical cases (the very kinds of cases from which the analogy derives its force), simply looks arbitrary and inconsistent.[44] And the territorial version of the Lockean proviso that Nine endorses, far from guaranteeing fair access for all to land and resources, simply reinforces this neglect. For Nine's proviso serves as a constraint not "on the acquisition of rights over territory," but only on "current territorial holdings" and only when other groups' holdings threaten the self-determination of some already-territorial collective (rather than, say, when persons or groups are denied the right to *become* self-determining).[45]

Further—and far more important—while the (pure) functionalist mandate of administering justice in a region certainly requires jurisdictional authority over resource-related *activities* in that area, as well as some sort of access to the funds necessary to support such administration, it pretty plainly does not *require* any *more* than that in the way of control or ownership of resources in the area. The need for jurisdictional authority in a region actually appears to imply *very little* in the way of a need for collective ownership of all things on and under that region, and Nine does not really adequately explain why we should think otherwise. Merely administering justice in an area need not involve "interacting" with the natural resources near that area (say, metals or oil reserves under it) in any way that would ground even quasi-Lockean rights over them. And respecting a group's right to *self-government*[46] (or self-determination) does not require us to accept as morally legitimate *all* of that group's choices or plans for itself. Its plans to do or control things that it has no special right to do or control are not somehow magically protected under the auspices of self-government. And the question here—that should not be simply begged by some tacit assumption of the moral legitimacy of international convention—is precisely whether discharging the function of administering justice *does* entail a special right over all locally located resources (and, if so, *why* it does). Appealing to the facts that my collective *wants* to maximize its wealth and *wants* to keep other groups from using or profiting from what is closer to us is simply not appealing to a morally interesting fact about it; nor are such wants in any obvious way relevant to the task of discharging the moral mandate to administer justice.

The apparent particularizing effect of societal *use* and *stewardship* of resources is, in fact, much better accounted for by the straightforwardly Lockean voluntarist

[44] Nine does allow that certain indigenous groups may achieve territorial rights over resources, and she allows as well the possibility of holding property rights outside the territorial domain of any group (see, e.g., ibid., 43). But she also seems unwilling to explore the implications of such concessions for her larger, functionalist project.

[45] Ibid., 163, 167.

[46] Ibid., 119.

theory of territorial rights than by any attempted quasi-Lockean addition to a functionalist theory (as I try to show in the next section). Nine rejects the Lockean approach to states' *resource* rights—the approach that she identifies as deriving resource rights from "legitimate political authority over persons" combined with those persons' "pre-political property holdings"[47]—at least partly because of its inadequate "coverage." The Lockean voluntarist theory (along with, Nine thinks, Kantian theories) "can justify only limited state authority over resources—a scope that is radically different from the full conception of resource rights." It cannot account for states' rights over undiscovered goods, over goods that are not owned by the state's citizens, over goods held by the collective in common, or over goods "held in a trusteeship for future generations."[48] While Nine is, I think, just mistaken about the implications of the Lockean theory in a couple of these cases (as I show below), it is certainly true that a thoroughgoing Lockean voluntarist *should* hold that the "full conception" of states' resource rights *cannot* be justified—especially with respect to many undiscovered goods and other goods not implicated in the individual or collective projects of states' willing members. But Nine, of course, now *also* concedes that many of the rights to land and other resources actually claimed by states cannot be justified, thus surrendering as well some of the "coverage" that she regards as a virtue of her own theory. Rights claimed in the Arctic and deep underground, rights claimed in Antarctica and deep undersea, and rights claimed in largely uninhabited wilderness areas or areas beyond the state's administration of justice (in, perhaps, the universe beyond our earth?) are now all said by Nine to be in fact indefensible.[49] These concessions, as we'll see, bring Nine's claims about resource rights largely into line with the—much better motivated—claims of the same kind made by the genuinely Lockean theory that she rejects.

In sum, all of the standard philosophical justifications for states' territorial rights thus look startlingly inadequate when we attempt to stretch them to cover the property-like claims over local natural resources actually made by the world's various states. It may, I suppose, seem that focusing on such systematic philosophical approaches to states' territorial rights has caused me (again) to disregard more obvious (or more "indirect") routes to justifying modern states' claimed resource rights. For instance, one might argue that it is sufficient for moral justification that international treaties and conventions have granted states legal rights to the resources they claim, at least when that fact is combined with another: namely, that a system of international law that permits such granting of rights to states is a morally defensible system. But I believe that whether

[47] Ibid., 122, 127.

[48] Ibid., 127, 126.

[49] Ibid., 27, 42, 178–9.

or not the current system of international law can be regarded as morally defensible is precisely the point at issue. The forces at work in the creation of international arrangements regarding resources have certainly not been fair to all who are affected by them. Many treaties and conventions have not been approved by all nations, or they have been approved only under pressure or for personal profit by corrupt national leaders; and they could certainly not be regarded as obviously in the interest of all nations—especially given the vast differences in national endowments of various kinds of resources. It seems clear, to me at least, that the international law currently governing state control over resources has been disproportionately influenced by wealthy and influential nations, along with those favorably endowed with natural resources or favorably situated to exploit the endowments of others.

Societies do, of course, quite naturally desire to maximally profit from those natural resources with respect to whose harvesting and use they turn out—or might turn out—to be especially well placed. Perhaps it initially seems—especially to those of us who live in affluent states—that legitimate states are simply entitled to reserve for themselves any such resources and to use them in whatever ways are consistent with not actively harming other persons or groups. This view, I think, brings us perilously close to embracing an outdated and unpersuasive Westphalian model of international moral relations and to abandoning altogether the idea that moral constraints ought to govern at all our uses of the earth and its limited resources. Even if we successfully resist such evil temptations, however, we ought to keep clearly in mind the plain limits of those (perhaps natural) first thoughts about states' entitlements. The claims states make are not *just* claims to property in those resources that they succeed in finding and harvesting *first*—these claims are not merely claims of the familiar "first-come, first-served" variety. State claims are to property in resources that are simply located in a particular geographical domain, regardless of whether or not they have been discovered or harvested by the citizens or agents of the state (or by anyone else) *at all*, let alone *first* discovered or harvested. And my arguments here have all pointed toward the conclusion that there is simply no good moral reason that can be given to justify anything very close to the full range of such claims.

Lockean Voluntarism and States' Property-like Rights

Once we give up the aspiration to justify something like the status quo of territorial claims by decent states, we may again find ourselves pushed away from the popular philosophical views I've just been considering and toward a more revisionist view—such as the older, individualist-Lockean version of voluntarism whose revisionist *jurisdictional* theory I supported above (in chapter 5). Just as that theory tells a plausible story about the source and extent of states' jurisdictional rights over their territories, I think it tells a plausible story about states' *property-like* rights over natural resources. Indeed, it seems to me to capture all of what is most plausible in the alternative theories of resource rights that we've just examined, but to do so without being committed to either their less plausible claims or their internal theoretical tensions. For the Lockean view I favor says precisely that legitimate states have rights over resources just to the extent that those resources actually figure in the morally acceptable plans and projects of their members (individually or collectively). This position will allow us to justify states' rights to use resources to enable their self-determination and their collective administration of justice—as plebiscitary voluntarists and functionalists insist—and to use what they add value to or what has played a central role in their history or cultural practices—as nationalists insist—but without committing ourselves to the deep problems from which these other theories suffer (as outlined in part II, above).

Locke, remember, argued that only those who have consented to membership in a political society are legitimately subject to its authority and have the obligations of citizens. And those who agree to be citizens, Locke claimed, must be understood to consent as well to submitting to the state's jurisdiction any land over which they have rights of occupancy or ownership. The Lockean account (or, at least, the kind of Lockean approach that I support) thus identifies the state's rightful territory with the land and resources that are rightfully lived on, worked on, and productively used by the state's willing subjects—all, of course, provided that enough and as good is left for all other groups and individuals to use. States' legitimate resource rights will thus be restricted to appropriate control over resources that are in some direct way implicated in those subjects' lives. Lockean voluntarists, for instance, should count those resources that have been legitimately harvested, developed, or actively stewarded by states' members (individually or collectively) as things over which that state has rights of regulation and control, just as the state will have the right to limit access by others to resources that cannot be developed or harvested without disrupting its subjects' legitimate projects.

That, of course, all concerns (one portion of) the Lockean ideal. The *nonideal* component of the Lockean voluntarist theory of states' resource rights (that is, the application of this ideal theory to the real, quite nonideal world) is—like *all* nonideal theory, in my view—considerably less clear and precise, simply because the principles of nonideal theory themselves are necessarily less clear and precise than those of ideal theory. Nonideal theory seeks politically feasible, morally permissible, efficient paths to full achievement of the relevant ideal. But balancing feasibility, permissibility, and efficiency will always be a difficult and nuanced matter, yielding nonideal principles that at most give us general, defeasible guidelines for individual action and collective policy. Pretending that this will not be the case with nonideal theory—for instance, pretending that our ugly pasts will simply be neatly superseded by changing circumstances or that trying to simply approximate "structural" justice is morally sufficient—is, as we have seen, an unacceptably comfortable and tidy solution to such deep and multidimensional moral problems.

Because of the content of the Lockean ideal, Lockean nonideal theory (with respect to states' territorial rights) will require that we first determine in some rough way what will count as the appropriate rectifications for past wrongs in states' histories of territorial and resource acquisitions, along with some rough guidelines for what now constitutes a fair share of the earth and its resources. State's claimed rights over lands and resources may need to be altered or "downsized" in order to satisfy these limits on legitimate state holdings. We saw (in chapter 7) some of the more specific content of the Lockean nonideal theory, with its central focus both on preserving those contemporary individual and collective holdings that are most central to our projects and productive lives, and on trying to honestly rectify (again with centrality to the projects and lives of the victims in mind) the historical wrongs done in the process of reaching the current distribution of portions of the world. Applying such principles will necessarily be rough and impressionistic, the clear moral vectors of ideal theory frequently pointing in conflicting directions. But we try to evade such rough, impressionistic philosophical (and social-scientific) work at our peril. For the branching tendrils of our past wrongs and our current overreaching are everywhere in evidence, winding through most features of our social and political lives.

Even independent of the considerable complexities of nonideal theory, though, many of the resource rights claimed by modern states just look straightforwardly suspicious from the Lockean perspective (as they do, as well, from some other of the perspectives we've examined). I think the Lockean approach, by asking us to think of states' property-like claims in roughly the same way that we think of individuals' property claims, points us in the correct direction here. After all, in defining states' territorial rights, international law has really done little more than follow the development of society's thoughts about the content and limits of individual landownership. States' property-like claims are strongest, the Lockean view argues, where they are claims to control the property-creating or property-preserving activities of their own willing subjects. And states' claims are weakest where they are claims over things that are not used or actively pursued in their subjects' lives—such as states' claims to resources that might be found in remote wilderness areas or to resources on or beneath the ocean floor. As for the resources under our feet (which are, of course, the ones to which modern states and their members feel *most* entitled): we should ask, from this Lockean perspective, what it is really reasonable to suppose that an individual landowner's projects entitle her to claim in the way of subsurface rights, once we think of those rights *in terms of* those projects. Answering that question will point the way to understanding over what things states can legitimately claim property-like territorial rights.

Lockean theories of individual property should limit legitimate appropriations and holdings not only by considerations of fairness—we are entitled to take and use no more than our fair share of the natural world and its resources—but as well by the *purposes or natures* of the individual projects in which external goods play essential roles. The land and other resources that I can legitimately take and use for farming, for instance, are constrained by what the activity of farming *is*. Rights in the land do not come naturally packaged with rights over all things over, around, or beneath that land, but only with rights to those things that are reasonably implicated in the specific kind of project that "incorporates" that land—and so on, *mutatis mutandis*, for all other kinds of projects involving the use of natural resources. So while I should be entitled to dig a cellar for my house or a well for my water supply without running into the shaft of (or having my water ruined by) your silver mine, there is simply no good reason—that is, a reason that can be plausibly derived either from the general point of individuals having rights over property or from the typical specific purposes of owning and living on a parcel of land—that I should be able to reserve for myself anything that I might happen to find beneath my land if I were to dig a miles-deep hole in it. This is especially true when I have no reason even to believe that there is anything worth digging for. Individual landowners are entitled to what (within their fair shares) they actively, productively use, to the objects of projects aimed at future use, and to what they responsibly and legitimately steward.

The Lockean voluntarist says: let it be the same for modern states and their property-like claims over resources, leaving Jules Verne's subterranean adventurers free of worries about violating states' rights to the interior of the earth. States may legitimately control and reserve only those things that their willing subjects may legitimately control and reserve, individually or collectively, always subject to the proviso's constraints. Because those subjects are entitled to self-defense and free movement without wrongful threats, states may legitimately control portions of their territorial subsurface and of the surrounding sea and air (on behalf of their members) in those ways required for national defense and traffic control. And states may claim (their portions of the rights over) the surface land and associated resources that figure in their members' individual projects or productive pursuits. Further, because individuals are entitled to act collectively to take for common purposes that which does not exceed the sum of their legitimate individual entitlements, states may also acquire territorial rights over the objects of *collective* productive labor (for things like roads, parks, places of worship, or public buildings) or make rights in things as part of a collective project for supporting future generations (again, all subject to the proviso's constraints). And states may legitimately serve as stewards for—but *not* as *owners* of—that which ought not to be owned or used at all and for which anyone may thus take on the role of steward. Everything, however, that is claimed and controlled by states that lies beyond such natural (Lockean) limits—including what is taken by states simply to deny it to other states, taken to establish "natural" or "manifested" boundaries, taken merely in the hope of somehow deriving from it future wealth—lies beyond a state's legitimate share of the earth and should be left open to rightful use by other individuals or groups.

Even, though, if one *rejects* this compelling, but admittedly revisionist Lockean position on states' justified territorial rights (as many people undoubtedly will), my arguments in this chapter should at least still have strongly suggested that the claims actually made by states to exclusive rights over natural resources extend far beyond those for which any compelling justification is available. This is true even if we *reject* cosmopolitan arguments from the moral arbitrariness of states' natural resource endowments, and even if we *reject* as well left-libertarian claims about equal natural entitlements to shares of the earth and its resources. Even absent such systematic grounds for skepticism, there appear to still be strong reasons to be deeply suspicious of modern states' claims over many of the resources located on, around, and far beneath their acknowledged territories. Many of the claims to resources made by states—and accepted by states' citizens and upheld in international law—appear in fact to be capable of no more defense than can be provided by appeal to naked national self-interest.[50] Especially in a world of widespread dire need and spectacular inequality, our political philosophies at least—even when they fail to influence our political practices—need to be far less casual about accepting states' claimed rights to whatever land, sea, and air they can defend and to whatever happens to lie beneath them, to the center of the earth.

[50] To be perfectly clear: my claim here is that what are indefensible are states' claims over resources without use or stewardship and beyond their fair shares. On the Lockean view, individuals or groups can (in principle, at least) make property in their fair shares of even (some of) what lies far beneath land or sea. And because of this, the states of which they are willing subjects can (in principle) hold territorial rights over those things. The limits on states' territorial rights in such locations are thus set primarily by the *practical* limits on successfully exercising jurisdiction and control and by requirements of fairness to other potential claimants. International agreements between legitimate states, of course, may also limit states' rights to take territory in the places covered by those agreements.

9

Borders

Boundary Lines and the Right to Exclude

Modern nation-states relate to their claimed territorial borders in many of the same ways in which individual landowners relate to their property lines. Both are in most cases permitted by applicable laws to fence (or wall) their holdings and otherwise govern movement by persons and things across their boundary lines. Both may legally (under international law and domestic property law) insist on acceptance of a wide range of requirements as conditions for being permitted to cross those lines.[1] States may even sometimes be *required* to control border crossings—to prevent the spread of an infectious disease, say—just as landowners are sometimes legally required to fence their lands (to confine livestock, for instance, or to deny outside access to dangerous sites). And both states and landowners are required to fence their lands only in ways that will not be directly harmful to innocent (and, perhaps, not-so-innocent) outsiders.[2] Federations of states—like gated neighborhoods of landowners—sometimes opt to control only the outer boundaries of their combined holdings. Friendly states or those with unfrequented borders—like neighborly or rural landowners—often choose to be casual about the extent to which they actually exercise such rights of border control. In all these ways, then, control over national borders is one of the claimed rights of states that seem *most* "property-like" in nature.

All of these similarities, however, so far concern only border *control*. While many may challenge the particular internationally accepted placements of particular national borders, few (as we saw in the last chapter) challenge the general right of autonomous states to responsibly *control* their legitimate borders

[1] Each state, Sidgwick says, has "the right to admit aliens on its own terms, imposing any conditions on entrance" (Sidgwick [1897], 248 [15, 2]).

[2] Property fences are often governed as well by local legal limits—on, e.g., height and style—that are motivated principally by aesthetic concerns and concerns for neighbors' interests. I know of no international legal restrictions of this sort on territorial border barriers.

for certain kinds of purposes—such as for security from outside threats to the state's viability or wellbeing. Most of the famous historic border barriers—such as the Great Wall of China, Hadrian's Wall, the Atlantic Wall, and the Maginot Line—were built to secure territorial holdings from threatened foreign military incursion, as were many of the most prominent contemporary examples (such as the Korean DMZ). Other contemporary barriers are just designed to funnel border crossings to monitored sites, another apparently legitimate purpose. But what of border barriers whose purpose is simply to keep outsiders out, to preserve the comfortable enjoyment of territory by members only (as with landowners in affluent, gated communities), or to preserve, unsullied by outside influences, members' preferred lifestyle or culture or racial/ethnic composition? Landowners, of course, are generally taken to have the right to simply *deny entry* to their land to all others, for reasons good, bad, or indifferent (except, perhaps, in various kinds of emergency situations or when states' jurisdictional activities require official entry). If you wish to be an antisocial curmudgeon, hidden away from the world on your own walled land, there are in most nations no legal obstacles to such a choice. Private property owners have quite sweeping rights to exclude others from their land and structures. Are states' (property-like, territorial) rights to control their borders—to determine who passes over the (tangible and/or juridical) national fence-line—similar to private property rights in this respect as well?

Most states, of course, do not choose to exercise any very stringent "right to exclude,"[3] preferring to permit entry and (at least) limited stays by aliens for tourism, education, employment, and a host of other reasons. Most also have legally defined pathways for aliens to secure more permanent statuses involving rights of long-term residence or citizenship (through "naturalization"). But legally speaking, the limits on states' rights to simply and unilaterally exclude from their territories all noncitizens and to expel all uninvited entrants, are impressively minimal—with the legal rights of refugees being perhaps the most salient exception.[4] And refugee law really amounts to little more than the kind of legal (and minimal moral) requirement that sometimes limits landowners' prerogatives: namely, the requirement that they accept (what would otherwise be) trespass under emergency conditions. So again, with respect to a "right to exclude"—in the eye of the law, at least—state territories and individual

[3] What Sidgwick calls "the right of each state to exclude foreigners" (Sidgwick [1897], 251 [15, 3]).

[4] Under the 1951 United Nations *Convention Relating to the Status of Refugees* (and under customary international law), qualifying refugees outside their countries of habitual residence (and with a "well-founded fear of persecution") may not be expelled or returned to a territory in which their life or freedom are threatened (under the so-called principle of "no forcible return" or "non-refoulement").

properties in land are treated much the same. Under international law, lawful residents of a state possess rights to *leave* their country, to return to it, and to move freely within it.[5] But there are no general rights to *enter* states in which one is not a legal resident, nor are there general duties on states not to simply exclude aliens from entering and using state territories.

When we shift our focus from legal rights to *moral* rights, however, many theorists believe that there is a sharp divergence between the "boundary rights" of landowners and those of states. Set aside for a moment some of the obvious parallel moral limits on those rights—such as those set by special obligations undertaken by the rightholder and humanitarian duties owed by the rightholder—and focus just on the right to exclude for "bad reasons." However unloveable (and unvirtuous) the antisocial curmudgeon may be, and however idiosyncratic or unpleasant or bigoted his reasons for doing so may be, most will still affirm his (defeasible) moral right to simply exclude unwanted (in his case, all) visitors from land that he legitimately owns. (This is one of those "rights to do wrong" that we accept in a variety of contexts.) But the parallel right for states is denied by many. States may not, they claim, without moral wrongdoing exercise their unquestioned rights of border *control* in ways that convert rights of control into robust rights to arbitrarily *exclude*.

Very few contemporary states have borders that are simply *closed* to outsiders (countries like Chad and North Korea perhaps currently come closest to this extreme). But between the extremes of closed borders and "open borders" (which are approximated, for instance, within the European Union), there is a wide and legally legitimate variety in the degrees of "hardness" or "softness" of the national borders in the world—that is, a wide variety in the kinds of border crossings (and the kinds and lengths of stays within the borders) that are permitted for those aliens who are taken to pose no criminal or security threats. This is just to say, of course, that the "right to exclude" is understood as a complex, *discretionary* right for states that can be exercised in any number of ways.

For our purposes here, states' claimed discretionary rights to exclude aliens are best understood as having three general components[6] (only the first two of which are closely analogous to the legal property rights of landowners): states claim the right to decide when aliens may *enter* their territories (the right to control border crossings), the right to decide when aliens may *remain* within their territories (the right to determine privileges of residence), and the right to decide when aliens may become *members* of the political community (the right to determine citizenship). States could, in principle, claim and exercise only one

[5] Under Article 12 of the *International Covenant on Civil and Political Rights.*

[6] See Fine (2013), 255.

or two, rather than all, of these rights. But existing states in fact claim and exercise all three, differences in state policies turning on how they choose to use the legal discretion these rights give them.

Because most states find that many state-monitored border crossings by aliens serve (or, at least, do no serious harm to) their national (e.g., economic or educational) interests, they choose to use their discretion in ways that result in reasonably broad legal permission for aliens to enter their territories. It is thus states' various choices regarding the *other* components of their claimed rights to exclude—those that issue in the ways they make available to aliens legal rights of residence and naturalization—that tend to be their more controversial choices, both politically and philosophically. So I next begin to assess such state choices by (very) briefly exploring a few of the central themes in contemporary debates (within political philosophy/theory) about the problem of *immigration*.[7] As we have seen, states' *legal* rights to determine their own immigration policies are virtually absolute, this being just one implication of international law's recognition of the autonomy of sovereignty entities. But our principal focus here, as always, will be rather on the *moral* question: what moral justifications, if any, can be given for states' claims to possess, if not absolute, at least robust rights to decide for themselves how they will secure their borders and under what conditions (if any) they will allow aliens to cross them and live within them?

Immigration and Self-Determination

The multiplicity of independent states in the world, of course, is what creates the problem of justifying the right to exclude aliens. In a single, global (or universal) state, there would instead be only the (still considerable) problem of explaining the moral legitimacy of nonvoluntarily subjecting individuals and groups to that one state's political authority. Indeed, even in a world of multiple states with viable land left free for appropriation by individuals or groups (including those groups aspiring to establish new territorial polities), justifying exclusion would be far easier than it is in our actual world. For in the actual world—the world in which states, individually or collectively, claim all livable spaces in the universe—the potential for deep helplessness and lack of autonomy (for individuals and groups) is omnipresent: if all states choose to close their doors to aliens, all persons are simply stuck in the countries where the natural lottery first

[7] Many recent discussions of immigration have included consideration of what is owed by states to the illegal or "irregular" immigrants who have resided for some time in state territories. I do not take up that problem here.

places them, however impoverishing, dysfunctional, inhospitable, or alienating those countries might be for them.[8]

The importance of autonomy or self-government thus factors centrally among the moral considerations that might appear to require of states that they adopt "soft" immigration policies. But the importance of autonomy or self-government *also* drives the opposed case, the case for state rights of unilateral discretion in matters of immigration. For we worry not only about the autonomy of persons trapped in unhappy circumstances (e.g., North Africans wanting to move to Western Europe), but also about the autonomy of established territorial groups (nations, states) and their abilities to control their own fates (e.g., the French and Italians, wanting to preserve their distinctive lifestyles and cultures). The strongest arguments for a robust right to exclude have mostly appealed to some version of the same principle appealed to in international law to justify virtually absolute rights for states to exclude aliens: namely, the principle of *self-determination* (or independence) for legitimate states.[9] As Michael Walzer puts it, "admission and exclusion are at the core of communal independence."[10] For Walzer, a group's right of self-determination includes the right to unilaterally close borders, in order that "communities of character," with their own particular ways of life, can be created or preserved.[11]

More recent theoretical appeals to rights of self-determination (in support of robust rights to exclude) have developed more fully some of Walzer's claims (often, however, without the communitarian trappings of his position). It is necessary, of course, to *analyze* the idea of a national right to self-determination[12]—rather than just to point to it or even to justify it—because the connection

[8] As Phillip Cole argues, the vaunted liberal "freedom to exit" one's own country is not worth much if there is no corresponding freedom to enter any other country (Wellman and Cole [2011], 197–207).

[9] Article 1, section 1 of the *International Covenant on Civil and Political Rights* reads: "All peoples have the right of self-determination. By virtue of that right they freely determine their political status and freely pursue their economic, social and cultural development."

[10] Walzer (1983), 61.

[11] According to Walzer, "communities of character" are "historically stable, ongoing associations of men and women with some special commitment to one another and some special sense of their common life" (Walzer [1981], 33).

[12] A group's right to self-determination is not, of course, on any analysis simply equivalent to its right to be self-governing (and so to craft and enforce exclusive immigration policies). The right to be self-determining is, in my view, the right to *choose* whether to be and act as a (political or nonpolitical) self-governing entity or to be ungoverned or externally governed. This is consistent with the distinction between "constitutive" self-determination (i.e., choice of political status) and "ongoing" self-determination (i.e., self-government) (used in Buchanan [2004], 332–3). For a different view of the relation between self-determination and self-government, see Margalit and Raz (1990), 126–7, 139, 144.

between a right of self-determination and a right to exclude is far from transparent. Nations may be entitled to be self-determining (just as persons have a right to freedom from interference by others), and so they may (both) be entitled to pursue policies that others regard as unwise or even bad. But a national right to self-determination (like a personal right to freedom) does not include any right to *wrong* others in the process of determining the self. Nations may not, under the banner of self-determination, choose, say, to annex or expel innocent neighbors; for in doing so, they would delegitimize themselves, thus forfeiting a legitimate state's right to be self-determining. Even, then, if we accept that nations' legal rights to self-determination are also moral rights, these rights imply discretionary moral rights to exclude aliens only if such exclusion does not wrong the excluded (or others). In short, we need an explanation of *why* discretionary self-determination in immigration policy does no wrong.

Recent attempts to link self-determination to exclusionary rights, though, concentrate less on showing that self-determination does no wrong to those excluded (unlike the Lockean approach that I defend below) and more on showing that self-determination advances important interests for the state doing the excluding. The most discussed of these arguments have invoked national rights to freedom of association and rights to preserve the value of national culture. Not surprisingly, these arguments have been advanced by many of the same theorists whose more general accounts of territorial rights we examined in part II. Kit Wellman, for instance, takes the best analysis of a legitimate state's right to self-determination to include robust national rights of associational freedom. And freedom of association importantly includes, Wellman argues, the freedom *not* to associate with others when one so chooses.[13] Self-determination must include the freedom not to associate because "an important part of group self-determination is having control over what the 'self' is."[14] So when the self in question is a legitimately established association, self-determination includes a (defeasible[15]) right to determine who the self will be by determining who will be admitted to and excluded from the association. Just as individuals (who are otherwise doing no wrong) have the right to marry whomever they please (or remain unmarried) and to admit to their club (or exclude from it) whomever they please, so legitimate states have a robust discretionary right to admit or exclude outsiders to their political society.

[13] Wellman and Cole (2011), 13. "Legitimate political states may permissibly refuse to associate with any and all potential immigrants who would like to enter their political communities" (36–7).

[14] Altman and Wellman (2009), 163. See also Wellman (2014), 186, Wellman and Cole (2011), 40–41.

[15] Wellman and Cole (2011), 34–6.

Prominent nationalist versions of the argument from self-determination to a right to exclude, not surprisingly, focus more on the idea of *cultural* self-determination (and thus more closely approximate Walzer's well-known arguments). National cultures play central roles in defining the identities of members, in providing contexts within which meaningful choices can be made by members, and more generally in making it possible for persons to experience a sense of belonging.[16] In interacting with their lands, nations make their cultures and their environments shape one another. Nations make laws to govern their relationships with the land, add value to the land through development and public works, imbue the land with various kinds of symbolic importance, bond their families to the land by burying deceased members in it, and so on. All of these kinds of ties to the land can be maintained only through autonomous jurisdiction over the land. But further, all of these sources of value for persons can be secured only if the borders of the land are secured; none can be reliably preserved if nations do not have the freedom to choose those national policies that they deem necessary for that preservation. And one clear aspect of this required national cultural self-determination, the argument goes, is immigration policy. Open borders would present a variety of severe obstacles to securing the values that a viable cultural context makes possible. And that kind of consideration is what justifies robust, discretionary rights for nation-states to exclude aliens.

Such cultural preservation is not only something in which citizens are typically (and justifiably) interested and which bears on their wellbeing,[17] David Miller argues, but also something that is a key to maintaining the level of social solidarity that makes it possible for states to accomplish their morally important goals. Without a reasonable cultural homogeneity in a society, members are unlikely to feel the kinds of identification with and trust in their fellow members that undergird the willingness to accept burdens and endure sacrifices in their shared political lives. And it is on such willingness that the success of democratic institutions and the achievement of social justice depend.[18]

Margaret Moore defends another kind of "self-determination theory" of territory (and of the right to exclude) that appears to fit somewhere between the positions of Wellman and Miller. According to Moore's account, "a 'people' has rights to jurisdictional authority over *the territory on which its members are legitimately residing* if and only if (a) there is a shared political commitment to establish rules and practices of self-determination on the part of *a wide majority of members*, (b) they have *the political capacity* to establish and sustain institutions of political self-determination, and (c) they possess an objective history

[16] Miller (1995), 85–6.

[17] Margalit and Raz (1990), 134.

[18] See Miller (1995), 90–98, and Miller (2005).

of political cooperation together, through, for example, state or sub-state institutions, or in a resistance movement."[19] The groups that qualify for territorial rightholding thus have much in common both with those described by Altman and Wellman (in their shared commitment to and capacity for political self-determination) and those described by Miller (in their shared histories, collective identities, and group solidarity).[20] And like most nationalist theorists (but unlike Altman and Wellman), Moore adds specific requirements of "attachment" to (portions of) their claimed particular lands that refer centrally to groups' identification with, projects that use, and symbolic or religious value conferred on those lands.[21] Importantly, it is, according to Moore, the value of collective self-determination that establishes for qualifying "peoples" not only their rights to jurisdictional authority over their territories, but also robust, property-like rights to control the natural resources in those territories and to (within limits) exclude would-be immigrants.[22]

The grand principle of national self-determination is thus very much at the center of recent attempts to justify robust discretionary rights for states to set their own immigration policies. There is also, of course, a host of more narrowly pragmatic reasons why states might be warranted in using their discretion to severely limit or to halt immigration—reasons that might apply only at particular times and/or in particular states. Massive or unexpected immigration could, for example, put intolerable strain on a state's economy, its social programs, its

[19] Moore (2014), 127–8 (all emphases mine); see also Moore (2015), 35–6. Moore's self-determining peoples are thus understood in both majoritarian and "capacitarian" terms, and (as in most of the views we have examined) there is a strong, but lightly defended, presumption of "legitimate residence" (through supersession of prior rights to the land). As noted above, these facts about it leave Moore's account vulnerable to the same arguments that I advanced (in chapter 4) against Altman and Wellman's voluntarist theory and that I advanced (in chapter 7) against the various Waldron-style "supersessionist" arguments.

[20] Moore tries to distinguish her position from Miller's chiefly by denying that the "shared political identity" required (on her account) to count as a "people" needs to involve a shared national *culture* (Moore [2015], 71, 79–80); and she distinguishes her position from Wellman's by not taking voting patterns to be sufficient to indicate a shared political commitment and by insisting instead on a shared past history of political cooperation (69 [nn25, 30]). But (on the first point) it seems very likely (though not, of course, necessary) that most (if not all) of the groups that satisfy Moore's conditions for rightholding will *also* share a culture. And (on the second) Moore's groups are still identified in majoritarian terms (like Wellman's), while the requirement of a shared political history seems mostly just to be an empirical indicator of likely future success in political endeavors (52)—and so to be just another way of determining the group's *capacity* for self-determination. So it is unclear to what extent (if any) the groups Moore's theory picks out for rights of self-determination will *in practice* differ from those picked out by Wellman or Miller.

[21] Ibid., 118–20. These arguments, Moore contends, are sufficient to identify groups' "heartlands," but may not be able to precisely identify the boundaries of groups' territorial authority.

[22] Ibid., 162, 166, 175, 189, 195–6.

physical infrastructure, or its ecology.[23] Those who argue against robust state rights to exclude typically do not deny these possibilities—though they often aver that appeals to such reasons for restricting immigration by particular (usually wealthy) states are usually merely self-serving rationalizations—nor do they deny that such reasons might justify limiting or halting immigration.[24] Rather, the claim is typically only that states lack the right to exclude aliens at will (or to impose highly restrictive conditions on admission[25]), that states instead have strong, but still *defeasible*, prima facie *duties to permit* immigration by those who pose no threat to the host state. In short, an important part of what is denied is just that honoring the self-determination of states requires acknowledging a robust discretionary right to exclude.

Much of the case in favor of *open* (or very soft) borders thus turns, *negatively*, on alleged weaknesses in the kinds of arguments we've just summarized—namely, those that purport to derive *robust* border rights from the idea of national self-determination. After presenting and questioning some of the arguments for open borders in the next section ("Open Borders"), I will argue in the following section ("Border Rights: The Implications of the Standard Views") that the defenders of open borders are in fact partly correct in thinking that simple appeals to the idea of national self-determination of this sort fail to establish a robust discretionary right to exclude. But I will argue as well (in this chapter's final section, "Lockean Voluntarism on Borders and the Right to Exclude") that there are other, better-principled arguments that *can* justify such a right. To foreclose *that* possibility, defenders of open borders require not just *negative* arguments against the purported implications of the self-determination principle, but *positive* arguments *for* open immigration that will defeat all *other* kinds of grounds for justified exclusion. The positive arguments offered in favor of mandatory open or soft immigration policies, however, strike me as unconvincing—or, more precisely, as arguments that would appear convincing only to those who have already *assumed* the failure of all of the possible principled arguments that might support justified exclusion.

[23] Indeed, even limited immigration might be thought to unfairly impose on the host society burdens of a different sort—namely, the burden of an imposed obligation "to create and support institutions capable of protecting and fulfilling the rights of the newcomer[s]" (Blake [2013], 114). See the similar suggestion in Wellman (2014), 186.

[24] See, e.g., Carens (1987), 260.

[25] Conditions such as the possession of wealth, of particular professional skills, or of a certain race or ethnicity. Many states currently give preferred consideration to groups of potential immigrants such as residents of former colonies, members of certain tribal or ethnic groups, family members of citizens, etc.

Open Borders

Of the main arguments for open borders that have been employed in recent theoretical debates on the subject, two sorts stand out: those that appeal to the moral arbitrariness of nationality, and those that appeal to rights of freedom of movement. We have, of course, already considered some aspects of Rawlsian arguments from moral arbitrariness (and their limitations) at several points in this book (most recently in chapter 8). The version of the arbitrariness argument at work here (most prominently in the writings of Joseph Carens) rests on the claim that *nationality* or *citizenship* (like gender or skin color) is an unchosen, arbitrary feature of persons' genetic and social inheritance. Public institutions that distribute important benefits or burdens on the basis of characteristics over which persons have no control are unjust, at least according to liberal democratic conceptions of justice. But existing states in fact do distribute extremely important benefits and burdens in this way, reserving for their own members benefits that outsiders are denied. And in doing so, even modern liberal democracies do little better than feudal societies, awarding to a select few a set of inherited "birthrights privileges" that greatly enhance their life chances (over the chances of those born into less fortunate states).[26]

As we saw in chapters 2 and 3, the "arbitrariness" of national boundaries lies not only in their historical contingency—that they could just as easily have been located here as there—but further in the fact that these boundaries have so often been established through unjust uses of force. The fact that lands and persons have been illegitimately subjected to states' political authority may require that state boundaries be adjusted in order to rectify such wrongs. And the equal claim to a fair share of the earth and its resources may require further adjustments. Those, however, are not normally the issues that concern defenders of arbitrariness arguments for open or soft national borders. They want to argue not for adjusting borders to rectify past rights violations, but rather for an ideal of justice that requires opening (or greatly softening) *existing* borders. Their primary appeal is to two simple (and indisputable) facts: (a) no person has any control over the country into which she is plunked at birth (any more than she does over her race or gender), and (b) states nonetheless assign membership or citizenship (and all that goes with them) differentially, according simply to which persons happen to be born where.

Should we take these facts to imply systematic injustice in "the state system," an injustice to which open or soft national borders are the appropriate remedy?

[26] Carens (1987), 262, 261–2; Carens (2013), 226. See also Phillip Cole's similar claims in Wellman and Cole (2011), 179.

It is important to remember that Rawls's arbitrariness argument, in its original formulation, was operating within a number of background assumptions (as we saw in chapter 8). The first is that the sense in which our starting places in life are "morally arbitrary" is simply that they are *undeserved*. It is just a matter of good or bad luck that we were born here or there or with this or that set of inherited genetic and social assets, not something for which we merit credit or blame (or larger or smaller shares of societal benefits or burdens). As Rawls puts it, "no one deserves his place in the distribution of native endowments, any more than one deserves one's initial starting place in society."[27] "We can be said to deserve" nothing that is a simple function of either "the outcome of natural chance or the contingency of social circumstances" (for instance, of our being "better endowed" or "more fortunate in . . . social position").[28] "From a moral point of view the two seem equally arbitrary."[29] Rawls's own principles of justice, then, "express the result of leaving aside those aspects of the social world that seem arbitrary from a moral point of view."[30]

But why does any of this matter? Saying that personal traits—say, gender or nationality—are arbitrary and undeserved in no obvious way implies that their possession is bad or wrong (so that such possession should be corrected) or that such traits or their uses are morally uninteresting (perhaps in ways having nothing to do with desert).[31] For Rawls, personal assets being undeserved calls for distributive shares (*within* societies) to be made (roughly) equal at least in part because Rawls thinks he has eliminated in advance all *other* possible bases

[27] Rawls (1971), 104. As has been frequently observed, Rawls comes close to denying the very *possibility* of personal desert by appearing to suggest that *everything* we are or do is a direct consequence of good or bad luck in the natural lottery, that nothing (good or ill) could be a product or an indication of individual merit.

[28] Ibid., 15.

[29] Ibid., 75.

[30] Ibid., 15.

[31] Risse (2012), 288–9. So-called luck egalitarians, of course, may argue that justice requires that societies "neutralize" the products of good or bad luck in the natural lottery. But apart from the obvious difficulties involved in distinguishing the results of brute luck from the results for which individuals' choices and efforts are responsible, it seems clear that it might be wrong to deprive people of advantages that societies assign them based on their possession of undeserved traits *if* those advantages constitute "compensation" for *disadvantages* imposed on them for possession of those same traits. Suppose for some reason that a society had to assign to all of its largest people its (socially necessary) dangerous or strenuous work. It might then not be unjust for the society to reward large people with higher pay—despite physical size being a morally arbitrary trait. (This kind of inequality, absent the duress, might, in fact, be one that Rawls's own Difference Principle would permit.) A similar argument can be made (see below) that the differential "rewards" societies give their own birth members are in fact fair compensation for the burdens to which members, but not outsiders, are (necessarily but nonvoluntarily) subjected by their societies—despite the arbitrariness of national birthplace.

(than desert) for distributive inequalities. If people had differential claims on society's resources, based on something *other than* personal desert, then unequal distributions might *not* be unjust.[32] It is not unjust for a society to allow an undeserving heir to inherit (a modest amount of) property, but only because it has determined in advance that heirs have special claims on certain goods, regardless of desert. If individuals (some of whom might nonetheless be undeserving) had special *natural* rights to larger shares of society's resources, then it might not be unjust to allow those claims to determine or influence (and thus make unequal) societal distributive shares.

But Rawls rejects on independent grounds claims of (logically prepolitical) natural rights over distributable resources.[33] The reasoning of which Rawls's claims about moral arbitrariness is a part is precisely designed to *determine* all bases for differential claims, not to rest on them. If all this is correct, though, the open-borders argument from the moral arbitrariness of nationality looks as if it must either be confused—supposing (as it often appears to) that the arbitrariness of nationality *by itself* calls for equal access for all to all societies' membership rights—or be tacitly accepting the entire body of Rawlsian (or similar) political philosophy, along with its (in my view, indefensible) rationale for dismissing all claims of natural rights to goods. Perhaps some who employ the argument from the arbitrariness of nationality confusedly suppose that moral claims of *desert* are the only kinds of moral claims there are—so that if national "birthrights" are undeserved, distributions based on them *must* be unjust—or perhaps they are simply assuming (without supporting the assumption with the requisite systematic argument) that all defenses of states' differential claims over lands, resources, and wealth have failed. Either problem would be fatal to the argument. And the latter problem would involve just assuming what must be

[32] This is part of what makes Nozick's well-known response to Rawls's arbitrariness argument both compelling and puzzling (see Nozick [1974], 213–27). Nozick seems right that desert is not *all* that matters to legitimating differential claims to things; but he also seems to ignore the fact that Rawls's reasoning presupposes that natural entitlements to things are not in play.

[33] In Rawls's later political philosophy, derivations from natural-right premises are excluded because natural-right claims can be reasonably rejected by adherents to other comprehensive doctrines. In his earlier political philosophy, Rawls might be taken to have accepted one broad (Kantian) natural right—namely, a right to be subject to a just basic structure—but he certainly could not accept natural rights to property that could exist prior to political society, since these would ground claims of justice in addition to (and possibly in conflict with) those generated under Rawls's two principles. Rawls does in a few places suggest that justice as fairness "has the characteristic marks of a natural rights theory" (Rawls [1971], 505–6n, 28, 32). But these claims seem to be based simply on the fact that justice as fairness derives from the two principles real *rights*, rights that both persist in the face of utilitarian arguments against them and that are independent of "social conventions and legal norms." Rawls never appears (in *A Theory of Justice* or earlier work) to argue directly against the possibility of (logically) prepolitical natural rights, rights of the sort that Nozick (with Locke) has in mind.

shown: namely, that states have no property-like territorial rights that might justify their choices to harden their borders and reserve (admittedly undeserved) citizenship for those they select.

It is also worth reiterating, second, that Rawls's arbitrariness claims are made by him quite explicitly as part of an argument for *domestic* distributive equality, *within* states. Arbitrariness arguments cannot be used to establish the injustice of "the state system" because there *is* no state system of a sort suitably analogous to a single bounded state. There are only separate states, dealing coercively with their own jurisdictional tasks. And there is, Rawls thinks, a special burden of justification that states owe their own citizens for the systematic coercion to which they, unlike outsiders, are nonvoluntarily subjected (as we saw in the introduction). States can justify their unsolicited use of coercion over, and adequately justify this *to*, their (nonvoluntarily subjected) "captive audiences" only by insuring that they are all treated as fairly as possible by the institutional structure that will inevitably shape their lives and determine their prospects. No such justification is owed to those who live outside the state's domain of direct coercion, to those whose life prospects, while obviously sometimes affected by the state's domestic policies, are not so directly, immediately, and intentionally determined by them. So the Rawlsian argument from moral arbitrariness to equal distributions is conceived by him as part of an especially strict and demanding justificatory requirement, one that is (arguably, at least, and certainly in Rawls's view) not at issue in the same way in the international context (as we will see below). One will need, then, a great deal more argument for open borders than simply citing the egalitarian conclusions that appear to flow from Rawlsian arbitrariness arguments.

Consider next the freedom of movement arguments for open borders. Again, Carens is perhaps the best-known proponent of such arguments. According to Carens, we liberals believe that "people should be free to pursue their own projects and to make their own choices about how to live their lives so long as this does not interfere with the legitimate claims of other individuals to do likewise."[34] Believing this, we also are committed to regarding freedom of mobility within a state's borders as a fundamental right in liberal societies, since restricting internal mobility would undermine this essential freedom. But the very same interests that support such a right of internal mobility, Carens argues, support a right of free movement *across* national borders. Each kind of reason a person might have for moving within a state's borders she could also have for moving across a state's borders.[35]

[34] Carens (1992), 26.

[35] Ibid., 28.

A natural way to resist such claims is to try to deny the analogy—between the interests at stake in domestic and international movement—on which the argument rests, perhaps using some of the same kinds of points employed above against arbitrariness arguments. When one's own state denies one freedom of movement, the freedom to formulate and pursue one's own life plans is also deeply and systematically restricted. By contrast, when one is denied the opportunity to move between countries, one still has access to the opportunities to pursue projects and make one's own choices that are available domestically (and in countries that opt not to exclude aliens from their territories). If conditions are sufficiently bad in one's home country that minimally acceptable opportunities for an autonomous life are *not* available there, then other arguments come into play that might ground obligations of international assistance or accommodation. But these new arguments would be ones that could be accepted even by those who defend broad (but defeasible) discretionary state rights to exclude aliens—especially given that such assistance can often be given in forms that do not involve opening one's borders to some or all of those aliens suffering from poverty and oppression.

Carens has responded to arguments of this sort, observing that most liberals would not be willing to accept the domestic analog of this stance—namely, that societies might acceptably restrict movement considerably *within* their overall territories, provided only that minimally acceptable opportunities for an autonomous life were available in smaller portions of those territories. If I can freely formulate and pursue a life plan without leaving my province (state, county, city, neighborhood), what would then be wrong with my state's hardening its *internal* borders to restrict my freedom of movement to movement within my province or town?[36] The importance of autonomy (for liberals), Carens holds, is simply too great for such domestic interference with free movement to be morally acceptable.

That might, in fact, all be true. But I do not think even an admission of that sort should be thought to compel acceptance of open borders. For this argument from freedom of movement *again* has force only if all *other* grounds for justifiably excluding aliens—grounds that might yield conflicting or superior moral claims for states to exclude aliens—have already been assumed away. Just as my discretionary rights to restrict others' movement on my own property are far more extensive than my rights to restrict their movement elsewhere, a state's right to restrict international movement onto its territories might be a *special* right, grounded in the nature of its history with the land in question. And this special right to secure its borders might be one that it simply cannot hold internally, against its own subjects—perhaps because those subjects (in legitimate

[36] Carens (2013), 236–49.

states) have surrendered to their state only rights to govern the state's *external* boundaries (as I will argue below). Only an assumption (that I do not accept) that such arguments are off the table from the start—an assumption that we have somehow accomplished a Rawlsian clearing of the moral decks before our real debate begins—allows analogical freedom of movement arguments to (appear to) yield the desired conclusions.

Arash Abizadeh has defended a slightly different version of a freedom of movement argument for soft borders, one that appeals to the need to justify the *coercion* involved in closing borders to aliens. Liberals (including Rawls) believe, as we have just seen, that the coercive political power exercised by states over their subjects requires special justification (*to* those subjects). But, argues Abizadeh, "the regime of border control of a bounded political community subjects both members and nonmembers to the state's coercive exercise of power. Therefore, the justification for a particular regime of border control is owed not just to those whom the boundary marks as members, but to nonmembers as well."[37] The only adequate justification of this sort requires inclusion for those excluded by closed borders, an expansion of the (presumed) *demos*. The state's supposed unilateral discretionary right to exclude is thus undercut from the start by the same kinds of moral considerations that undercut domestic injustice and tyranny.

One obvious way to challenge claims like these is to dispute either the technical idea of "coercion" at work within the argument or the assumption that all kinds of "coercion" equally require moral justification. David Miller, for instance, responds to Abizadeh's argument by distinguishing between "coercion" proper and mere "prevention." Prevention, Miller claims, does of course in one way reduce freedom to act; but it does so without undermining autonomy (and so without requiring the kind of democratic justification that coercion requires).[38] Now I do not, myself, believe that any of the various technical accounts of coercion on offer (including the one employed by Abizadeh) can be counted as simply the best account, *tout court*—as opposed to just being the best account for illuminating some particular set of philosophically interesting distinctions. But even if, against Miller, we do insist that one account of coercion (namely, the one preferred by Abizadeh) is correct, and that what Miller calls "prevention" is really just "coercion," Miller is surely right at least about this: there is a morally interesting difference between *kinds* of coercion—that being "stopped from" doing some specific act (such as crossing a border) is different from being "forced to" do a specific act (such as serving in your country's military), at least partly because a wide range of viable, related options remains in former case,

[37] Abizadeh (2008), 45. See the similar claims in Cole (2000), 186.

[38] Miller (2010), 114–15.

but not in the latter.[39] While a state's closing its borders does involve threatening with a coercive response those who attempt unpermitted border crossings, it also straightforwardly involves *declining* to use state coercion to compel any other particular conduct by aliens.

More generally (and as Miller's arguments also suggest), the plausibility of coercion-based arguments (of the sort used by Abizadeh) depends on two assumptions, neither of which seems true. It depends first on there being no differences in the kinds of required moral justifications for using coercion that turn on how wide-ranging or systematic the coercion in question is. And it seems obvious that there *are* such differences. Isolated or minimal coercion is simply easier to justify than is more enduring, more extensive coercion. The relevance of this point is obvious, and it is part of what drives the Rawlsian distinction between the domestic and the international political conditions. The coercion to which aliens are subjected by the presence of closed borders is of a completely different kind and order from the wide-ranging, systematic coercion to which states subject their subjects. Aliens are denied the opportunity to make one particular choice (or set of choices)—namely, to cross the particular closed border and reside in that particular country. This may, of course, have a considerable impact on would-be immigrants, by denying them things of great importance (or of great importance to them). But citizens subject to their own states' laws, even under the least intrusive existing legal systems, are subject to coercion across an enormous range of the most central areas and activities of life. It is this more systematic coercion that grounds for states a special, different burden of justification owed to their own subjects than is owed to any excluded aliens.[40] (This is, roughly, the position of many theorists who defend broadly Rawlsian views, such as Thomas Nagel and Michael Blake.[41]) And the lesser burden in the latter case (of excluded aliens), of course, means that states may well be able to meet it by offering less than they offer their subjects—that is, by offering things far short of simply opening their borders, or opening their society's system of political participation, to those who are excluded.[42]

[39] Ibid., 116.

[40] Pevnick objects that such systematic state coercion "requires no further justification" than the state's provision of the important public goods citizens reap by being subject to it (Pevnick [2011], 70–71). But even *beneficial* coercion requires justification when it is imposed on persons without their consent—and Pevnick admits that most citizens even in good states are not consenters (28–9). This is the point of our objections to political paternalism. And the more extensive such coercion is, the greater the burden of justification on the coercer.

[41] Nagel (2005), Blake (2001).

[42] Abizadeh elsewhere attempts to answer such objections—objections from what he calls "the coercion theory," supplemented "with elements from the pervasive impact theory" (Abizadeh

But the case for exclusion does not need to be made in such relative terms, comparing two kinds of burdens of justification; because, second, coercion-based arguments for open borders again depend on there being no *special, direct* moral justifications available for coercive exclusion of aliens. But such direct justifications are, in fact, a commonplace in what appear to be analogous cases. Landowners, for instance, while perhaps precluded from using certain kinds of coercion against trespassers, are certainly permitted to lock their gates against them. Homeowners may lock their doors against would-be intruders, even against those who seem likely to be harmless and those who are not fellow citizens. (Indeed, my own view is that this would be true even in a state of nature.) If such "coercion" is simply directly defensible (without the necessity of including would-be intruders in some sort of "justifying process")[43]—say, because of the kinds of important interests at stake in legitimate claims to property—why may states not lock their border gates with similar warrant? The coercion at issue in property cases is *disanalogous* to that used by states in excluding aliens *only if* we assume in advance that states can *have* no special property-like claims to their territories. And that—again—is precisely one of the central points at issue in the debate. No argument that must in this way simply *assume* the falsity of state claims to property-like rights can have any *independent* force in a debate about the moral justification of states' rights to exclude. It can at best just illustrate the hypothetical moral consequences of states' *lacking* property-like territorial rights.

Border Rights: The Implications of the Standard Views

Those who have written about states' territorial rights have, by and large, had considerably less to say about states' border rights—and states' property-like rights generally—than they have about states' jurisdictional rights. This is not surprising. Most recent discussions of territorial rights have (as we've seen) either been functionalist through and through or built around a functionalist account of state legitimacy. And functionalism operates most naturally and

[2007], 349)—by simply asserting that closed borders "*do* 'profoundly and pervasively' affect human beings' life chances in our world" (350). But this response (apart from being factually true of only that minority of persons in the world who both want to and could, in the absence of closed borders, emigrate) appears to beg the crucial normative question: namely, whether border closure is *responsible* for the "life chances" of those outside the border *in the same way* that the state's more systematic and pervasive coercion of its subjects is responsible for their life prospects.

[43] See, e.g., Wellman and Cole (2011), 97–8; Wellman (2014), 203.

plausibly when it is attempting to explain states' core jurisdictional authority. Certain kinds of territorial control do indeed seem essential to states successfully discharging their morally mandated functions (such as doing or making possible justice).

What is far less clear is why we should think that the more property-like aspects of states' claimed territorial rights—such as robust rights of control over (or "ownership" of) natural resources in (or around) the effectively governed territory, or a robust discretionary right to exclude aliens from crossing or living within the borders of the effectively governed territory—*also* are essential for fulfilling states' moral mandates. Indeed (and again, as we've seen throughout this book), functionalist theories have struggled to plausibly locate the moral boundaries of legitimate states at all—that is, struggled to explain why we should identify the morally legitimate borders of states' political authority with the de facto reach of their effective, justice-administering institutions. How states *came to* administer justice over particular lands and people seems vitally important to the legitimacy—and, hence, to the valid extent—of their territorial claims. And this fact piles worries about functionalist justifications for robust (property-like) border control upon the more basic worry that the functionally specified borders themselves are not even the legitimate boundaries of states' mundane jurisdictional activities.

Can functionalism deal with these problems? We have already seen (in our discussion of resource rights) some strong reasons to think it cannot. Even if we simply *disregard* the boundary problem for functionalist theories (detailed in part I)—by supposing for the moment that functionalism can somehow identify specific and morally legitimate borders over which states may justifiably exercise discretionary control—there is no apparent reason why discharging a moral mandate to do justice or promote utility requires that states possess a unilateral right to exclude aliens. Doing (or making possible) justice, by instituting and enforcing a particular regime of property rights or by making holdings more equal, say, does appear to require jurisdictional rights over (some) territory. But it does not obviously require unilateral state discretion to exclude aliens who pose no threats to justice-administering institutions. And the promotion of utility (the concern of utilitarian functionalists) may often in fact require substantially curtailing such state discretion.[44] There may, of course, be circumstantial

[44] Sidgwick, despite his apparent acceptance of states' rights to exclude, acknowledges that if states possess territory that is "under-peopled," or if they possess "waste land suitable for cultivation," immigration must be permitted to remedy this inefficiency (Sidgwick [1897], 255 [15, 4]). And it is, of course, easy to imagine a host of other broadly utilitarian reasons why permitting immigration might be required (e.g., immigration by those whose talents will otherwise be seriously underutilized in their native countries). See Risse's related "underuse" arguments for an obligation on states to admit immigrants (in Risse [2012], chap. 8).

limits to the numbers or kinds of immigrants that states can absorb while still effectively administering justice to all members (or successfully promoting social utility). But these limits establish no *principled* reason—of the sort necessary to ground a *right* of pure discretion—why states require the power to unilaterally exclude aliens.

The very same problems appear to face those accounts of territorial rights that rest on functionalist theories of state legitimacy, but that are not functionalist through and through (such as Altman's and Wellman's plebiscitary voluntarism or Nine's "Lockean" account of territorial rights). It is at this point, of course, that the arguments from self-determination (introduced above) are supposed to enter to save the day. Respect for collective self-determination, for an incorporated group's free political choice, is supposed to require that states be able to exclude aliens according to their own, procedurally legitimated immigration policies.[45] Otherwise, groups are not genuinely self-determining, not able to control their own fates by their own choices, not able to express their chosen ways of life in their rules and policies.

But why—short of eagerness to embrace whatever definition of "self-determination" yields the desired conclusions here—should we accept such claims? Can we not respect an autonomous state's right to be self-determining without also permitting it to simply choose as it pleases in the matter of excluding aliens? Can't it count as self-determining in virtue of its having independently constituted itself as a political entity, combined with the self-governing practices of its members, practices operating independent of outside interference, without also needing to have that membership itself determined solely in accordance with its own will? Whether we count a group as self-determining—just as whether we count an individual as free or autonomous—clearly depends on which areas of activity (or "determination") we think important to the group's functioning and on the extent to which activity in those areas "flows" acceptably from the "self" in question. Thus, self-determination is also plainly a matter of kind and degree, rather than a simple, all-or-nothing concept. Theorists trying to extract conclusions about territorial rights from the very idea of group self-determination—an idea of which, of course, we all enthusiastically approve (without, though, agreeing on a definition of it)—often find themselves

[45] To be clear: virtually nobody in these debates thinks that states owe no obligations at all to aliens, and virtually nobody thinks that there could not be circumstances in which states were morally obligated to accept unchosen immigrants. Legitimate states' rights to exclude are not supposed to be *absolute* with respect to such matters. Indeed, such rights are not fully absolute even under applicable international law (as we have seen). Those who defend a unilateral right to exclude instead typically hold that where states can discharge their moral obligations to aliens *without* admitting them as immigrants—as they hold to be often or normally the case—they are entitled to unilaterally decide to do so.

legislating among the possible understandings of self-determination, insisting that it is groups' rights to "genuine" or "true" or "robust" self-determination that imply the desired conclusions.

But surely, even if we thought (as I do not) that there were one "genuine" way in which a group could qualify as fully self-determining, there are obviously (and as we have seen) other weighty moral considerations in play that argue *against* group rights of full self-determination. Our concern should not be to ask what makes a group *fully* (genuinely, robustly) self-determining—as if self-determination were the *only* value of interest—but rather what makes it adequately or acceptably self-determining (in the same way that we insist that individuals, in order to count as free or autonomous, require an adequate or acceptable—but not necessarily the maximal possible—range of real options in important areas from which to choose). After all, no group in a world of multiple sovereign states can expect to be *entirely* self-determining, can expect not to have other groups' (e.g.) economic or political choices at all affect and limit their own range of available economic or political choices. So our question(s) here should be: can states or nations or peoples be acceptably or adequately self-determining *without* holding property-like territorial rights over all resources in and around their places of residence and *without* holding property-like discretionary territorial rights to exclude aliens? In the last chapter, I defended an affirmative answer to the former question. And I have seen no very good reasons offered to support a negative answer to the latter.

It is true, of course, that settled groups often have an "interest" in restricting immigration, in order to "prevent unwanted changes in their environment" and preserve the "character of their community." Setting their own rules concerning entry and exit is undoubtedly one way in which groups foster their "own conception of how they want to organize their society."[46] But why should we suppose that groups have a moral right to simply legislate their tastes and preferences in these ways? Not, I think, because they would fail to count as having a real or adequate right to be self-determining if they did not. If affluent nations were required to accept some reasonable quota of unwanted immigrants, it would seem a bit hysterical to assert that they, as a result, no longer counted as self-determining polities (any more than their accepting the authority of the World Court would count as rendering them interestingly non-self-determining). The vaunted right of self-determination is thought by almost nobody to be an *unlimited* right to act according to the group's expressed will, a will which could, of course, dictate human rights violations, the expulsion of desperately endangered refugees, and so on.

[46] Moore (2015), 195–6.

"Unwanted changes" in our communities are, of course, unwanted. But we enjoy no general moral right to be free of unwanted changes, either individually or collectively.[47] When old folks (like me) lament the passing of "the good old days," the lament may seem pathetic. But it is a lament that sometimes flows from genuine, even quite serious, feelings of alienation, irrelevance, loss, or outrage. When the young no longer value what we value, no longer feel about their countries, neighborhoods, or families the way we feel, no longer dress, talk, or eat as we do, the changes in lifestyle to which we are then forced to adjust are, for many, mostly "unwanted." Yet we rightly feel nonetheless that it would be deeply wrong to use the coercive powers of the state to prevent such change. Much of the threat posed by immigration to culture or collective identity is of this same order. And we should feel it similarly wrong in the latter case to use the jurisdictional authority of the state to "protect ourselves" from such change.

While we no doubt tend to romanticize a bit the cultures and lifestyles of aboriginal or exotic peoples, it is undoubtedly true that many unwanted changes to those cultures have had profound and enduring negative impacts on the quality of life of group members. But most contemporary cultures are far less unique and vulnerable; they overlap significantly with others and are far less fragile in the face of change.[48] Distinctive, sacrosanct practices that might be undermined by "cultural dilution" grow fewer and fewer with the homogenization wrought by global society. And many of the most contentious differences between contemporary cultures are based in ethnic or racial biases and in histories of hatred and warfare, differences that we should be happy to see lessened (and changed in ways that are no doubt "unwanted" by insiders), rather than scrupulously preserved.

In this context, we should also remember that most of the "supersessionists" who advance arguments proceeding from (collective or cultural) self-determination to a group's right to exclude are happy enough to follow Waldron in allowing that aboriginal peoples were obligated as a matter of justice to share their lands with settlers, thereby permitting (very unwanted) changes in the (much more vulnerable) "characters of *their* communities."[49] The majority groups that are said by self-determinists to possess rights of jurisdictional

[47] As Waldron suggests, once we examine the actual arguments in favor of cultural integrity, "its being properly protected comes to seem more like a preference than a necessity" (Waldron [2010], 406).

[48] "Life in a modern multicultural society includes elements of many different cultures, but their boundaries tend to blur, they are each permeable to influence from the others and their purity and independence are inevitably compromised" (ibid., 402).

[49] And it is, of course, not contemporary, more homogenized cultures, but aboriginal and exotic cultures—such as those of the Maori or the Lakota or the Bedouin—that are typically used by these theorists as illustrations of how outside influences can destroy a way of life.

authority in "their" territories have, by contrast, relatively little to fear (and stand a good chance of reaping unexpected enrichment) from reasonable levels of unwanted immigration. The majority controls the laws, the politics, the social and economic policies of their states. Their "collective identities" seem certain to survive a fair bit of unwanted immigration. That they want to control more, to be still more "self-determining" than this, exercising unilateral control over their immigration policies, is perhaps unsurprising, but surely does not describe plausible grounds for asserting a moral right to do so.

Perhaps, though, the appeals to self-determination at work in the specific plebiscitary voluntarist and nationalist positions described above will be found more effective. Wellman, remember, fills out his notion of group self-determination in terms of freedom of association. If groups are compelled to admit unchosen outsiders to their group, they are not free to create or sustain a group that reflects their own values or preferences—that is, they are not being permitted to *not* associate. Hence, they do not really count as enjoying a right to freely associate, hence to be self-determining, at all. Wellman supports these claims, as we've seen, largely by citing analogies to our understandings of other kinds of associations, like families[50] and clubs.[51] But it seems plausible to respond to such claims that states are not really much like clubs or other local associations of this sort, at least given the ways in which the state system currently operates.

If you decide to reject my proposal and marry someone else (or remain unmarried), there are still, as they say, plenty of other fish in the sea for me. If you and your associates exclude me from your club, I can always go and (at least try to) make a club of my own (from which *I'll* then exclude *you*). But states, unlike clubs, control all of the viable land on which new, rival states might be established.[52] And even if they did not, the difficulties and costs involved in finding, organizing, and relocating the like-minded potential members of a new state—along with the difficulties of establishing a brand new basic structure of institutional rules for them—would be prohibitive (especially when compared to the possibly quite minimal costs of simply joining the already established society). An even more obvious disanalogy between marriages or clubs and states, of course, is that marriages and clubs are (typically) fully voluntary associations, where modern states never are (including any states that might be counted as legitimate by Wellman, who [remember] characterizes legitimate states as "nonconsensual

[50] Wellman draws analogies both with the rights of parents to "dominion" over their children (e.g., Wellman and Cole [2011], 23–4) and with the rights of any individual "to determine whom (if anyone) he or she would like to marry" (54). Interestingly, Miller also employs this analogy between an individual's right to marry and a nation's right to exclude (Miller [2007], 209).

[51] Wellman and Cole (2011), 34–5; Wellman (2014), 189.

[52] Fine (2014), 263.

associations"). And given that legitimate states are supposed to operate according to majority rule, many "members" of political "clubs" can thus both be trapped (nonconsensually) within the claimed borders of functionally legitimated states and systematically outvoted on crucial matters by stable majorities of fellow citizens (like the kidnapped club member discussed in chapter 3). Such "members" don't in the end really much resemble the members of the nonpolitical clubs, marriages, or other kinds of voluntary associations with which we are familiar.[53]

Could the right to *secede*, whereby trapped minorities might use for their new association some of the territory claimed by some state(s), solve any of the problems here? Not if (as we also saw in chapter 4) existing states may simply stop groups from acquiring those characteristics (such as territorial contiguity, wealth, or political capacity) on which the right to secede is said to rest. Worse, of course, while I set it aside momentarily (in order to explore functionalism's additional problems), the boundary problem persists as a continuing defect of all theories built on functionalist foundations. Unless we just assume with them (without compelling reasons) that the mere effective reach of contemporary states' institutions, no matter how despicably achieved, is what determines states' legitimate territorial extent—and that the rights to land of all prior occupants have been conveniently superseded—functionalist accounts of state legitimacy seem to lack the resources to explain what it is that "attaches" functional polities to any specific, bounded territorial domain. And trying to justify the use of nonfunctionalist additions to their theories to handle this problem, as we've seen, appears to be a losing proposition.

When all is said and done, then, it may seem that nationalist theories of territorial rights are the best positioned (of the three standard views on the subject) to answer skeptical concerns about justifying states' border rights, states' rights to exclude—just as nationalism at least appeared to be better positioned (than its rivals among the standard accounts) to justify the particular claimed borders of particular states and their rights of resource control within those borders. The alleged *essential* connection between particular nations and particular territories seems to be an especially natural argumentative route to justifying the property-like territorial rights claimed by states. But we have already seen some of the problems that appear to block that route.

David Miller, for instance, says that using his own nationalist account to motivate states' *jurisdictional* rights is easy:

> [it is] not difficult to justify rights of jurisdiction on the basis of what has been said. Rights of private property alone will not do the job of

[53] A point also made in Pevnick (2011), 28–30.

> protecting . . . this added cultural value because a) such rights are always susceptible to being redrawn by whoever holds rights of jurisdiction and b) much of the embodied value that the group has created is likely to be located in public space—in public architecture, landscapes of historic significance, and so forth. The group needs to maintain overall control over the territory in order to secure that value over time, and for that it needs rights of jurisdiction such as those normally exercised by a state.[54]

Suppose we allow this, arguendo; so far, so good, we might say. But what is it that justifies the property-like territorial rights that extend beyond such merely jurisdictional rights? We have already seen (in chapter 8) that nationalist reasoning does a poor job of justifying anything like the full range of rights over natural resources that are claimed by modern states—and that the Lockean approach offers a more internally consistent and intuitively compelling account (indeed, an account from which nationalists tend to borrow) of the kinds of resource rights (and of claims to "added cultural value") that nationalist reasoning does seem capable of motivating. What about states' rights to exclude aliens?

Here, remember, the standard nationalist moves echo Walzer's appeal to the importance of "communities of character": nationalists tend to point to the value of particular national cultures and the "contexts of choice" that they provide their members, along with the vital ways in which members' very identities turn on the preservation of those particular cultures. Without the right to decide unilaterally to exclude (all or specific) aliens, nations cannot preserve these important goods for or with their members. It is thus rights of "cultural self-determination" that are alleged to underlie states' discretionary rights to exclude aliens. Miller, for instance, says that "a common public culture . . . in part constitutes the political identity of [states'] members."[55] And insofar as undermining the features essential to peoples' capacities for self-identification is a great harm to them, cultural self-determination is a legitimate interest of national groups. Nation-states cannot protect their cultures and their members' access to it (e.g., through preserving a common first national language) without the right to restrict invasive, pluralizing or homogenizing immigration.[56]

But it is hard, first, to see how such nationalist reasoning will yield anything like clear borders for states to control. Since national groups, including groups with political ambitions and identities, often spill across state borders or lay rival claims to the same border areas, it appears that nationalist reasoning must appeal

[54] Miller (2012), 263.
[55] Miller (2005), 199.
[56] Ibid., 200.

to either functionalist or conventionalist reasoning—neither of which, as we've seen, deals well with the boundary problem either—to try to resolve this difficulty. More obviously perhaps, the idea of "culture" is something of a moving target in such nationalist arguments. Nobody thinks, of course, that there is a clear, all-purpose definition of "culture" available for use here. But the nationalist argument tends to equivocate between two quite different notions of culture, sliding from one to the other as the immediate rhetorical need dictates.[57] As we have seen (in chapter 4), Miller, with many other liberal nationalists, acknowledges the point that modern nation-states are simply *not* culturally uniform in the sense of "way of life culture," culture that involves shared traditions, religion, language, history, lifestyles, and so on. Modern states are irreversibly culturally pluralistic in this sense of "culture." That fact by itself threatens to short-circuit from the start nationalist arguments for self-determination—or to unhelpfully limit their applicability to multiple, possibly "layered," substate groups, typically with overlapping, conflicting, or interstate territorial claims.

So Miller (with others) slides in his arguments to the idea of a statewide *public political culture,* and it appears to be the value of national "culture" so understood that is said to ground national rights of self-determination. But shared public political cultures (in liberal polities) will both tend to be quite similar to one another in important ways—compare the political cultures of the various Western liberal democracies—and to consist primarily in shared commitments to certain broad political principles and to shared reverence for certain defining political events and foundational documents—such as principles of democratic proceduralism or respect for human rights and reverence for the society's political constitution and the events commemorated by national holidays.[58] It is simply unclear why "culture" understood in this way should be thought capable of playing the same role in nationalist arguments for a right to exclude that "way of life culture" appeared to play in communitarian arguments like Walzer's.[59]

A particular shared public political culture—while undoubtedly important in a variety of ways (e.g., to maintaining societal "stability for the right reasons") and implicated in various ways in our senses of "who we are"—is still merely a "foreground" behind which operate a host of other nonpolitical societal features (such as family, language, work, neighborhood, friends, church, lifestyle, cuisine, economic class, etc.) that provide independent contexts of meaningful choice

[57] See Moore (2015), 79–82.

[58] Rawls defines the "public political culture of a democratic society" as "the political institutions of a constitutional regime and the public traditions of their interpretation (including those of the judiciary), as well as historic texts and documents that are common knowledge" (Rawls [1993], 13–14).

[59] Here my argument follows, at least in broad outline, that in Laegaard (2007), 292–4.

and bases for self-ascriptions of identity. Some groups' "way of life cultures" (say, the culture of an aboriginal people in a colonized land) can perhaps plausibly be said to be vital to sustaining the very identities or contexts of meaningful choice for those groups' members. But a state's public political culture seems much less the kind of thing that would be naturally threatened by soft immigration policies than does a particular, distinctive "way of life culture." In the latter case, but not the former, it is easy to imagine a "culture" being diluted, altered, or corrupted by a steady flow of immigrants, immigrants who bring with them their new and different languages, lifestyles, and histories. "Way of life cultures" thus might seem sensitive to immigration in the right way—that is, in the way the nationalist arguments require—but they are plainly not uniform across modern states (or even across substantial regions) in the right way to yield the desired nationalist conclusions concerning states. Political cultures, by contrast, are (or, at least, may be) uniform across states in the right way, even if they may not yield clear moral boundaries for states; but they seem not to be the kinds of things that are inevitably affected (to their detriment) by an influx of immigrants, at least in the right ways for nationalist arguments from cultural self-determination to succeed.[60]

A state's public political culture in fact appears to be far more vulnerable to internal and generational (as well as international) forces for change than it does to the influence of typical immigrants, who are often eager to fit into their new communities and avoid calling unwanted attention to themselves or rocking the boat. And public education concerning the political culture, not the systematic exclusion of alien influence, seems the natural (and far more obviously morally defensible) strategy for addressing any undesirable threats to "culture" (understood politically). Immigration seems to genuinely threaten a state's public political culture primarily when excessive immigration threatens the state's very viability, by overwhelming its social programs, infrastructure, police, or governmental and legal structures. And in that kind of case, nationalists are far from being the only ones with plausible arguments supporting a state's right to restrict or halt immigration. Arguments for states' rights to exclude that appeal to the importance of cultural self-determination thus seem to me to fail on their own terms. It is, I think, only a kind of equivocation on the idea of culture (or, less charitably perhaps, the kind of desperate conservatism that we all sometimes experience in the face of lost ways of life) that makes such arguments seem initially compelling.

So, to summarize the results of this section: all of the standard approaches to territorial rights seem unable to convincingly defend robust rights for states to exclude aliens—just as they seemed unable to defend other aspects of states'

[60] See the related argument in Pevnick (2011), 140–41.

claimed property-like territorial rights. This failure can, of course, be taken in two different ways. We might conclude, first, that all of these theories are simply defective. And perhaps many of these theories' defenders would agree that my arguments, *if* they were successful, should be understood to have that conclusion. Alternatively, we might conclude that states simply *lack* many of the property-like territorial rights that they claim for themselves, and that the standard approaches in fact successfully converge to confirm that truth. I believe that this latter conclusion is partly correct. As my arguments in this book have suggested, many of the property-like rights that states claim, like some aspects of their jurisdictional claims, are simply incapable of moral justification (according to the dictates of *any* plausible political philosophy). But even once that is conceded, many will no doubt be left with the sense that this cannot be the whole story. Surely legitimate states, even if they lack *some* of the property-like rights they claim, must still at least have *more* of a discretionary right to exclude aliens than any of the standard approaches has been able to demonstrate. The Lockean theory that I support shows us, I think, the rest of that story.

Lockean Voluntarism on Borders and the Right to Exclude

The border rights for states that can be justified within a Lockean voluntarist theory of territory are far from absolute rights to pure discretionary exclusion. But the Lockean theory I support does at least show how such state rights *could be* relatively robust (while the competing accounts we've just considered seem unable even to show that). And it shows this by according precisely with commonsense intuitions about *why* it seems acceptable for states to decide to exclude outsiders. That, I think, is yet another indication of the fact that the Lockean theory best articulates the principles that actually structure our ordinary view of states' territorial rights—principles that are often co-opted, without adequate justification (and sometimes in ways that are inconsistent with their cores), in theories that utilize "Lockean" elements or analogies.

The Lockean ideal of the legitimate state (or civil/political society), remember, is that of a substantial group of persons who willingly create (or join) a group committed to persisting as a viable, governed territorial polity. Agreement to be a member of such a group implies agreement to (among other things) "join" any holdings in land (that is, land over which the member has moral rights of exclusive use) to the political territory over which the group will collectively exercise jurisdiction. Provided that this accumulated territory does not exceed the quality and amount that the proviso dictates must be left for others, its creation and preservation do no harm to the freedom of others. States of this sort may expand their legitimate territories by adding new, consenting members along with their just holdings, or by additional mixing of labor with land by either individual members or members acting collectively, on behalf of the whole (provided, as always, that the additions satisfy the proviso). The state may create public spaces by collective labor or by lawful appropriation of portions of private holdings, making room for roads, bridges, schools, parks, and so on. And it will inevitably create as well formal institutions of government and law, through which the state's jurisdictional and property-like territorial rights will be administered.

What is distinctive about this Lockean ideal of the legitimate state, of course, is not only that such a state governs no unwilling subjects, but that it claims territorial rights over no land or resources over which its members, individually and/or collectively, do not have strong exclusionary rights. Land that is privately owned in such a state will be protected by both the rights reserved for individual landowners and the rights landowners are required to surrender to the state (such as those rights which permit the state to exercise jurisdiction, control national boundaries, regulate uses of resources, etc.). The rights over land that are thus shared between landholders and state add up to (since they were derived from splitting the incidents of) the strong ownership rights over land which individuals may naturally acquire by their labor (subject to the proviso's constraints). Further, land that is public in such a state will be owned in just as strong a fashion by the people as a whole (holding their rights as an incorporated, collective agent), along with the public spaces, buildings, roads, schools (etc.) built on public land.

A state, so conceived, is entitled to fence, control, and exclude in the same ways that an individual landowner is. Moreover, of course, the members are collectively entitled to exercise unilateral control over whatever nonterritorial products flow from their individual and collective labors—including control over the institutions and practices that they create and sustain. The society may (as a landowner may) decide to allow some (or all, or no) outsiders to reside in its territories or become members of the society, as these policy decisions flow from the society's chosen mechanisms for dispute resolution (to whose operations all members have necessarily consented, explicitly or implicitly, in becoming members). And all of this, I think, accurately reflects the reasoning that would likely be cited by most to support the ordinary belief that good states are morally permitted to (e.g.) set their own immigration policies. That from which the members of legitimate political societies exclude the alien is, quite simply, *theirs*, and they may decide for themselves when and how to share what is theirs. A compassionate state, like a compassionate property owner, will share freely. But no legitimate state is *obligated* to share what is theirs with whoever requests it. They may use their own discretion in such matters—at least within limits, limits that are *also* effectively captured by Lockean ideal theory.

For there are several natural limits to what may be held under claims of Lockean territorial right, even beyond those established by the proviso's constraints on legitimate appropriations and holdings. We saw in chapter 8 what some of those limits are with respect to state claims over resources. Further, in my view, the legitimacy of private appropriation of portions of the world—and hence also that of collective jurisdictional and property-like territorial rights for states—turns on the fact that appropriation of portions of the common must be possible if individuals are to have an effective right to be genuinely self-governing and independent. Hence, the Lockean theory I support holds that those who are incapable of such independence, even when they are left enough and as good by the appropriations of others, have rights to what they need to lead self-governing lives. There are thus individual natural duties on us to do our fair share of the work required to assist the world's less fortunate inhabitants—duties that must be discharged either individually by societies' members or collectively by their societies.

Legitimate states' rights to exclude—and to be clear, we are still discussing only *ideal theory* (and are still assuming full compliance with the demands of morality by all parties)—are thus not absolute, since it may be necessary for a state to admit its fair share of those willing aliens who cannot otherwise (i.e., without admission) be assisted in living self-governing lives. But states' border rights are certainly *robust* discretionary rights on this model, identical to those that an individual with exclusive property rights in land may exercise with respect to that land. Once all obligations to aliens have been met (by required assistance to outsiders and by satisfying the proviso's requirements), no alien has any valid basis for complaint about being excluded. Nor may outsiders reasonably complain because they are not permitted to control or participate in the institutions and practices that the state's members have collectively created. This all assumes, of course, that the states in question have not entered into any (binding) special agreements concerning these matters with other states, groups, or persons. On the Lockean model, absent such agreements states (and their rightful members) remain in the state of nature with respect to all alien persons and groups, bound to them only by the rules of natural morality (to which all remain always subject). Further, because legitimate states' territories are possessed with the force of property rights, not only are states generally at liberty to exclude aliens, but aliens (like would-be trespassers) usually have moral duties to refrain from unpermitted border crossings.[61]

[61] See the discussion in Laegaard (2010), esp. 255–6, 260. Most of my discussion here has been aimed at illuminating the nature of states' discretionary rights to control residence (and rules governing citizenship) in their countries. Rights of free movement, when we understand them more generally, are also more complicated. Because (I believe) individual self-government requires rights to

Lea Ypi is among those who argue that while such Lockean reasoning might be able to explain states' *liberty* rights to *use* portions of the world, it cannot ground states' rights to exclude others from the portions they use, their rights to employ coercion to exclude aliens (in the manner of an owner of property). This is true, she contends, even of Lockean theories that acknowledge limits to states' rights set by some version of the Lockean proviso.[62] Her principal example to illustrate the problem for Lockeans is that of a public bench in a pleasant spot, used regularly by friends. No matter how attached the friends may become to "their" bench, no matter how regularly they use or even maintain it, they cannot by such means acquire any right to exclude others from using it as well.[63] But as the example makes clear, the force of Ypi's argument depends on our simply accepting her Kantian assumption that in state-of-nature relationships, persons (and hence ultimately states, depending for their territorial rights on portions of persons' state-of-nature rights over things) can acquire at most only (provisional?) moral rights to use things, not property-like claim rights with legitimately controlled boundaries. Ypi, for instance, says that Lockean-style "acquisition-based" theories of territory try to explain states' rights to exclude aliens by asserting individual (and state) property claims that illegitimately "disrupt" the regime of "communal use" with which such theories begin their reasoning.[64]

A properly developed Lockean theory, though (as we have seen), has the resources to answer such objections. The relevant background regime of communal use of the world, in a Lockean theory like my own, is one of (limited) unilaterally divisible positive community. Permissible unilateral divisions result in property rights that are (also within limits) fully exclusionary. The relevant regime of communal use, while in some sense "disrupted" by private appropriation, is in no sense *corrupted* by it, since all continue to enjoy the same opportunities to use their fair shares of the world or to appropriate holdings as good and as extensive as those already appropriated. If, for instance, instead of one public bench in a lovely spot, there were as many such benches as people who wanted

reasonably free movement in the pursuit of legitimate projects, it may also sometimes ground moral rights to necessary "easements" or "rights of way" on land owned by others. Because any such rights held by nonmembers could not be extinguished simply by members joining together in political society, aliens may continue to possess moral rights to pass through (or over) the collected individual property that constitutes the basis of state territory (and so, aliens may possess moral rights to limited use of other states' infrastructures and institutions). States' general exclusionary rights may thus be somewhat constrained, even if their more specific rights to deny residence or citizenship to aliens are confirmed, by Lockean reasoning. Free *domestic* movement (i.e., by members) on the Lockean view is a matter to be either left as in the state of nature or regulated by consensual domestic arrangements.

[62] Ypi (2013), 246.

[63] Ibid., 248.

[64] Ibid., 245.

to use them, all equally pleasant and convenient, there would be no obvious reason why the use, attention, and labor lavished on one such bench by friends should *not* give them exclusionary claims over it. Others' objections to being excluded from using that particular bench (and thus from benefiting from the labor the friends have invested in it) would in that case just look like an unreasonable demand to ride (sit?) free.

The Lockean (ideal-theoretical) claim that legitimate states' territories are simply *theirs* may, at first, seem similar to another position that has been recently defended in discussing immigration theory. Ryan Pevnick, in defending his "associative ownership view," also characterizes legitimate states as associations that possess (broadly) Lockean rights over their societal accomplishments (including their political institutions, their public infrastructure, economy, educational system, etc.).[65] Those who contribute to the creation and maintenance of such things have a (limited) right to determine who will have access to them—that is, a (limited) right to exclude the alien from the kinds of presence in their territories that will give the alien access to those societal creations. And Pevnick, like the Lockean, locates some of the limits to this right to exclude in our moral duties of rescue to those in dire need, such as asylum seekers and the desperately poor.[66] While Pevnick emphasizes societies' collective ownership of their institutional achievements—rather than their collective rights over their territories, as is central to the Lockean view[67]—the positions seem, at least initially, to be similar in basic orientation.

One kind of objection that has been raised against Pevnick's view is that the "associative ownership" view in fact yields the wrong collections of associate owners—that is, the wrong ones to support legitimate states' discretionary rights to exclude. Not all insiders or residents of a state (for instance, young children) actually contribute to their own societies' accomplishments, while many outsiders or aliens may have contributed quite a lot to other societies (especially in cases of outside disaster relief, postwar rebuilding efforts, and colonial development).[68] I think such complaints can probably be answered by Pevnick.[69] But I have more basic concerns of my own about his position, concerns that

65 Pevnick (2011), 13, 33–5.

66 Ibid., 12.

67 Pevnick does not appear to treat the land itself as something over which associations have strong, exclusionary rights. Borders matter morally in his theory because those within them can gain unfair access to societal accomplishments.

68 See, e.g., Fine (2013), 264.

69 The rights of some resident noncontributors can be covered by thinking of the ownership rights as genuinely collective rights; and collectives can simply opt to include the infirm, the native-born who rise to adulthood (etc.) as full associates. Some other noncontributors (like career criminals) perhaps ought not to be viewed as associate rightholders at all. As for outside or alien contributors,

(by now, predictably) involve the ways the Lockean elements of Pevnick's view are detached from their Lockean motivations.

At times Pevnick seems content to characterize his position weakly, as holding merely "that it is *possible* for a group to have legitimate claims of collective ownership over the institutions they construct" or that "the view that states *cannot* claim territorial rights" is (as a result of his arguments) unconvincing.[70] And a Lockean political philosopher, of course, should agree with these claims. A Lockean would add, however, that they are correct only provided that the group in question is a consensual association and that its members and territories were acquired legitimately. Pevnick, however, seems eager to distance his own view from any Lockean insistence that political societies be consensual or that territories not be wrongfully subjected to political authority. He says, for example, that while the "not fully consensual" nature of political societies might bear on the question of "whether or not a citizen has the right to disobey the government," it should not "be thought to call into question the rights citizens hold against *outsiders*."[71] And while "particular historical injustices . . . must be considered when we consider the legitimacy of restrictions on immigration," the fact that "all claims in our world lie on a bed of injustices" means that some claims resting on that bed must be accepted as legitimate.[72]

But it is important to remember here just *why* the Lockean stresses issues of political consent and wrongful subjection. Where persons or land are illegitimately subjected to a society's political authority, they simply do not count (morally) as members or territory of the state in question, and the state is morally bound to refrain from exercising control over those persons or lands. The legitimate boundaries of the state's authority are then other than the claimed boundaries. The *state's* right to exclude aliens cannot be unaffected by this, since it *has* no right to exclude aliens from lands that are not part of its rightful territories (which, of course, includes that land over which nonconsenting persons have *individual* rights of control). Nonconsenters have (limited) rights to exclude others from their just holdings, but these are neither *collective* rights nor rights held *as citizens*.[73] So from a Lockean perspective, the contours of the

some of their contributions (such as disaster relief) should surely be regarded as either morally required or as freely given charity, acts which normally result in no rights over the "product"; and other contributions (by postwar rebuilders or colonial powers) are at least often owed to the society for prior harms or wrongs—which again would yield no rights over the product.

[70] Pevnick (2011), 41 (my emphasis), 59.

[71] Ibid., 58. See also 37.

[72] Ibid., 58, 42; see also 41, 119. Pevnick takes no stance on the question of Waldron-style supersession of rights.

[73] Pevnick's argument that "lasting claims of ownership can originate in non-voluntary associations" (ibid., 36–7) is thus misleading. Because the "association" in Pevnick's example is produced

association that can assert associative ownership over anything will be crucially determined by precisely the Lockean considerations (concerning consent and wrongful subjection) that Pevnick tries to deemphasize in his account. In the end, then, I think the associative ownership view again involves grafting intuitively compelling Lockean parts onto a theory that in fact fails to acknowledge the sources of the intuitive force of those very parts.

Let us turn finally (in closing) from ideal Lockean theory to more of the principles to which Lockean voluntarism is committed for guiding our practical political lives in the real world, the nonideal world replete with its wrongdoings and injustice—that is, to Lockean principles of the *nonideal theory* of state territoriality, primarily now as these concern border control and exclusion of aliens.[74] We have seen the target Lockean ideal toward which nonideal theory must guide us—nonideal theory (remember) being understood here as a transitional theory, consisting in rules for achieving the target ideal in ways that are morally permissible, likely to be effective, and politically feasible. The nonideal theory of property-like state territorial rights, like that of state jurisdictional rights, will not yield conclusions about policy that are deeply radical or dramatic. Nonideal theory in this domain is by its very nature both reasonably imprecise and reasonably conservative. It is imprecise both because (as we saw in chapters 7 and 8) morally required rectifications for past wrongs will often involve rights to rectifications "within an acceptable range," rather than rights to a specific outcome, and because which policies are politically feasible and likely to be effective tends not to be something that can be determined with much exactitude (even supposing that all the facts of a particular state's societal, political, and international condition are well understood). Nonideal theory is also, of course, by its nature reasonably conservative: the best path forward toward the moral ideal will be the one that can effectively circumvent the often considerable real-world obstacles to achieving an ideally rightful condition (since the path must be politically

by kidnapping, its creation in no way morally limits its "members'" rights. Any "claims of ownership" that flow from its members' labors will thus be *individual* claims, not collective ones (as required by Pevnick's claims about nonconsensual political associations).

[74] This, again, will concern just a portion of Lockean nonideal theory. But it is a portion that will include elements of all three branches of nonideal theory (as these are outlined in chapter 2): the relevant noncompliance with ideal principles of right (in establishing borders and in dealing with aliens—as in claiming resources) has been a function of wrongful actions by individuals, by states within their own borders, and by states interacting with those outside their borders. Further, this noncompliance has typically fallen within the category of deliberate, not merely unfortunate, wrongdoing, thus calling for more severe moral requirements of restitution or compensation in our transition to an ideally rightful condition. While some individuals (such as aggressive "settlers") may in fact owe *personal* duties of restitution to wronged persons and peoples, the principal culprits in these matters have plainly been states. So I will focus here primarily on the principles of nonideal theory that govern the conduct of noncompliant states.

feasible and likely to be effective). Such obstacles will tend to be substantial, because real societies' institutions will typically be wrongfully structured and real peoples' expectations will be correspondingly distorted (with their lives built around those expectations).

All that acknowledged, we can still give some substantial content to Lockean voluntarist nonideal theory. In the real world, the kinds of standard departures from the Lockean target ideal—that is, the things that make real-world territorial claims by states wrongful according to these Lockean standards—are (for our purposes here) primarily four. First, the land possessed by individuals and incorporated into state territories is often not *innocently* possessed, possession instead resting on a history of unjust and violent seizures or deceptive negotiations (by individuals, groups, and states). Second, real states subject to their political authority many unwilling persons and groups. Third, the land and resources held as property by individuals and/or as territory by their states often do not satisfy the proviso's requirement that a fair share of the earth be left available for all. And fourth, private landowners claim rights over things they are not productively using, while states claim rights over things not being productively used by their members.

The required moral remedies for such wrongs have already been partly described. The specific policies that will be required in particular states (in order to eventually fully accomplish such remedies) will partly turn on local political feasibility and likely effectiveness. But real states are always morally required to be honestly working toward full rectification. As we have seen, the most natural rectifications of historical wrongs in the acquisition of subjects and territories—including wrongful seizure of land or resources and wrongful subjection or expulsion of persons or groups (including, but not limited to, those innocently in residence on wrongfully seized lands)—involve granting full or partial autonomy to those wrongfully subjected and/or downsizing of the relevant territorial claims (along the lines detailed in chapter 7), in order to provide access to unsubjected land for those wronged by the state.[75] It may be necessary for states

[75] The Lockean voluntarist theory of permissible and justified *secession* that follows from such reasoning has two essential parts. The first part concerns the binding duration of the consent that subjects persons to the authority of legitimate states. If (as I believe) such consent cannot be "in perpetuity," but requires periodic reaffirmation, individual or group "secession" from a legitimate state may be permissible when that consent's binding force lapses. The second part concerns the right of wrongfully subjected or internally abused persons or groups to form their own autonomous political society (on the lands the state wrongfully seized or on lands over which the state forfeited its rights by abuse). In both cases, secession will be permissible if it can be accomplished without wronging innocents (such as newly trapped minorities or individuals) and will be justified on balance in terms of the severity of the wrong being righted and the weight of the likely consequences of secession in the particular case.

(instead or as well) to offer those who were unwillingly subjected (or wrongfully expelled), or their heirs, favorable terms of membership; and it may be necessary for states to tolerate the existence of independent political (or nonpolitical) territories within their legitimate domains or to contract their outer boundaries in order to create external space for such territories.[76]

Wrongs by states may also relate to the proviso's requirement of fair shares for all or to the Lockean requirement that others be excluded only from that part (of the share permitted by the proviso) that is being productively used. In such cases, the required remedies again flow naturally from the arguments of the preceding chapters. Downsizing territorial holdings and relinquishing control over resources—by removing state-created obstacles to use by others—is again the most obvious remedy. But it is also possible to remedy under-use of land and resources by recruiting additional productive users as willing members of the political society in question, since the extent of justifiable territorial claims by states expand (all else equal) with the numbers of those who employ the land and resources in their life projects. Thus, softer, "targeted" immigration policies may be another way in which states can satisfy the requirements of the Lockean proviso.[77]

There is a final aspect of nonideal theory on which I have not yet commented in this book (and on which I will comment now largely only in order to distinguish it from other aspects). Suppose we stretch our imaginations to consider a state that is has made itself fully legitimate by Lockean standards, exercising its political authority exclusively over willing subjects and over land and resources legitimately held. All rectifications of past wrongs have been fully accomplished, and the state has done its share (or more) in assisting the desperate and the oppressed outside its boundaries. In those circumstances, what are the (fully legitimate) state's obligations when other states are *not* doing their morally required parts?

Must a legitimate state liberate the unwilling subjects of other states, redistribute the territories or resources they hold that were unjustly seized or that now exceed their fair shares, remedy other states' failures to assist those beyond their borders? This, of course, is a part of nonideal theory that concerns neither the state's obligations to those it has *itself* wronged in its history (which I have emphasized in this book) nor its obligations to reform its institutions and laws in order to do domestic justice for its members (as emphasized in Rawls's early

[76] This concerns, of course, only rectification for wrongs actually done by the state. Those to whom such responses are owed may *themselves* have obligations to rectify wrongs that *they* have done to prior occupants.

[77] While at the same time satisfying utilitarian (and Risse's version of contractualist) requirements to avoid inefficient under-use.

work on civil disobedience, discussed in chapter 2). Rather, the problem more closely resembles, though in international terms, the kind of moral problem that occupies Liam Murphy in his discussion of (primarily interpersonal) nonideal theory.[78] In situations of partial compliance with morality's demands, must we do more than we would be morally required to do were all others fully compliant with those demands?

On the one hand, of course, it seems unfair that those (persons or states) that willingly conform their conduct to morality's requirements must then sacrifice still more simply because others decline to do their parts. On the other hand, when others don't do their parts, people (and peoples) suffer unjustly, often desperately, and simple decency seems to require that we help those suffering if we can, at least if we can do so without great loss to ourselves—even if we *have* already done "more than enough." Consider, for instance, the kind of case that causes Murphy such discomfort.[79] Imagine a shallow (Singer-style) pond in which six children are drowning, the pond surrounded by six competent adult (potential) rescuers. Five of the adults do their fair shares of the moral work, saving a child apiece, while the sixth walks away, leaving one unrescued child in the pond. Any of the five who remain could relatively easily save that sixth child as well; but all have already done (what ideal, full-compliance theory specifies as) their duties. May they, without wrongdoing, simply leave the sixth child to his desperate fate?

Consider now an international analog of Murphy's case: some or most states are not doing what morality requires of them, increasing the need for action by legitimate states (that have done what they should, according to ideal theory). Murphy's interpersonal case, I'm afraid, is simple by comparison with this international one. For the international case involves numerous additional considerations, not (typically) present in cases of drowning children. States do wrong not only by failing to help others when they need help (or by failing to maximize overall social utility), but also by wrongfully subjecting people and territory to illegitimate political control. So doing the moral work that should be done by illegitimate states will inevitably involve not just additional efforts to help the world's needy, but may require coercively intervening in the domestic affairs of illegitimate states, in the process possibly destabilizing the political/legal order there and jeopardizing international peace. Such international intervention would thus be more closely analogous (in interpersonal cases) to forcing other people to do their morally required tasks (say, by coercing at gunpoint the sixth potential rescuer) than it would be to doing those tasks in their steads. But the

[78] Murphy (2000).

[79] Ibid., 127–33.

stakes involved in the international case would almost certainly be vastly higher than in such a coercion-filled interpersonal case.

My inclination in such cases is to say that states that satisfy Lockean standards of legitimacy are morally required to do no more than their fair shares of helping the world's desperate denizens. Doing that fair share may sometimes involve selectively opening their borders and may sometimes involve participating in interventions in other states. But legitimate states are not morally required to take up all morally imperative tasks, even if those tasks are roundly ignored by others. As we conclude in the individual case, so we should conclude in the international case: legitimate societies, on the Lockean model, can owe no more to others than the sum of their members' moral debts. And the natural moral duties of individual persons to help others and to combat injustices are, I believe (and as Murphy believes for slightly different reasons), only to do a fair share of the overall moral task. It may be that caring people simply cannot stand by, even after doing what morality demands, in the face of further human suffering (caused by the moral failings of others). But people would breach no clear natural duties by turning away at that point. Given that few of us ever really approach doing our fair shares of the moral work that would be required in even a fully compliant world, of course, this is perhaps a conclusion of only limited practical relevance. And I will not, in any case, attempt here to defend it any further.

Lockean nonideal theory thus requires that contemporary states (and their subjects) make sincere efforts to do their parts in moving us toward a fully rightful world, one that contains no states that are not voluntary political associations on legitimately controlled territories. The actual policies this will mandate, for both individuals and their societies, will depend deeply on specific societal conditions and the socially available opportunities for change. But the Lockean target ideal offers a distinctive guiding beacon for these policies. The Lockean ideal also demands in this distinctive way, I think, much of what its rival ideals demand. It requires that justice be done for all—not merely by creating and maintaining basic institutions to resolve disputes over rights, but also by respecting the rights of those outside our polities—including even the rights of those residing in *no* polity—and by rectifying the wrongs done by our states in their bloody-handed transformations into their contemporary forms. The Lockean ideal requires as well that choices to be self-determining be respected, whether those are choices to make self-determining political societies or choices to remain self-governing outside them. And it requires that we permit peoples to practice and protect their inherited cultures, traditions, and lifestyles, that we permit them to be culturally self-determining. But the Lockean ideal requires all this only on the condition that none are trapped, forgotten, compelled to subjection, denied their fair shares, or robbed of their just heritages along the way. It demands a political universe that contains only those districted "common worlds" that are *genuinely* common, not ones that are only really common for the numerous and the powerful. And in that sense, I think, the Lockean ideal may be truer to the political ideals that have guided rival theories than those theories have been themselves.

BIBLIOGRAPHY OF WORKS CITED

Abizadeh, A. (2007). Cooperation, Pervasive Impact, and Coercion: On the Scope (not Site) of Distributive Justice, *Philosophy and Public Affairs* 35, 318–58.

Abizadeh, A. (2008). Democratic Theory and Border Coercion, *Political Theory* 36, 37–65.

Altman, A., and Wellman, C. (2009). *A Liberal Theory of International Justice* (Oxford: Oxford University Press).

Anscombe, G. E. M. (1990). On the Source of the Authority of the State, in J. Raz (ed.), *Authority* (New York: New York University Press), 142–73.

Armstrong, C. (2014). Against "Permanent Sovereignty" over Natural Resources, *Politics, Philosophy and Economics* (online), 1–23.

Baldwin, T. (1992). The Territorial State, in H. Gross and R. Harrison (eds.), *Jurisprudence: Cambridge Essays* (Oxford: Oxford University Press), 207–30.

Barry, B. (1999a). Self-Government Revisited, in R. Beiner (ed.), *Theorizing Nationalism* (Albany: SUNY Press), 247–77.

Barry, B. (1999b). Statism and Nationalism: A Cosmopolitan Critique, in I. Shapiro and L. Brilmayer (eds.), *Nomos XLI: Global Justice* (New York: New York University Press), 12–66.

Bedau, H. (1991). Civil Disobedience and Personal Responsibility for Injustice, in H. Bedau (ed.), *Civil Disobedience in Focus* (London and New York: Routledge), 49–67.

Beitz, C. (1980). Tacit Consent and Property Rights, *Political Theory* 8, 487–502.

Beran, H. (1987). *The Consent Theory of Political Obligation* (London: Croom Helm).

Blackstone, W. (1765–9). *Commentaries on the Laws of England*, 1st ed. (Oxford: Clarendon Press).

Blake, M. (2001). Distributive Justice, State Coercion, and Autonomy, *Philosophy and Public Affairs* 30, 257–96.

Blake, M. (2013). Immigration, Jurisdiction, and Exclusion, *Philosophy and Public Affairs* 41, 103–130.

Branch, J. (2014). *The Cartographic State* (Cambridge: Cambridge University Press).

Brilmayer, L. (1989). Consent, Contract, and Territory, *Minnesota Law Review* 74, 1–35.

Brownlie, I. (1998). *Principles of Public International Law*, 5th ed. (Oxford: Clarendon Press).

Buchanan, A. (1991). *Secession* (Boulder, CO: Westview).

Buchanan, A. (1997). Theories of Secession, *Philosophy and Public Affairs* 26, 31–61.

Buchanan, A. (1999). Recognitional Legitimacy and the State System, *Philosophy and Public Affairs* 28, 46–78.

Buchanan, A. (2003). The Making and Unmaking of Boundaries: What Liberalism Has to Say, in A. Buchanan and M. Moore (eds.), *States, Nations and Borders* (Cambridge: Cambridge University Press), 231–61.

Buchanan, A. (2004). *Justice, Legitimacy, and Self-Determination: Moral Foundations for International Law* (Oxford: Oxford University Press).

Carens, J. (1987). Aliens and Citizens: The Case for Open Borders, *Review of Politics* 49, 251–73.
Carens, J. (1992). Migration and Morality: A Liberal Egalitarian Perspective, in B. Barry and R. Goodin (eds.), *Free Movement: Ethical Issues in the Transnational Migration of People and of Money* (University Park: Pennsylvania State University Press), 25–47.
Carens, J. (2013). *The Ethics of Immigration* (Oxford: Oxford University Press).
Christiano, T. (2004). The Authority of Democracy, *Journal of Political Philosophy* 12, 266–90.
Christiano, T. (2006). A Democratic Theory of Territory and Some Puzzles about Global Democracy, *Journal of Social Philosophy* 37, 81–107.
Christiano, T. (2008). *The Constitution of Equality: Democratic Authority and Its Limits* (Oxford: Oxford University Press).
Christiano, T. (2013). Authority, in E. Zalta (ed.), *The Stanford Encyclopedia of Philosophy*. http://plato.stanford.edu/archives/spr2013/entries/authority/.
Cole, P. (2000). *Philosophies of Exclusion: Liberal Political Theory and Immigration* (Edinburgh: Edinburgh University Press).
Copp, D. (1999). The Idea of a Legitimate State, *Philosophy and Public Affairs* 28, 3–45.
Davis, L. (1976). Comments on Nozick's Entitlement Theory, *Journal of Philosophy* 73, 836–44.
Dworkin, R. (1977). *Taking Rights Seriously* (Cambridge, MA: Harvard University Press).
Dworkin, R. (2011). *Justice for Hedgehogs* (Cambridge, MA: Harvard University Press).
Estlund, D. (2005). Political Authority and the Tyranny of Non-consent, *Philosophical Issues* 15, 351–67.
Estlund, D. (2008). *Democratic Authority: A Philosophical Framework* (Princeton, NJ: Princeton University Press).
Feinberg, J. (1978). Voluntary Euthanasia and the Inalienable Right to Life, *Philosophy and Public Affairs* 7, 93–123.
Fine, S. (2013). The Ethics of Immigration: Self-Determination and the Right to Exclude, *Philosophy Compass* 8, 254–68.
Gans, C. (2003). *The Limits of Nationalism* (Cambridge: Cambridge University Press).
Gaus, G. (1991). Does Compensation Restore Equality?, in J. Chapman (ed.), *Nomos XXXIII: Compensatory Justice* (New York: New York University Press), 45–81.
Glendon, M. (1991). *Rights Talk* (New York: Free Press).
Godwin, W. (1976). *Enquiry Concerning Political Justice* (Harmondsworth: Penguin).
Goodin, R. (2007). Enfranchising All Affected Interests, and Its Alternatives, *Philosophy and Public Affairs* 35, 40–68.
Green, L. (1988). *The Authority of the State* (Oxford: Oxford University Press).
Grotius, H. (2004). *The Free Sea*, ed. D. Armitage (Indianapolis, IN: Liberty Fund).
Grotius, H. (2005). *The Rights of War and Peace*, ed. R. Tuck (Indianapolis, IN: Liberty Fund).
Hampton, J. (1997). *Political Philosophy* (Boulder, CO: Westview).
Hart, H. L. A. (1982). Commands and Authoritative Legal Reasons, in *Essays on Bentham* (Oxford: Oxford University Press), 243–68.
Hobbes, T. (1968). *Leviathan* (Harmondsworth: Penguin).
Hobbes, T. (1972). *Man and Citizen* (Garden City, NY: Anchor).
Hohfeld, W. (1964). *Fundamental Legal Conceptions as Applied to Judicial Reasoning* (New Haven, CT: Yale University Press).
Kant, I. (1991). *The Metaphysics of Morals* (Cambridge: Cambridge University Press).
Kavka, G. (1986). *Hobbesian Moral and Political Theory* (Princeton, NJ: Princeton University Press).
Kolers, A. (2009). *Land, Conflict, and Justice* (Cambridge: Cambridge University Press).
Kolers, A. (2012). Justice, Territory, and Natural Resources, *Political Studies* 60, 269–86.
Koskenniemi, M. (1999). The Politics of International Law, in K. Culver (ed.), *Readings in the Philosophy of Law* (Peterborough, ON: Broadview), 494–521.
Ladenson, R. (1980). In Defense of a Hobbesian Conception of Law, *Philosophy and Public Affairs* 9, 134–59.
Laegaard, S. (2007). David Miller on Immigration Policy and Nationality, *Journal of Applied Philosophy* 24, 283–98.

Laegaard, S. (2010). What Is the Right to Exclude Immigrants?, *Res Publica* 16: 245–62.
Lefkowitz, D. (2014). Autonomy, Residence, and Return, *Critical Review of International Social and Political Philosophy* 18: 529–46.
Lewis, D. (1973). *Counterfactuals* (Cambridge, MA: Harvard University Press).
Locke, J. (1960). *Two Treatises of Government* (Cambridge: Cambridge University Press).
Lomasky, L. (1987). *Persons, Rights, and the Moral Community* (New York: Oxford University Press).
Lomasky, L. (1991). Compensation and the Bounds of Rights, in J. Chapman (ed.), *Nomos XXXIII: Compensatory Justice* (New York: New York University Press), 13–44.
Lyons, D. (1977). The New Indian Claims and Original Rights to Land, *Social Theory and Practice* 4, 249–72.
Lyons, D. (1998). Moral Judgment, Historical Reality, and Civil Disobedience, *Philosophy and Public Affairs* 27, 31–49.
Mack, E. (1981). Nozick on Unproductivity: The Unintended Consequences, in J. Paul (ed.), *Reading Nozick* (Totowa, NJ: Rowman and Littlefield), 169–91.
Margalit, A., and Raz, J. (1990). National Self-Determination, in J. Raz (ed.), *Ethics in the Public Domain* (Oxford: Oxford University Press, 1994), 125–45.
Meisels, T. (2009). *Territorial Rights*, 2nd ed. (Dordrecht: Springer).
Miller, D. (1995). *On Nationality* (Oxford: Oxford University Press).
Miller, D. (1998). Secession and the Principle of Nationality, in M. Moore (ed.), *National Self-Determination and Secession* (Oxford: Oxford University Press), 62–78.
Miller, D. (2005). Immigration: The Case for Limits, in A. Cohen and C. Wellman (eds.), *Contemporary Debates in Applied Ethics* (Oxford: Blackwell), 193–206.
Miller, D. (2007). *National Responsibility and Global Justice* (Oxford: Oxford University Press).
Miller, D. (2009). Democracy's Domain, *Philosophy and Public Affairs* 37, 201–28.
Miller, D. (2010). Why Immigration Controls are Not Coercive: A Reply to Arash Abizadeh, *Political Theory* 38, 111–20.
Miller, D. (2011). Property and Territory: Locke, Kant, and Steiner, *Journal of Political Philosophy* 19, 90–109.
Miller, D. (2012). Territorial Rights: Concept and Justification, *Political Studies* 60 (June), 252–68.
Mokrosinska, D. (2007). "Political Obligation." PhD dissertation, University of Amsterdam.
Moore, M. (1998). The Territorial Dimension of Self-Determination, in M. Moore (ed.), *National Self-Determination and Secession* (Oxford: Oxford University Press), 134–57.
Moore, M. (2001). *The Ethics of Nationalism* (Oxford: Oxford University Press).
Moore, M. (2012). Natural Resources, Territorial Rights, and Global Distributive Justice, *Political Theory* 40, 84–107.
Moore, M. (2014). Which People and What Land? Territorial Right-Holders and Attachment to Territory, *International Theory* 6, 121–40.
Moore, M. (2015). *A Political Theory of Territory* (Oxford: Oxford University Press).
Morris, C. (1984). Existential Limits to the Rectification of Past Wrongs, *American Philosophical Quarterly* 21, 175–82.
Morris, C. (1998). *An Essay on the Modern State* (Cambridge: Cambridge University Press).
Murphy, L. (2000). *Moral Demands in Nonideal Theory* (New York: Oxford University Press).
Nagel, T. (2005). The Problem of Global Justice, *Philosophy and Public Affairs* 33, 113–47.
Nine, C. (2008a). A Lockean Theory of Territory, *Political Studies* 56, 148–65.
Nine, C. (2008b). Territory Is Not Derived from Property: A Response to Steiner, *Political Studies* 56, 957–63.
Nine, C. (2012). *Global Justice and Territory* (Oxford: Oxford University Press).
Nozick, R. (1974). *Anarchy, State, and Utopia* (New York: Basic Books).
O'Neill, O. (1987). Rights to Compensation, *Social Philosophy and Policy* 5, 72–87.
Paul, J, (1990). Property, Entitlement, and Remedy, *The Monist* 73, 564–77.
Perez, N. (2011). On Compensation and Return: Can the "Continuing Injustice Argument" for Compensating for Historical Injustices Justify Compensation for Such Injustices or the Return of Property?, *Journal of Applied Philosophy* 28, 151–68.

Pevnick, R. (2011). *Immigration and the Constraints of Justice: Between Open Borders and Absolute Sovereignty* (Cambridge: Cambridge University Press).

Pogge, T. (1992). Cosmopolitanism and Sovereignty, *Ethics* 103, 48–75.

Pogge, T. (1994). An Egalitarian Law of Peoples, *Philosophy and Public Affairs* 23, 195–224.

Pufendorf, S. (1934). *De jure naturae et gentium libri octo* (Oxford: Clarendon Press).

Pufendorf, S. (2003). *The Whole Duty of Man, According to the Law of Nature* (Indianapolis: Liberty Fund).

Pufendorf, S. (2009). *Two Books of the Elements of Universal Jurisprudence* (Indianapolis: Liberty Fund).

Rawls, J. (1971). *A Theory of Justice* (Cambridge, MA: Harvard University Press).

Rawls, J. (1993). *Political Liberalism* (New York: Columbia University Press).

Rawls, J. (1995). Reply to Habermas, *Journal of Philosophy* 92, 132–80.

Rawls, J. (1999a). *The Law of Peoples* (Cambridge, MA: Harvard University Press).

Rawls, J. (1999b). *John Rawls: Collected Papers* (Cambridge, MA: Harvard University Press).

Rawls, J. (2001). *Justice as Fairness: A Restatement* (Cambridge, MA: Harvard University Press).

Raz, J. (1979). *The Authority of Law* (Oxford: Oxford University Press).

Raz, J. (1986). *The Morality of Freedom* (Oxford: Oxford University Press).

Raz, J. (1990). Introduction, in J. Raz (ed.), *Authority* (New York: New York University Press), 1–19.

Richardson, H. (2011). Estlund's Promising Account of Democratic Authority, *Ethics* 121, 301–34.

Ripstein, A. (2009). *Force and Freedom* (Cambridge, MA: Harvard University Press).

Risse, M. (2012). *On Global Justice* (Princeton, NJ: Princeton University Press).

Rosenblum, N. (1996). Introduction, in *Thoreau: Political Writings* (Cambridge: Cambridge University Press), vii–xxxi.

Rousseau, J. (1997). *The Social Contract and Other Later Political Writings* (Cambridge: Cambridge University Press).

Sarkar, H. (1982). The Lockean Proviso, *Canadian Journal of Philosophy* 12, 47–59.

Scott, J., ed. (1916). *The Hague Court Reports*, vol. 1 (New York: Oxford University Press).

Selden, J. (2004). *Mare Clausum: Of the Dominion or Ownership of the Sea, Two Books* (Clark, NJ: Lawbook Exchange).

Shapiro, S. (2002). Authority, in J. Coleman and S. Shapiro (eds.), *The Oxford Handbook of Jurisprudence and Philosophy of Law* (Oxford: Oxford University Press), 382–439.

Shaw, M. (1997). *International Law*, 4th ed. (Cambridge: Cambridge University Press).

Sher, G. (1979). Compensation and Transworld Personal Identity, *The Monist* 62, 378–91.

Sher, G. (1981). Ancient Wrongs and Modern Rights, *Philosophy and Public Affairs* 10, 3–17.

Sidgwick, Henry (1897). *The Elements of Politics* (London: Macmillan).

Simmons, A. (1979). *Moral Principles and Political Obligations* (Princeton, NJ: Princeton University Press).

Simmons, A. (1983). Inalienable Rights and Locke's *Treatises*, *Philosophy and Public Affairs* 12, 175–204.

Simmons, A. (1991). Locke and the Right to Punish, *Philosophy and Public Affairs* 20, 311–49.

Simmons, A. (1992). *The Lockean Theory of Rights* (Princeton: Princeton University Press).

Simmons, A. (1993). *On the Edge of Anarchy: Locke, Consent, and the Limits of Society* (Princeton, NJ: Princeton University Press).

Simmons, A. (1994). Original-Acquisition Justifications of Private Property, *Social Philosophy and Policy* 11, 63–84.

Simmons, A. (1995). Historical Rights and Fair Shares, *Law and Philosophy* 14, 149–84.

Simmons, A. (1998). "Denisons" and "Aliens": Locke's Problem of Political Consent, *Social Theory and Practice* 24, 161–182.

Simmons, A. (2001a). Justification and Legitimacy, in Simmons, *Justification and Legitimacy* (Cambridge: Cambridge University Press), 122–57.

Simmons, A. (2001b). Philosophical Anarchism, in Simmons, *Justification and Legitimacy* (Cambridge: Cambridge University Press), 102–21.

Simmons, A. (2001c). Makers' Rights, in Simmons, *Justification and Legitimacy* (Cambridge: Cambridge University Press), 249–70.

Simmons, A. (2002). Political Obligation and Political Legitimacy, in R. L. Simon (ed.), *The Blackwell Guide to Social and Political Philosophy* (Malden, MA: Blackwell), 17–37.

Simmons, A. (2005). Consent Theory for Libertarians, *Social Philosophy and Policy* 22, 330–56.

Simmons, A. (2007). The Particularity Problem, *A.P.A. Newsletter on Philosophy and Law* 7, 18–27.

Simmons, A. (2008). *Political Philosophy* (Oxford: Oxford University Press).

Simmons, A. (2010). Ideal and Nonideal Theory, *Philosophy and Public Affairs* 38, 5–36.

Simmons, A., and Wellman, C. (2005). *Is There a Duty to Obey the Law?* (Cambridge: Cambridge University Press).

Simon, M. (1984). Thoreau and Anarchism, *Michigan Quarterly Review* 23, 360–84.

Sprankling, J. (2008). Owning the Center of the Earth, *UCLA Law Review* 55, 979–1040.

Sprankling, J. (2014). *The International Law of Property* (Oxford: Oxford University Press).

Spruyt, H. (1994). *The Sovereign State and its Competitors* (Princeton, NJ: Princeton University Press).

Sreedhar, S. (2010). Anarchism, Historical Illegitimacy, and Civil Disobedience, *Boston University Law Review* 90, 1833–46.

Steiner, H. (1996). Territorial Justice, in S. Caney, D. George, and P. Jones (eds.), *National Rights, International Obligations* (Boulder, CO: Westview), 139–68.

Steiner, H. (2005). Territorial Justice and Global Redistribution, in G. Brock and H. Brighouse (eds.), *The Political Philosophy of Cosmopolitanism* (Cambridge: Cambridge University Press), 28–38.

Stilz, A. (2009a). *Liberal Loyalty: Freedom, Obligation, and the State* (Princeton, NJ: Princeton University Press).

Stilz, A. (2009b). Why Do States Have Territorial Rights?, *International Theory* 1, 185–213.

Stilz, A. (2011). Nations, States, and Territory, *Ethics* 121, 572–601.

Stilz, A. (2013). Occupancy Rights and the Wrong of Removal, *Philosophy and Public Affairs* 41, 324–56.

Thoreau, H. (1996). *Thoreau: Political Writings* (Cambridge: Cambridge University Press).

Thoreau, H. (2000). *Walden and Other Writings* (New York: Modern Library).

Van der Vossen, B. (2014). Locke on Territorial Rights, *Political Studies* 63, 713–28 (online, 1–16).

Waldron, J. (1988). *The Right to Private Property* (Oxford: Oxford University Press).

Waldron, J. (1992). Superseding Historic Injustice, *Ethics* 103, 4–28.

Waldron, J. (1993). Special Ties and Natural Duties, *Philosophy and Public Affairs* 22, 3–30.

Waldron, J. (1999a). *Law and Disagreement* (Oxford: Oxford University Press).

Waldron, J. (1999b). *The Dignity of Legislation* (Cambridge: Cambridge University Press).

Waldron, J. (2002). Redressing Historic Injustice, *University of Toronto Law Journal* 52, 135–60.

Waldron, J. (2004). Settlement, Return, and the Supersession Thesis, *Theoretical Inquiries in Law* 5, 237–68.

Waldron, J. (2010). Two Conceptions of Self-Determination, in S. Besson and J. Tasioulas (eds.), *The Philosophy of International Law* (Oxford: Oxford University Press), 397–413.

Waldron, J. (2015). Supersession and Sovereignty, New York University School of Law, Public Law and Legal Theory Research Paper Series, Working Paper No. 13–33.

Wallace, R. (1997). *International Law*, 3rd. ed. (London: Sweet and Maxwell).

Walzer, M. (1981). The Distribution of Membership, in P. Brown and H. Shue (eds.), *Boundaries: National Autonomy and Its Limits* (Totowa, NJ: Rowman and Littlefield), 1–35.

Walzer, M. (1983). *Spheres of Justice* (Oxford: Blackwell).

Weber, M. (1947). *The Theory of Social and Economic Organization* (New York: Free Press).

Wellman, C. (2014). *Liberal Rights and Responsibilities* (Oxford: Oxford University Press).

Wellman, C., and Cole, P. (2011). *Debating the Ethics of Immigration* (Oxford: Oxford University Press).

Wenar, L. (2008). Property Rights and the Resource Curse, *Philosophy and Public Affairs* 36, 2–32.

Whelan, F. (1983). Prologue: Democratic Theory and the Boundary Problem, in J. Pennock and J. W. Chapman (eds.), *Nomos XXV: Liberal Democracy* (New York: New York University Press), 13–47.

Wolff, R. (1981). Robert Nozick's Derivation of the Minimal State, in J. Paul (ed.), *Reading Nozick* (Totowa, NJ: Rowman and Littlefield), 77–104.

Wolff, R. (1998). *In Defense of Anarchism* (Berkeley and Los Angeles: University of California Press).

Ypi, L. (2013). Territorial Rights and Exclusion, *Philosophy Compass* 8, 241–53.

Ypi, L. (2014). A Permissive Theory of Territorial Rights, *European Journal of Philosophy* 22, 288–312.

INDEX

www.ingramcontent.com/pod-product-compliance
Ingram Content Group UK Ltd.
Pitfield, Milton Keynes, MK11 3LW, UK
UKHW021135160926
475595UK00020B/58